Crisis and Conciliation

In memory of my father

Crisis and Conciliation

A year of rapprochement
between Greece and Turkey

JAMES KER-LINDSAY

Published in 2007 by I.B.Tauris & Co Ltd
6 Salem Road, London W2 4BU
175 Fifth Avenue, New York NY 10010
www.ibtauris.com

In the United States of America and Canada distributed by Palgrave Macmillan
a division of St. Martin's Press, 175 Fifth Avenue, New York NY 10010

Copyright © 2007 James Ker-Lindsay

The right of James Ker-Lindsay to be identified as the author of this work has been asserted by him in accordance with the Copyright, Designs and Patent Act 1988.

All rights reserved. Except for brief quotations in a review, this book, or any part thereof, may not be reproduced, stored in or introduced into a retrieval system, or transmitted, in any form or by any means, electronic, mechanical, photocopying, recording or otherwise, without the prior written permission of the publisher.

ISBN: 978 1 84511 504 3

A full CIP record for this book is available from the British Library
A full CIP record is available from the Library of Congress

Library of Congress Catalog Card Number: available

Printed and bound in Great Britain by TJ International Ltd, Padstow, Cornwall
From camera-ready copy edited and supplied by the author

CONTENTS

Acknowledgements *ix*
Abbreviations *x*
Preface *xi*

Introduction 1
1. Historical Background 11
2. Bilateral and Regional Crises 34
3. The Start of Rapprochement 44
4. Disaster Diplomacy 57
5. Next Steps 73
6. The Path to Europe 89
Epilogue 102
Conclusion 110

Appendix A: Cem and Papandreou Letters *123*
Appendix B: Helsinki Conclusions *127*

Notes *130*
Bibliography *153*
Index *163*

ACKNOWLEDGEMENTS

My first debt of gratitude goes to the members of the Greek-Turkish Forum. Over the course of the two years I worked with them, they provided me with a wealth of background information on Greek-Turkish relations and were able to put into context many of the developments taking place in Athens and Ankara throughout the period covered here.

Secondly, I would like to thank my colleagues at RUSI and PRIO. In particular, I would like to mention Admiral Richard Cobbold, Dr Jonathan Eyal, Dan Smith and Eline Oftedal. However, a special thank you must go to Jamie Bruce-Lockhart from the Roberts Centre. More than anyone else, he deserves credit for turning the idea of dialogue into action. The eventual success of the Greek-Turkish Forum was in no small measure the result of his hard work and dedication.

Finally, I am extremely grateful to Hubert Faustmann and Robert Holland for their extremely helpful comments on drafts of this work and to Matthew Brown at Bookcraft for his assistance with the preparation of the text. Needless to say, I take full responsibility for any omissions and errors that remain. Special thanks also go to Joe Bailey and Philip Spencer at Kingston University for their support and to Liz Friend-Smith at I.B.Tauris for all her invaluable comments, suggestions and advice. However, my greatest thanks go to my wife, Biljana, for all her love and support.

ABBREVIATIONS

AKP	Justice and Development Party (Turkey)
AKUT	Search and Rescue Association (Turkey)
ANAP	Motherland Party (Turkey)
CHP	Republican Peoples Party (Turkey)
DSP	Democratic Left Party (Turkey)
DYP	True Path Party (Turkey)
EMAK	Greek Special Disaster Unit
EU	European Union
ICJ	International Court of Justice
KKE	Communist Party of Greece
MHP	National Action Party (Turkey)
MIT	Turkish National Intelligence Service
NATO	North Atlantic Treaty Organisation
ND	New Democracy (Greece)
PASOK	Pan-Hellenic Socialist Movement (Greece)
PKK	Kurdish Workers Party
TRNC	Turkish Republic of Northern Cyprus
UN	United Nations

PREFACE

This book is an account of how, in the course of just one year, relations between Greece and Turkey underwent a major transformation. In 1999 a remarkable series of events led the two countries from a major diplomatic crisis to an unexpected and unprecedented thawing of tensions.

But while the work is primarily intended to provide a detailed outline of the political developments that took place over that twelve month period, it is also a very personal project. In the autumn of 1998 I was appointed to co-ordinate an initiative that eventually became known as the Greek-Turkish Forum. As a result, I was therefore extremely fortunate to be able to observe many of the events recounted here at first hand.

The first steps towards the formation of the Forum had taken place in early 1998. At that time, bilateral relations between the two countries were at a low point. Two years earlier, in 1996, Greece and Turkey had again come to the brink of armed conflict in the Aegean. Meanwhile, in December 1997, Turkey's EU accession had once again been blocked by Athens at the Luxembourg European Council, which led to further recriminations. On top of this, a decision by the Cypriot Government to purchase a Russian-made air defence system threatened to cause another crisis in the Eastern Mediterranean. It was against this backdrop that a number of prominent Greeks and Turks – drawn from politics, academia, business and the media – saw an opportunity to create an unofficial and informal process of dialogue. Starting out from a conference held at Wilton Park, the Forum secured institutional support from the Royal United Services Institute (RUSI) in the United Kingdom and the International Peace Research Institute, Oslo (PRIO) in Norway, and received funding from the Roberts Centre, a British charity.

The underlying aim of the effort was to avoid discussions on the main points of difference between the two countries and instead examine areas of mutual interest. The key to this process was to focus efforts on developing a common approach to joint problems. This would be underpinned by the formulation of practical confidence building measures that could then be put to the two governments. In the eyes of many taking part, the main hindrance to improved relations was the degree of focus placed on trying to deal with the various disputes that existed between Athens and Ankara. While these certainly needed to be addressed, it was felt that this should be supplemented by efforts to improve contacts between the two countries over non-controversial areas. If this could be done, or so the thinking ran, it would produce an improved climate of co-operation that might in turn allow for meaningful discussions on the more thorny issues. This innovative approach, though by no means first articulated by the Forum, was nevertheless relatively untried when the Forum was founded. However, the value of this approach was soon recognised. Indeed, as will be seen, it was precisely this mode of thinking that shaped the process of rapprochement established between Greece and Turkey in 1999.

Despite the obvious merits to the idea, I must admit that when I first started in the post I was sceptical about the prospects for peace between the two countries. Having lived in Cyprus, I had witnessed the scale of the problem confronting the region. However, the two years I spent working with the Forum changed my mind. During that time I was immensely fortunate to be able to work with a number of remarkable people – almost all of whom were highly respected in their fields – who sincerely believed that a good working relationship was possible between the two countries. Importantly, their views were not based on an unrealistic idealism. Many of the participants had held high office in their countries and had first hand experience of the practical limits facing politicians and decision-makers. Still, each of them had nevertheless come to the conclusion that better relations were possible. Even if few felt that a great friendship would ever develop between Greece and Turkey, they all believed that the poor state of relations could be improved significantly.

At the same time as the Forum eschewed idealism for pragmatism, it also sought to avoid the glare of publicity. Unlike many other groups working to promote Greece and Turkey rapprochement, the Forum chose to keep a fairly low profile in the two countries. Despite allegations from some quarters that it was a secret process, the Forum never actively tried to conceal its activities. Moreover, accusations that it was pursuing a hidden agenda of some sort were equally groundless. There was never an ulterior motive to its work beyond the desire of the participants to see a greater understanding develop between the two countries. Instead, the relatively low-key approach adopted by the Forum was the result of a deep-seated belief shared by the participants that by quietly concentrating on the task at hand they would be able to achieve the best results.

In many ways this policy paid dividends. The fact that they had not sought to publicise their work meant that following the arrest of Abdullah

Öcalan, when relations between the two countries sank to their lowest since 1974, the Forum was able to continue its work free from public pressure to break off contacts. When other, more high-profile teams were forced to suspend their activities, the Forum continued to meet. It is also to the credit of the participants that they followed this same principle in the good times as well as the bad. For example, in the aftermath of the earthquakes, when there was a rush to initiate or resume contacts, the Forum still avoided the limelight. While others made great show of their efforts to promote reconciliation, the participants continued to believe that the Forum's energies were better directed towards work than towards publicity.

In the months after the earthquake the Forum intensified its efforts and looked to new horizons. Rather than promote mere messages of understanding and friendship, the group focused its work on how to ensure that the progress made at the time could not only be sustained, but could also be enhanced by encouraging the two governments to take bolder and more concrete measures to improve bilateral relations. It was truly a remarkable effort, and it is one that I feel very fortunate to have been involved with. For anyone wishing to learn more about the history and work of the Forum, an account of its activities has been written by Soli Özel. A reference for this can be found in the bibliography of this volume.

Lastly, while this work is essentially a positive story of how two long time adversaries pursued peace and reconciliation, it is also tinged with sadness. On 24 January 2007, İsmail Cem, one of the protagonists in the process, died following a battle with cancer. Having managed Turkey's external relations under three administrations, holding the portfolio from 1997 until 2002, he was one of the longest serving foreign ministers in the history of the Republic. He was also regarded as one of its most successful. However, almost every tribute and obituary viewed his efforts to improve relations with Greece as his greatest achievement and his lasting legacy. In one of the most poignant moments at his state funeral, George Papandreou, the other key figure in the process, and who was by now the leader of the opposition in Greece, laid an olive branch from a tree they had planted together in Athens to mark the rapprochement between the two countries.

James Ker-Lindsay
Kingston-upon-Thames

INTRODUCTION

On 15 February 1999, Abdullah Öcalan, the leader of the Kurdish Workers Party (PKK), was captured in a daring raid conducted by a team of Turkish commandos and intelligence officers. As Turkey's most wanted man, held responsible for the bitter fifteen year civil war in the country's south eastern provinces that had left over 30,000 dead, and reviled as the mastermind behind numerous terrorist attacks, his arrest was greeted with jubilation.[1]

However, there was also a public outcry when it emerged that he had been captured as he left the Greek Embassy compound in Nairobi, Kenya. In Turkey this was seen as definitive proof that Greece had been aiding and abetting the PKK – an accusation that successive Turkish Government had made against Athens. Nevertheless, few could quite believe that the Greek Government would be willing to provide shelter and support to Öcalan. Many saw it as an act of outright hostility and aggression and calls soon emerged for the Turkish Government to respond, with force if necessary. Even the resignations of three senior Greek ministers shortly afterwards did little to stem the tide of anger and many felt that an armed confrontation might indeed develop between the two countries.[2] Although this did not happen, in the days and weeks that followed the arrest, relations between the Aegean neighbours sank to their lowest level since the summer of 1974, when the two countries had come to the brink of war over Cyprus.

By the end of the year, however, the picture could not have been more different. An improbable series of events that included a regional conflict, two major disasters and the death of a senior Greek politician had led to a complete transformation in the relations between the two countries. Instead of proclaiming their historical enmity, people on both sides of the Aegean were now declaring their fraternal solidarity with one another. At the same time, the two governments had initiated a process of dialogue that aimed to foster a new spirit of co-operation and promote mutual co-operation on a range of issues. But perhaps the most significant change to have taken place was the decision taken by Greece that December to overturn its long-standing objection to Turkish candidacy for membership of the European Union. In the eyes of many this represented the clearest indication possible that the strained relations between the two countries had turned a corner. While the outstanding issues between the Aegean neighbours would still need to be solved – a task easier said than done – it nevertheless appeared as if a new era in relations had begun that had the potential to transform the situation in the wider Eastern Mediterranean region.[3]

This work is an account of how this transformation occurred. It is the story of how two countries started down a path to peace after decades of tension and hostility and how, over the course of that monumental year, relations between Greece and Turkey went from the brink of conflict to an unprecedented outpouring of friendship and solidarity. But behind the account of events the work also sheds light on why the process took place. As will be shown, rapprochement was in large part the result of new thinking driven by wider imperatives. For the principal figures behind this process, George Papandreou and İsmail Cem, the foreign ministers of Greece and Turkey respectively, as well as for the number of people around them who acted as the architects of rapprochement, the arguments in favour of the détente were clear. Most importantly, an improvement in relations would lead to a reduction in tension and mistrust, which would in turn reduce the likelihood of conflict. On several occasions over the previous two decades the two countries had teetered on the verge of armed confrontation through lack of communication. By opening a channel of dialogue between Athens and Ankara, the belief was that the chance of crises erupting in the future would be significantly reduced.

However, the process had a far bigger aim. The hope was that in time the process might offer up an opportunity to resolve the various differences that exist between the two countries, most notably the Aegean disputes.[4] By generating greater mutual confidence by tackling issues that were not contested, the architects of the process hoped that an atmosphere would be created that would facilitate efforts to settle the main problems that existed. Meanwhile, better relations between Greece and Turkey might open the way for movement towards a comprehensive settlement on the island of Cyprus.

But rapprochement was not only about trying to reduce tensions and find ways of solving the long-standing issues of difference. It was also about confronting new challenges. While the two states had spent decades locked in disputes centred on traditional notions of sovereignty and the regional balance of power, the world had moved on around them. The end of the Cold War, as well as the wars that raged across the Balkans in the 1990s, had created a complex range of new threats across Southeast Europe. Terrorism, organised crime and illegal immigration represented the regional security challenges of the new era. Rather than pit Athens and Ankara against each other, and therefore exacerbate the existing tensions, these new threats and problems represented a challenge to both countries. In this regard they served to emphasise the need for mutual co-operation. As one analyst put it, 'it became clear that one's own security depended on the security of the other.'[5] Similarly, there was an appreciation of the need for joint action to confront other important issues, such as environmental concerns.

And yet rapprochement was not just about confronting problems, of either the traditional or new varieties. It was also about generating opportunities for economic development, such as increasing trade and promoting joint tourist ventures in the Aegean. All the while, the process of European integration was increasingly challenging traditional notions of identity and proving that the old patterns of confrontation between countries – most notably the long standing conflict between France and Germany – could be transformed into a productive partnership. In this regard, the architects of rapprochement realised that co-operation was not just desirable, it was essential. Indeed, it was probably inevitable.

Similarly, the effects of the rapprochement would be felt far beyond the borders of Greece and Turkey. Any steps that the two countries could take to challenge some of the most pressing issues confronting Southeast Europe, such as stemming the tide of illegal immigration and drug smuggling, would necessarily have a wider impact across Europe as a whole. The emerging détente was therefore welcomed by the international community. However, it also marked a welcome opportunity to secure peace and stability in the Eastern Mediterranean. For almost fifty years, the tensions that existed between Greece and Turkey had been a major source of international concern. Indeed, throughout the Cold War, a war between two NATO partners posed a serious threat to the security of the West as a whole. Indeed, fearing that any major conflict between the two countries would be exploited by the Soviet Union, Washington spent most of the 1960s, when the East-West confrontation was at its height, trying to keep a lid on the growing tensions between the two countries, which were mainly driven at that time by the dispute over the island of Cyprus.[6] The most serious chance of conflict came in 1974 when Turkey invaded the island in response to a coup on the island ordered by the military junta in Athens, resulting in the *de facto* partition of the island. Thereafter, the threat of conflict in Cyprus subsided somewhat. Instead, Greece and Turkey came close to confrontation in the Aegean, most notably in 1987. Even in the post-Cold War era it has been argued that a conflict between Greece and Turkey, either in the Aegean or over Cyprus, could fundamentally destabilise NATO.[7]

But it was not just NATO that has had reason to be concerned about Greek-Turkish relations. The tensions that have existed between the Aegean neighbours have also affected the European Union. Following the decision to accept Greece as a member of the European Economic Community, in 1980, the question of relations between the two countries has been a wider European issue. Although many in Turkey argue that when Greece joined Europe Turkey was given an assurance that this would not affect their own hopes of joining, Athens soon made it clear that it hoped to use its membership as leverage over Ankara. This position was further strengthened in 1987, when Turkey formally applied to join the European Community.[8] Despite this, until 1995, the main tactic used by the Greek Government was to block a customs union between the EU and Turkey and prevent financial aid from being distributed to Turkey under the Fourth Additional Protocol. All this served to cause tension between Greece and its EU partners, who felt that Athens was obstructing the EU's relations with Turkey for its own national interests.[9]

These objections were eventually lifted following a decision by the EU to open formal membership talks with Cyprus. Thereafter, the point of contention became Turkey's efforts to join the Union. This came to the fore at the Luxembourg European Council in 1997, which led to another crisis in Greek-Turkish relations as well as a crisis in Turkish-EU relations.[10] Greece paid a high price for this approach. Every time it vetoed Turkey, it increased tensions between the two countries. Turkey, rather than relenting, would become ever more obstinate. At the same time, the number of airspace violations in the Aegean, each of which posed a danger of escalation, increased. By the late-1990s it was becoming clear that something had to be done. The question was how a peace process could be initiated. Turkey would not offer concession to Greece, nor would Greece offer concession to Turkey. Meanwhile, in the background, Cyprus's impending membership of the EU threatened to spark yet another, this time possibly disastrous, crisis between Athens and Ankara. The fact that something needed to be done was recognised by all parties – Greece, Turkey, the European Union, NATO and the United States. The question was how to start a process of dialogue.

Greek-Turkish conflicts

As is usually the case with international conflicts, the tensions between Greece and Turkey stem from a number of factors. First of all, there is the realm of bilateral relations. This is largely shaped by the differences that exist over the Aegean. For its part, Greece has asserted that the question of the continental shelf, which sparked major crises in 1976 and 1987, is the only issue of contention.[11] However, Ankara has argued that the range of issues in the Aegean is in fact greater and includes questions over territorial waters and airspace. At present Greece claims six nautical miles of territorial waters and ten nautical miles of airspace. However, it reserves the right, as laid down under the UN Convention of the Law of the Sea, to extend both to 12 nautical miles. In response, the Turkish Grand National Assembly has passed a resolution declaring that the Turkish Government may initiate hostilities in the event that any attempt is made by Greece to extend its territorial waters beyond the six miles currently in force.[12]

In order to press its claims, Turkish aircraft frequently mount incursions into claimed Greek airspace. Often these aircraft fly within the ten mile limit, but nevertheless remaining outside the six miles – the extent of territorial airspace recognised by Ankara. In addition, there are also disagreements over the militarization of a number of Greek islands that Turkey has argued should remain demilitarised.[13] Then there is the contentious issue of the Grey Zones. These are areas in the Aegean where the Turkish Government does not specifically lay territorial claim, but instead argues that Greek sovereignty is not automatic and is open to question. It was a dispute over one of these areas, the small islets of Imia, known as Kardak in Turkish, which sparked a major crisis between Greece and Turkey in early 1996 that almost led to armed conflict.[14]

While the issues relating to the Aegean have dominated bilateral relations, the situation has also been complicated by several other issues. For Greece, concerns centre on the Greek minority in Turkey and the position of the Patriarch of Constantinople – widely regarded as the leader of the World's 300 million Orthodox Christians.[15] Since the 1950s the number of Greeks living in Turkey has steadily dwindled and is now at an extremely low level, numbering no more than a couple of thousand. This has raised deep concerns about the future of the Patriarch, who, under the terms of the Treaty of Lausanne, must be a Turkish citizen. At the same time, the failure of the Turkish Government to reopen the seminary located on the island of Halki, which was closed in 1971, has also been a source of tension as any Greeks wishing to train for the priesthood are forced to go abroad. The whole issue has also been exacerbated by occasional attacks on the Patriarchate by Turkish nationalists. Many in Greece believe that the Turkish Government is not doing enough to provide protection. Indeed, some even argue that the moves are an attempt by the Turkish Government to intimidate the Patriarch. While this has not been proven, the Turkish Government nevertheless closely monitors the activity of the Patriarchate.[16]

For Turkey, attention has been focused on the Muslim minority in Western Thrace. As with the case of Greeks in Turkey, the Muslim community in Greece has also faced persecution and human rights abuses over the years.[17] Similarly, there have been questions raised about religious freedom as successive Greek governments sought to exercise control of religious appointments. However, these questions have tended to be rather secondary in recent years. On the one hand, this is due to Greece's willingness to see the question of the Patriarch dealt with by the Greek community in the United States, which comes under the spiritual authority of the Patriarch, and therefore has put considerable pressure on the US Congress and the successive administrations to act on this matter. As for Turkey, while concerns still exist about religious freedom, the conditions for the Muslim minority in Greece have steadily improved in recent years. This is in part due to increased public spending in the region and as a response to Greek membership of the European Union, which has also provided infrastructure funds but has also put in place safeguards to protect minorities and ensure greater respect for human rights. For these reasons, these issues might best be regarded as irritants that serve to exacerbate the negative climate, rather than as direct causes for tension.

Apart from the range of bilateral disputes, the relationship has also been fundamentally shaped and affected by the island of Cyprus.[18] Although the dispute is officially an issue to be solved between the Greek and Turkish Cypriot communities, the fact that both Greece and Turkey, along with the United Kingdom, are vested with the constitutional responsibility to guarantee the sovereignty, territorial integrity and independence of the Republic of Cyprus necessarily means that Athens and Ankara are inextricably involved with the Cyprus dispute. In reality, however, their respective involvement in the issue has been far deeper than this. Indeed, as a result of Turkey's decision to intervene in 1974, following a coup ordered by the military regime ruling Greece at the time, Turkey has been regarded as an integral part of the Cyprus issue. This has since been confirmed by the European Court of Human Rights (ECHR), most notably the Loizidou Case, which found that Turkey was in military occupation of the northern third of the island.[19]

In contrast, since 1974, Greece has been careful not to be seen as a protagonist defining and shaping Greek Cypriot policy, let alone take an initiative on Cyprus over the heads of the Greek Cypriots. As a result, there is a fundamental imbalance in the way that Greece and Turkey are involved in Cyprus. In fact, a more logical negotiation would therefore seem to be one between Nicosia and Ankara. Nevertheless, while the issue is not a matter to be discussed between the Greek and Turkish governments directly, it has long been argued by Greek policy makers that there could never be a full normalisation of relations between Greece and Turkey until such time as a settlement had been found to the Cyprus Issue.

In turn, over the years, the mistrust caused by these differences has led both countries to see the hidden hand of the other in a wide variety of problems that they face. The fact that there are a number of perceived differences, coupled with the fact that the level of mistrust is so great, has prompted many external observers to view the problem as being embedded in historical antipathy and, therefore, without hope of resolution. Such a view is misguided. Contrary to widely held views, relations between Greeks and Turks have not always been bad. There were times within living memory when the two countries lived peacefully side-by-side and approached the bilateral relations in a positive atmosphere free of concern over territorial differences and minority rights. However, it has always been a sad feature of relations that these periods of peace have never lasted. This has led some to argue that there has in fact been a cyclical nature to Greek-Turkish relations.[20] The question now being asked is whether this pattern can at last be broken? We will not know whether the events of 1999 truly marked a turning point for some time yet. However, as this work will show, it can certainly be argued that the basis for this process of rapprochement is firmer than ever before.

Wider issues for consideration

In addition to providing a detailed account of the events that took place over the course of 1999, and an analysis of the domestic factors that drove rapprochement in Greece and Turkey, there are also a number of important wider issues that this work will address. First, and perhaps most importantly, it will seek to assess the degree to which the European Union, either directly or indirectly, acted as a catalyst for the process of rapprochement. It has been argued that the process of EU enlargement presents a chance to transform and resolve long-standing and apparently intractable conflicts. One of the most powerful arguments in favour of this view has been the case of Cyprus. In advance of the island's accession in May 2004 there had been a significant debate about the degree to which the process leading to membership had created the conditions for yet another attempt at reunification.[21] On the one hand, there was a body of opinion that agreed with the European Union's position that accession would provide an impetus for a settlement.[22] Balanced against this view were those who took the view that the island's accession would hinder or complicate efforts to reach a solution,[23] or might even raise the possibility of conflict in the region.[24]

In the end, however, the view taken by the EU was broadly correct. In view of the fact that it had been Turkish and Turkish Cypriot intransigence that was generally seen to be the primary problem preventing a solution,[25] the island's accession process did provide the impetus for the peace process that took place from 2002 until 2004. The fact that this ultimately ended in failure following the decision of the Greek Cypriots to reject a UN peace plan (often referred to as the Annan Plan) for reunification, does not diminish the fact that the prospect of Cypriot accession to the EU encouraged Turkey to take an active stance in favour of a settlement, thereby vindicating those who took the view that EU accession would act as a catalyst for a settlement of the Cyprus Problem.

However, what has not been sufficiently recognised is the degree to which the events that took place in Cyprus were directly shaped by the developments that took place between Greece and Turkey in 1999.[26] There is an important argument to be made in favour of the view that, had it not been for Greece's decision to drop its longstanding veto on Turkish candidacy of the EU, Ankara would not have had an interest in seeing a resumption of talks. In fact, it could well be argued that had it not been for the prospect of membership of the European Union, the response to Cyprus's accession to the European Union may well have sparked a major crisis in the Eastern Mediterranean, as had been widely predicted. After all, on numerous occasions the Turkish Government stressed that any move to incorporate the island would result in serious consequences that may even have resulted in the annexation of the northern third of the island by Turkey. Had this happened the consequences may well have been dire. For a start, it may well have ended Turkey's accession hopes once and for all. In all likelihood it would also have led to perpetual tension in the region. Meanwhile, quite apart from the fact that this would have made solving the Aegean issues almost impossible, the lingering question of Cyprus would have prevented the full normalisation of relations between Athens and Ankara.

It is in the context of the catalytic effect that EU had on developments in Cyprus that the events recounted in this book take on an added and specific significance. Had it not been for the process of rapprochement, which resulted in the confirmation of Turkey's EU candidacy at the December 1999 Helsinki European Council, it is highly likely that the moves to resolve the Cyprus dispute would not have come about. However, can we take this logic one step further back? Could it also be argued that the European Union also provided the necessary conditions for the improvement in bilateral relations between Greece and Turkey that opened the way for the Cyprus peace talks? This work will also seek to identify the degree to which the prospect of Turkey's EU accession was also a catalyst for the process of rapprochement. Specifically, the question can be broken into two different parts. On the one hand, it seeks to assess the extent to which the dynamics of 1999 were shaped by Turkey's desire for membership of the European Union. This is perhaps the obvious question to ask. However, the position of the Greek Government must also be considered.

The events of 1999 appeared to mark a fundamental change in Greek thinking on the question of Turkish membership of the European Union. This is a second strand of the analysis that has not been scrutinised so closely. In fact, as will be seen, this is the far more pertinent question. In reviewing the events of that year, it becomes very clear that the main driving force behind the process of rapprochement was to be found in Athens. While the first steps were initiated by Ankara, it was the counter-response by the Greek Government, and the fundamental change in thinking that took place in Greece, that provided the impetus for the process. In large part, this explains the significant emphasis that this work gives to developments in Greece over those that took place in Turkey. As will be shown, the truly fascinating element of rapprochement was the degree to which the EU transformed the Greek-Turkish relationship by changing Greek, rather than Turkish, attitudes and positions. Naturally, this has profound, and rather positive, implications. Rather than providing leverage in their conflicts with states that are not members of the EU, European Union membership can actually serve to moderate and transform the behaviour of member states in ways that are rather unexpected.

Secondly, and related to the question of the dynamics of Greek and Turkish politics in the events that unfolded in 1999, the work will examine the role of the two main protagonists in the process, George Papandreou and Ismail Cem, the foreign ministers of Greece and Turkey respectively. They have been widely credited with responsibility for the rapprochement. Notwithstanding the points made above about the degree to which the process of rapprochement was driven by decisions taken by Greece, the work will also examine the different political contexts within which the two foreign ministers operated. In large part the degree to which Papandreou was able to respond to the opening presented by Cem was shaped by the particular political situation that existed. Similarly, there is a case to be constructed that the more limited response from Cem was a direct result of the difficult, and nationalist, environment that prevailed in Ankara. Indeed, as will be shown, there is a case to be constructed that Cem achieved far more than might have been expected given the competing pressures he faced, both from within his own party and from other external sources, such as the coalition partners and the military.

A final avenue of analysis in this work relates to the much vaunted process of 'disaster diplomacy', sometimes referred to as 'earthquake diplomacy', that emerged in the aftermath of the earthquake that struck the western Turkish city of Izmit, in the Marmara province, in August 1999. This process was further strengthened when a far smaller, but nevertheless deadly, tremor hit Athens the following month. Even though examples of assistance between the two countries in the aftermath of disaster had been recorded before, most notably following the Ionian earthquake in 1953, on this occasion there was an unprecedented outpouring of popular emotion in both countries. For several months after the disaster, the world watched as the people of Greece and Turkey came together to help one another and then tried to find ways to ensure that the new found spirit of reconciliation and friendship at a popular level flourished. This in turn encouraged political leaders on both sides of the Aegean to act with greater boldness than would otherwise have been the case. Indeed, it was the level of public engagement, coupled with the significant results that this brought on the political stage, which in many ways acted as a spur for the development of the study of 'disaster diplomacy' in international relations.

Even now, when a major incident strikes that it may lead to a breakthrough in political relations between conflicting states, the media still refers back to the case of Greece and Turkey in 1999. Recent examples of this included the earthquake that struck Iran in 2002, which led many to ask whether it could lead to a thawing of relations with the United States.[27] Similarly, when earthquakes struck northern India and Pakistan in 2001 and 2005, many observers felt that it might lead to results on the disputed region of Kashmir.[28] Despite the fact that neither of these cases resulted in the transformation in bilateral relations seen between Greece and Turkey, it is emblematic of the strength of the results achieved between Athens and Ankara that the concept of 'disaster diplomacy', and the belief that horrific natural disasters can produce beneficial political results, has now been established as an area of study in international politics. This work will analyse how and why the earthquakes shaped the process of rapprochement and provide insights into the lessons that can be learned from those events.

1

HISTORICAL BACKGROUND

The first problem that confronts anyone trying to write a history of Greek-Turkish relations is when to begin. As has been pointed out, the relationship can in some manner or another be traced back to the first major interactions between the Byzantines and the Seljuks in the eleventh century or to the conquest of Constantinople by the Ottomans in 1453.[1] But while it is certainly tempting to view contemporary Greek-Turkish relations as just the latest chapter in a long history of antagonism, looking so far into the past is fraught with problems. Specifically, there is a danger that one will simply cement the widespread view that the modern differences between the two countries are just the most recent developments in a long-running ethnic conflict. This is problematic for a number of reasons.

For start, until relatively recently the term 'Greek' and 'Turk' had little real meaning to ordinary people in the lands that now make up Greece and Turkey. As has been stated, 'Greekness and Turkishness were fluid and imprecise concepts, with no specific legal or political implications, which were applied to a fluid and imprecise reality.'[2] For the 'Greeks' of the multinational Byzantine Empire the term 'Hellene' signified the ancient, pagan Greeks. It had no meaning to ordinary citizens of Byzantium, who saw themselves as 'Romans' until the very last stages of the Empire.[3] Similarly, no unifying notion of 'Turkishness' emerged until the formation of the Turkish Republic in the twentieth century. Prior to that, 'Turks' represented just one particular element of the diverse Ottoman Empire. But looking beyond these points, it should also be recognised that ascribing an inherently ethnic dimension to a conflict that can also be so readily steeped in history risks creating the impression that conflict in the contemporary era is somehow natural, if not inevitable. Such a view also encourages observers to believe that the 'Greek-Turkish conflict' is intrinsically beyond resolution.[4]

However, balanced against the need to treat history with caution, one cannot simply ignore the past altogether. In spite of the shortcomings and dangers associated with reading a modern conception of ethnicity into the past, the Byzantine and Ottoman periods cannot be entirely discounted as a reference point. Correctly or not, history has played an important part in shaping the mindset of those who shaped the modern relationship between Greece and Turkey. As one leading Greek academic put it, 'tension between Greece and Turkey is implicit in their perceptions of one another. Most Greeks identify Turkey with an Ottoman legacy that they have learned to reject, while those in Turkey who believe in its European orientation are confronted with a stumbling block placed in their path by a former subject of their fallen empire.'[5]

In this sense, the perception of a historical legacy is in many ways just as important as the reality in the terms of its ultimate consequences. As two long-standing observers of the politics of Greece and Turkey have explained about the difficulty of improving relations, 'the mutual suspicion is so deeply rooted in 1,000 years of common history that overcoming differences will require a big shift in mentality on both sides.'[6] Regardless of whether people 500, let alone 1000, years ago would have understood their interaction in the way that Greeks and Turks do today, the fact remains that lingering perceptions of a deep historical ethnic antipathy has had a powerful effect on the contemporary perceptions both nations have towards each other.[7]

Ottoman decline and the growth of the Greek Kingdom

The modern relationship can be traced back to the start of the nineteenth century. On 25 March 1821, an uprising began in the Peloponnesus that aimed to end four hundred years of Ottoman rule over Greece. Bringing together an unlikely combination of church leaders, European-educated nationalists and brigands, the rebellion soon gathered support in parts of the Aegean, as well as in Cyprus. However, it was not universally acclaimed. Many of the Greek merchants and Church leaders in Constantinople viewed it with concern, fearful that it could jeopardise their comfortable existence in the Ottoman hierarchy. Elsewhere, many Greeks decided to remain neutral, fearful of the reprisals that would follow if the uprising was defeated. By 1827 their caution appeared to have been well placed. With the support of Egyptian forces, the revolt appeared to have been all but crushed.[8] However, the uprising was saved when France, Britain and Russia rallied to the Greek cause. Five years later, in July 1832, the Ottoman Sultan was forced to recognise the Kingdom of Greece as a sovereign and independent state.

Although economically weak, the new kingdom had major aspirations. By the 1850s, Greek politicians were actively seeking to unite all Greeks in one country, a policy known as the *Megali Idea*. A period of territorial growth soon followed. In the 1860s Greece gained the Ionian Islands from Britain. In the early 1880s, the Ottoman Empire gave up Thessaly and parts of Southern Epirus. Crete, which had gained its independence from the Ottoman Empire in 1898, joined in 1908. But the Kingdom's largest expansion came during the Balkan Wars of 1912–13. Allied with Bulgaria, Montenegro and Serbia, Greece conquered vast swathes of territory in Macedonia and Thrace, including the city of Thessalonica, from the increasingly weak Ottoman Empire. But while the new lands marked an important step forward to realising the national goal of unifying all Greeks under a single flag, the Kingdom's main ambitions lay elsewhere. Attention now turned to the Greeks living in Asia Minor and to the greatest prize of all: Constantinople.

Capitalising on the weakness of the Ottoman Empire following its defeat in the First World War, and having received a green light at the 1919 Paris peace conference, Prime Minister Eleftherios Venizelos ordered Greek forces to invade Asia Minor. On 15 May 1919, the first troops landed in the Aegean coastal town of Smyrna.[9] From there, the Greek Army pushed outwards along the Aegean coastline and then inland. At first they met very little resistance and by 1920 they had occupied large parts of south west Anatolia. They also occupied Thrace. Indeed, it was only as a result of pressure from Britain, France and Italy that refrained from trying to occupy Constantinople.[10]

However, Greek fortunes soon began to wane. By late-1921 the tide had begun to turn. Turkish nationalist forces led by General Mustafa Kemal, one of the Ottoman Empire's finest military commanders during the First World War, started to beat back the Greek forces. Overstretched and badly led, the Greek army was eventually defeated in September 1922. A formal armistice was signed the following month, on 11 October.

On 20 November a peace conference began in the Swiss town of Lausanne. By now, Greek hopes of reclaiming Asia Minor and Constantinople had vanished entirely. Instead, attention was focused on the best way to avoid future conflict. To this end, the Greek and Turkish delegations reached a monumental decision. They decided to institute a compulsory population exchange. Almost every Christian would be required to leave Asia Minor and almost all Muslims would have to leave Greece. Certain key exemptions would, however, be made. The large number of Moslems living in Thrace would be allowed to remain in Greece. Similarly, the Greeks living in Istanbul and on the islands of Imvros and Tenedos would also be allowed to stay put. This arrangement was confirmed in the Treaty of Lausanne, signed on 24 July 1923. The agreement also laid the foundations for the Republic of Turkey, which formally came into being three months later, on 29 October. Meanwhile, over the course of that year almost one and half million Greeks and Turks were uprooted and forced to settle in their 'home' countries.[11]

Greek-Turkish friendship, 1923–55

Despite the legacy of the past, relations soon began to warn between Greece and Turkey. But it was not a smooth process. For example, General Pangalos, during his brief rule in 1925, made several threats against Turkey.[12] In 1928, Venizelos returned to power and was determined to build a new relationship between the two countries. Although Lausanne had addressed almost all the major issues of contention, tensions remained over the question of compensation payable to refugees for immovable property left behind at the time of the population exchanges. This needed to be addressed and by 1930 relations had improved enough as to allow Venizelos to visit Turkey to discuss the issue directly with Kemal, who was now president of Turkey.

Following negotiations, the two countries concluded the Ankara Convention. Although the agreement failed to meet the main demands of the refugees for full compensation, it was nevertheless an important step forward. At the same time, the meeting allowed the two leaders to discuss a range of other matters. One of the more radical ideas to emerge during their talks was a tentative suggestion by Venizelos that some form of political union could be established between the two countries. In the end, however, the two leaders settled on signing a more modest, though still highly important, treaty of friendship. This agreement, which many felt could only have been concluded by Venizelos and Kemal,[13] was widely regarded as marking a new beginning in relations between the two countries.[14]

In the years that followed the relationship was cemented by further agreements. In 1934, the two countries, along with Romania and Yugoslavia, signed the Balkan Entente. This sought to provide mutual security and ensure the inviolability of regional borders. Two years later, in 1936, Athens and Ankara signed the Montreux Convention.[15] This modified the Treaty of Lausanne to give Turkey full sovereignty over the Bosporus and the Dardanelles. At the same time, and as a side consequence, Greece was permitted to refortify some of the islands in the Aegean that had been demilitarised as a part of the Treaty of Lausanne. This removed the final issue of contention between Greece and Turkey and two years later another treaty of friendship was signed by the two countries.[16]

In 1940, Greece was invaded, first by Italy and then by Nazi Germany. Despite the agreements in place, Turkey chose to remain neutral.[17] Although the Greek Government felt that Turkey should have intervened, Ankara nevertheless assisted Greece in several important ways. For example, it aided Greek resistance fighters to make their way out of Greece to join the Greek Government in exile in Egypt. It also supplied food aid to the Greek populations during the famines of 1941–42.[18] Both these efforts were welcomed by the Greek Government, which had by this stage realised that it was far more important to the Allied war effort for Turkey to remain neutral than for it to be invaded and occupied,[19] or ruled by a government sympathetic to Nazi Germany.

More serious tensions arose, however, over the introduction of a capital tax by the Turkish Government. Although designed to prevent profiteering from wartime shortages, the new levy particularly affected the minority communities. It is estimated that 55 per cent of the tax was eventually paid by Greeks and Armenians, who were charged a rate up to ten times higher than the levy placed on Muslim citizens. Those who could not pay were forced to sell their businesses or sentenced to hard labour. This severely dented the confidence of the minorities in the Turkish state.[20]

These issues were, however, quickly forgotten at the end of the war. As a result, the transfer of the Dodecanese islands from Italian to Greek sovereignty, under the terms of the 1947 Treaty of Paris, was completed with no opposition from Turkey. Meanwhile, relations between the two countries were strengthened by when they were both drawn into the western fold with the start of the Cold War. In 1950, both governments sent troops to fight in Korea as part of the United Nations Force. And two years later, in 1952, they were accepted as members of the North Atlantic Treaty Organisation (NATO).

In 1954, the two countries signed the Balkan Pact alongside the Yugoslav Government of Marshal Tito, which had broken away from Soviet influence in 1949. By now thirty years had passed since the Treaty of Lausanne and it appeared as if Athens and Ankara had formed a solid and enduring friendship. This was seemingly underpinned by their commitment to mutual defence agreements and by their integration within the wider western political sphere. However, in 1955, the two countries found themselves drawn into a situation that would eventually destroy the good relationship that had developed and would come to dominate their foreign policies for the rest of the century.

Cyprus in Greek-Turkish relations, 1955–74

In 1878 Britain took administrative control of the Eastern Mediterranean island of Cyprus from the Ottoman Empire. Almost immediately, the Greek Cypriot community, which represented four-fifths of the total population, began to demand union with Greece (*enosis*). These calls continued even as Britain cemented its rule over the island, first by annexing Cyprus in 1914 and then by declaring it a crown colony in 1925. In 1950 the Orthodox Church organised a referendum on the issue, which purported to show that 96 per cent of those who had taken part wanted Cyprus to become a formal part of the Greek state. But Britain flatly refused to discuss the issue, either with the Greek Cypriot political leaders or with the Greek Government.

On 1 April 1955, a series of bomb explosions marked the start of a campaign to end colonial rule and unite Cyprus and Greece. Despite efforts to allay their concerns, EOKA, the Greek Cypriot body organising the uprising, quickly came to be seen as a threat by the Turkish Cypriot community, representing 18 per cent of the population. By autumn fears were growing about the possibility of a civil war on the island. In response, Britain convened a conference with representatives of the Greek and Turkish Governments to discuss security issues in the eastern Mediterranean. However, the Greek Cypriot leader, Archbishop Makarios, refused to attend on the grounds that the meeting was attempting to reawaken a Turkish interest in the island that had been dormant since the signing of the Treaty of Lausanne just over thirty rears earlier. Against this backdrop, the conference 'fell apart in disarray'.[21] This led to major anti-Greek riots in Istanbul, on 6–7 September, instigated by the Turkish Government. In response, many tens of thousands of Greeks left Turkey.[22] The first major tensions between Athens and Ankara since 1923 had just emerged.

Over the next few years a number of efforts were made to try to resolve the fighting on the island and find an acceptable political formula that would satisfy both communities. However, all attempts to reach an agreement failed. While Britain was prepared to consider options for a high degree of self-rule under continued British sovereignty, the Greek Cypriots would accept nothing less than *enosis*. Meanwhile, the Turkish Cypriots had begun to agitate for the partition of the island between Greece and Turkey (*taksim*). All the while, the situation on the island continued to become more unstable. This naturally led to increased tensions between Greece and Turkey, which were supporting their respective national communities.

By late 1958, Britain had all but given up efforts to try to find a settlement. It had also come to terms with the fact that it would not be able to maintain its rule over the island. Greece and Turkey decided to take matters into their own hands and reach an acceptable solution. Rather than haggle over *enosis* or *taksim*, they instead decided that Cyprus would become an independent sovereign state. In February 1959 all the sides met in London to thrash out a final agreement. Their answer was to put in place a complex constitutional structure that would balance power between the two communities. At the same time, under a set of associated treaties, Britain, Greece and Turkey were vested with responsibility for guaranteeing the sovereignty, independence and territorial integrity of the new state. On 16 August 1960, the Republic of Cyprus came into being.

Athens and Ankara now tried to normalise their relations once again, and a short lived period of détente emerged as both countries sought to put the tensions of the previous few years behind them.[23] However, the complicated constitutional arrangements in Cyprus soon started to unravel. In November 1963, and against the advice of Greece,[24] Makarios proposed thirteen constitutional amendments. These were almost immediately rejected by Turkey and, on 21 December, fighting erupted in the streets of Nicosia, the island's capital. Within days incidents were reported in other towns and Turkey began to mobilise its forces for a military intervention.

In an attempt to avert a major regional conflict, London proposed the creation of a peacekeeping force made up of contingents from Britain, Greece and Turkey. This was accepted by Athens and Ankara. At the same time, a peace conference was convened. However, this failed to bridge the differences between the two communities. As a result, tensions between Greece and Turkey continued to rise. This was exacerbated by the election of George Papandreou as Greek prime minister in February 1964. As a wholehearted supporter of the Greek Cypriot cause of *enosis*, Papandreou abandoned the caution of the caretaker administration and threw his full support behind Makarios. On 16 March, Prime Minister İnönü abrogated the Treaty of Friendship, signed by Venizelos and Atatürk in 1930, and started to expel many thousands of Greek citizens living in Istanbul. By the end of the year, an estimated 40,000 people had been deported, or had otherwise chosen to leave voluntarily with family members who had been forced out.[25] The Cyprus issue had finally brought about the end of three decades of good relations between Athens and Ankara.

Meanwhile, despite the fact that a UN peacekeeping force had been established, sporadic fighting was still taking place in Cyprus.[26] In August Turkey launched a series of air strikes against Greek Cypriot positions following an attack on a Turkish Cypriot enclave. In response, Greece insisted that the Turkish Government cease its attacks immediately or face the consequences. It was only through the timely intervention of the UN Secretary-General that a conflict between the two countries was avoided. The following year, 1965, the UN appointed Mediator, Galo Plaza, submitted his report on Cyprus. As well as opposing both *enosis* and *taksim* as solutions, the report was also critical of the 1960 agreements that formed the constitutional basis of the Republic. Turkey immediately rejected the report, condemning it as misrepresenting the situation on the island. Instead, Ankara proposed bilateral discussions with Athens. The offer was accepted by Greece and the two governments met under NATO auspices in June 1966. However, no agreement was reached.

In April 1967 the Greek military seized control of the government. Five months later, in September, the Greek and Turkish prime ministers held a series of discussions on either side of the border in Thrace. Although they agreed that Cyprus was harming relations, they could not agree on a solution to the problem. In fact, the meeting itself exacerbated tensions after a new proposal for *enosis*, put forward by the Greeks at the suggestion of the US, was rejected out of hand by the Turkish government. Soon afterwards there was yet another outbreak of fighting on the island. The Turkish army was mobilised once more and the Turkish Grand National Assembly authorised the government to go to war if the situation deteriorated any further.

However, a crisis was averted when the Greek Government agreed to withdraw many of its troops from the island. This marked the last major outbreak of fighting between the two communities for a number of years. Instead, tensions grew within the Greek Cypriot community. By this point, Makarios appeared to have abandoned *enosis* as a political goal and was instead focused on a solution within the framework on an independent Cypriot state. This option was rejected by a hard core of Greek nationalists on the island, who began to mount a violent campaign against his administration. The situation became increasingly tense in late 1973, following a coup within the Greek military administration that had brought harder-line elements into power.

On 15 July 1974 the Greek military ordered the overthrow of Makarios. In his place they installed Nicos Samson, a virulently anti-Turkish supporter of *enosis*. To most observers, unification appeared to be the next step.[27] At this point, Turkey tried to encourage Britain to participate in a joint intervention. But London refused. Therefore, on 20 July, the Turkish Prime Minister, Bülent Ecevit, ordered the armed forces to intervene unilaterally and within hours a full-scale invasion had started.[28] In response, the Greek government ordered a general mobilisation. It now appeared as if a full scale war was imminent. However, it soon became clear that despite of years of military rule the Greek armed forces were simply unprepared for combat.[29] In the face of this realisation, the military government collapsed.

On 24 July Constantine Karamanlis returned to Greece to take up the head of a new civilian government. A ceasefire was called and over the next few weeks a series of peace talks were held in Switzerland. However these eventually failed when Turkey issued an ultimatum to the Greek Cypriots to accept a federal settlement.[30] On 14 August, the second wave of the invasion began. Breaking free of the narrow land corridor that they had established in July, Turkish troops now spread out to the east and west. Within days Cyprus lay divided, with 36 per cent of the island under Turkish military control.

The policy of the Greek military government had been a disaster. As a result, Greece was now forced to take a back seat on Cyprus. No longer would Athens decide on a policy and expect Nicosia to follow. Henceforth, it would defer to the wishes of the Cypriot Government. Similarly, the days when Greece and Turkey could hammer out a settlement over Cyprus were over. The Greek Government now gave its full support to the UN process.[31] However, Cyprus also had a profound effect on Greek-Turkish relations.[32] Athens made it clear that there could be no normalisation of relations with Turkey until such time as the Cyprus issue had been solved.

The emergence of the Aegean disputes

Although the Cyprus issue had brought about the end of the good relations forged in the 1920s and 1930s, by the mid-1970s the first strains of a new set of bilateral differences were emerging. Although the Treaty of Lausanne had settled the borders between Greece and Turkey, at the time it was signed international law was still at a nascent stage. Over the course of the fifty years since then, a number of new developments had taken place that had opened up new areas of dispute between the two countries.

In 1958 the United Nations Conference on the Law of the Sea (UNCLOS) resulted on the Convention) of the Continental Shelf. This specified that a state could claim a continental shelf that covered the seabed adjacent to its coastline, including islands, to a depth of two hundred metres. Alternatively, a state could claim to a depth that could be feasibly exploited. These provisions were, however, deemed to relate to the continental shelf and did not affect the six-mile limit that had been set for territorial waters. Therefore, under the terms of the convention a state could claim a continental shelf that extended beyond the boundaries of its territorial waters and into international waters. With regard to disputes arising between states on the basis that the two respective continental shelves conflicted, the convention stated that the two states should try to work out an acceptable regime between themselves. If this were not possible the point of demarcation would be the meridian line between the two.

Greece signed up to the convention. But the Turkish Government, concerned about the implications of the agreements given the large number of Greek islands in the Aegean Sea, refused to agree. Instead, it argued that the Turkish continental shelf should be considered to be the seabed that constituted the natural prolongation of the Anatolian peninsula.[33] Under this definition, the Turkish continental shelf stretched westwards into the Aegean past a number of Greek islands. At first this difference did not pose a problem. Given the good relations between the two countries, the matter remained dormant. However, at the start of the 1970s, the Greek Government issued a number of licenses to petroleum companies to start exploring for oil reserves in the Aegean.[34] This was followed, in early 1973, by a report stating that there was reason to believe that there were significant mineral deposits in the Aegean. And later that year it was confirmed that oil had been found in the northern Aegean Sea, close to the

Greek island of Thasos. Suddenly the Aegean had become a source of potential tension between Greece and Turkey.

This was confirmed on 1 November 1973, when Ankara published a map showing the limits of the Turkish continental shelf extending beyond the eastern Greek island in the Aegean and announced that the Turkish State Petroleum Company (TPAO) had also been granted a licence to explore for minerals in the Aegean.[35] At the same time the Gazette of the Turkish Government published a map in which it showed the delineating line of the Turkish continental shelf to the west of a number of Greek islands lying in the eastern Aegean. The Greek Government officially protested and asked for talks. Three months later, in February 1974, the Turkish Government agreed to open negotiations. However, within days, it announced that it would start explorative operations on what it regarded as its continental shelf. Soon afterwards, a seismological survey ship entered the international waters of the Aegean accompanied by thirty-two warships of the Turkish Navy. Despite the strong protests from Athens, the ship spent six days exploring before returning to port. The following month, Turkey issued further licences, this time in the region close to the Dodecanese. Again Greece protested. However, at this stage the events in Cyprus took centre stage.

At the start of the next year, a new effort was made to try to address the areas of bilateral difference. On 27 January 1975, Prime Minister Karamanlis proposed that the two countries take the question of the continental shelf to the International Court of Justice at The Hague. Turkey at first responded positively to this idea. However, on 16 April, the new Turkish Prime Minister, Süleyman Demirel, announced that Turkey would prefer to deal with the matter through direct bilateral negotiations rather than have the matter adjudicated upon by the ICJ.[36] As a result, the two governments entered into talks, all of which proved fruitless. This failure led Ankara to announce, in February 1976, that it was permitting another survey ship to explore for oil near to the Greek island of Thasos.

Just a few weeks later the ship set sail. However, it remained in a region that was clearly Turkish territorial waters. This therefore did not cause any tensions with Greece. Nevertheless, realising the danger of a conflict posed by such activities, Prime Minister Karamanlis proposed that Greece and Turkey conclude a non-aggression pact. The hope was that this would prevent an escalation of hostilities in the event that a difference of opinion arose. However, the Turkish Government turned the idea down.

Over the next few months, Greece continued to watch warily as the ship appeared to edge closer to Greek territory. Eventually, on 6 August, the ship finally entered an area claimed by Greece. Despite being seen as a highly provocative step, Athens nevertheless refrained from taking any retaliatory action and for three days the ship continued to survey the area unmolested. After several days of watching the vessel, Athens decided to act. On 10 August Greece formally brought the matter before the United Nations Security Council under the terms of Article 35 of the UN Charter, which governed threats to international peace and security. In the ensuing debate Greece and Turkey levelled accusations and counter-accusations against one another. In response, the Council avoided placing blame on either party. Instead it passed a resolution calling on the two countries to reduce tensions in the region and adopt a framework for further discussions. It also called upon them to consider taking their case before the International Court of Justice.[37]

In fact, Greece had put two separate applications before the ICJ on the same day as they took the matter to the Security Council. The first application asked the Court to rule on the issue of sovereignty over the continental shelf. The second application appealed to the Court to issue an injunction against Turkey, to prevent it from continuing with its exploratory activities. On the second question, the ICJ delivered a swift judgement. On 10 September, it ruled that it could not issue an injunction on Turkey because the purely exploratory nature of the Turkish ship did not in itself prejudice any Greek claim to the shelf.[38] This decision effectively forced Greece to come up with some means by which to prevent tensions in the event of further Turkish activity in the area. After a series of meetings in Berne, a declaration was signed between the two countries that, among a number of other provisions, prohibited the two countries from using military force or aggression in the respective dealing over the Aegean.[39] This document now allowed the two parties to resume their discussions over the issue with one another free from the concern that a major conflict could arise.

In January 1978, the Greek leader met with Prime Minister Ecevit at Montreux to discuss a range of issues that were dividing the two countries, including both the Aegean question and the Cyprus issue. For the first time since the Aegean dispute first came to the fore in 1973, and was followed by the Cyprus crisis the following year, tensions between the two countries seemed to be easing. To many observers the meeting of the two Prime Ministers was seen as the first step towards normalising relations and resolving the disputes that had arisen between the two governments over the previous five years. Indeed, despite the fact that there were no agreements reached, the Greek Government felt that the talks had nonetheless managed to reduce tensions between the two countries. Similarly, the talks were welcomed by NATO.[40] However, the benefits achieved in Montreux were soon overshadowed by other events. In particular, the lifting of the US arms embargo against Turkey, which had been instituted in the aftermath of the Turkish action against Cyprus in 1974, proved to be a real source of concern for Athens, which now felt that

Ankara would re-arm and thus return to making claims in the basis of military threats.

Meanwhile, on 19 December 1978, the ICJ finally returned its judgement on the application made by Greece two years earlier for a ruling on the sovereignty of the continental shelf. In a blow to the hopes of the Greek Government the Court ruled that it was not able to produce a result as the matter had not, despite Greek assertions to the contrary, been brought before it by all parties concerned. Under these circumstances, the ICJ ruled that it did not have the competence to decide the matter.[41] As a result of this ruling, the two countries once again entered into discussions.

However, the resumption of talks met with severe criticism from the opposition parties. In particular the Pan Hellenic Socialist Party (PASOK) of Andreas Papandreou regularly challenged the extent to which Greece was giving up its rights under the terms of the 1958 Geneva Convention by engaging in the talks. This opposition to the talks was further bolstered in May 1981 when the Prinos oil field off the island of Thasos began production of crude oil. Although it was of low quality the 28,000 barrels produced each day was a significant contribution to the Greek economy as it met 10 per cent of the state's oil requirements, which in turn added a greater importance to future discussions over the continental shelf.

A return to tensions

In 1981 the pattern of slow rapprochement that had been developing since the Berne Declaration changed dramatically. The first major development, which would shape the long-term pattern of relations between the two countries, was Greece's accession to the European Economic Community. This decision, which was shaped by a desire in Western Europe to consolidate Greece's return to democracy, would fundamentally affect the relationship between the two states in the years ahead as it would now become Greece's main source of leverage against Turkey. Meanwhile, on 18 October, Papandreou's PASOK won the Greek general elections, thereby replacing the New Democracy administration which had ruled Greece since the return to civilian control seven years earlier. PASOK's victory was greeted with trepidation. During his period in opposition, Papandreou had taken a hard line towards Turkey and had often challenged the efficacy of talks with the Turkish Government. In his view, Ankara was simply using the talks to engage in expansionist activity and that Greece had made a mistake by even acknowledging any issues other than the continental shelf.[42]

Once in power, Papandreou stressed that Greece would make it clear, 'both to our neighbours and to the Atlantic Alliance that our land, sea and air borders are not negotiable – they are safeguarded by international treaties as well as by international practice.'[43] Emphasising that the Greek sovereignty over the continental shelf had been defined by relevant international conventions, and that he could not talk with Turkey while it was in occupation of Cyprus and failed to recognise Greek rights in the Aegean,[44] Papandreou called a halt to the discussions that had been established by his predecessor and ordered a resumption of exploratory activity around Thasos.

In response, the military led government of Prime Minister Ulusu stated that if Greece was not prepared to abide by the decisions taken in Berne then it would not either. Tensions between the two countries began to escalate once more. However, by July 1982, Papandreou appeared to realise the dangers inherent in his policy. He therefore called a halt to further exploration, ordered all activity to stop and called for a general moratorium on all actions likely to create tensions between the two countries. A few days later, the Turkish Government responded by proposing new talks. The offer was accepted by Athens. In many ways this new dialogue process closely mirrored the talks that had come about as a result of the Berne Declaration. However, the discussions proved to be very short lived as in November that year Greece pulled out of the talks claiming that during a NATO exercise Turkish military aircraft had wilfully violated Greek airspace.

Although a meeting took place between the Greek and Turkish Foreign Ministers in Strasbourg, the following April, little was achieved other than a statement that the two countries would refrain from provocative actions and that they would renew their efforts at reconciliation. However, the Turkish Cypriot declaration of independence, in November 1983, which appeared to have taken Turkey by surprise,[45] nevertheless created new tensions between the two governments. The Turkish government recognised the new state, the Turkish Republic of Northern Cyprus (TRNC), despite a UN Security Council resolution declaring the move illegal.

Soon afterwards, however, Turkey returned to civilian rule. The new Prime Minister, Turgut Özal, quickly made clear his intention to seek a solution to the Greek-Turkish disputes. He also took the unilateral step of lifting the visa requirement for Greeks visiting Turkey.[46] Despite this, little of substance occurred either over the Aegean or with regard to Cyprus. In fact relations between the two countries continued to fluctuate between bad and dire. In particular, an incident on 8 March 1984, when five Turkish warships fired upon a Greek destroyer patrolling the Aegean showed once again how fragile the peace between the two countries truly was. As a result of the continued hostility between the two countries, and no doubt exacerbated by this incident, Papandreou shocked his western allies in December 1984 by announcing that under the terms of the new defence doctrine that had been adopted by the Greek Government, Turkey, and not the Warsaw Pact, would be regarded as Greece's main external threat.

In the view of the Turkish Government, this new doctrine was ill founded. Özal, holding true to his stated desire to improve relations between the two countries had made several overtures to the Greek Government. For example, in July 1984, the Turkish Prime Minister stated that Turkey did not covet one inch of Greek territory and offered to supply water and electricity to several Greek islands lying off the Turkish coast. The following March, he made another attempt to promote dialogue by stating his willingness to meet with his Greek counterpart 'anywhere, anytime' to discuss the issues of difference. The next year he went further still, calling for the two countries to sign an agreement of friendship, good neighbourliness, conciliation and cooperation.[47] Thereafter he gave the Patriarchate the long-awaited permission to start restoration work on a number of buildings,[48] and rescinded the 1964 decree limiting Greek property rights in Istanbul.[49]

However, despite his calls for improved relations, Özal was unwilling or unable to meet Greek demands that Turkey give up all its claims to the various parts of the Aegean. In view of this, Papandreou rejected Özal's overtures on the grounds of insincerity and refused all attempts to convene a face-to-face meeting. Meanwhile, relations were strained by the continued Turkish attempts to explore for oil in the Aegean and by the fact that the third UN Conference on the Law of the Sea (UNCLOS III) had opened the way for countries to declare twelve nautical miles of territorial waters. If Greece opted to do this after ratifying the treaty – it signed the Convention on 10 December 1982 – then the percentage of the Aegean in Greek hands would rise from 35 per cent to 65 per cent. On the other hand, Turkey's share would rise by just one percentage point, from nine percent to ten per cent.[50] In the eyes of the Turkish Government, the agreement would effectively turn the Aegean into a Greek lake.[51] This therefore created yet another source of antagonism in the relationship.

The 1987 Aegean Crisis

However, it was the ongoing question of oil exploration in the Aegean that was to be the cause of the next crisis in Greek-Turkish relations. On 6 March 1987, the Papandreou Government presented legislation before the Greek Parliament for the compulsory purchase of a majority stake in the predominantly Canadian owned and operated North Aegean Petroleum Company (NAPC). This private operation had been responsible for drilling in the Prinos oil field and was by now producing one million tonnes of crude oil annually.[52] The stated reasons for the nationalisation of the company was that its calls for oil exploration to be conducted outside of Greek territorial waters presented serious implications for relations with

Turkey and that any such decision must remain solely in the hands of the Greek Government.

In Turkey, however, the decision to purchase the NAPC was seen as proof that the Greek Government was about to start surveying areas under dispute. Stating that such moves would be contrary to the Berne Declaration, Ankara made it clear that it would adopt whatever means necessary to prevent Greek attempts to explore outside of its own waters. For its part, Athens claimed that following the termination of the talks in 1981, the Berne Declaration ceased to be valid and that Greece alone had the right to decide, 'when, where and how to conduct exploration on the Greek continental shelf.'[53]

Soon afterwards, the Greek Government authorised the, now state-owned, company to begin exploration in the in international waters off Thasos. Turkey, arguing that the absence of a delimitation treaty meant that the area being explored by Greece was also open to Turkish exploration, issued a licence, on 25 March 1987, to its own state petroleum company to begin work in international waters. Once again a survey ship was sent to begin seismological work, this time off the coasts of the Greek islands of Lemnos, Lesbos and Samothrace; all of which Greece regarded as being constituent parts of its own continental shelf. In response to Turkey's move, Athens called for the two countries to take the matter to the ICJ for adjudication. At the same time, Papandreou issued a stern warning to the Turkish Government that if the ship entered into any areas that Greece regarded as being either its territorial waters or part of its continental shelf, then it would take all 'necessary measures' to halt the ship's work.

Despite this threat it appeared that the Turkish Government was intent on sending the ship into the area. Papandreou once again repeated his warning. However, this time it was couched in far stronger language. The Greek Prime Minister now made it clear that he was prepared to use military force to prevent the ship's activities. In response, the Chief of the Turkish General Staff laid down the gauntlet and stated that if Greece attempted to prevent the vessel from carrying out its assigned operation then the Turkish armed forces would respond accordingly. By this stage it was clear that both countries were equally determined to carry out their threats against each other, even if this meant going to war. International attention was once again focused on the two countries, which now appeared to be once again on the brink of conflict.

Against the backdrop of growing tensions, the US Government and NATO acted to persuade the two countries to moderate their behaviour and back down. At the same time, the Prime Minister Özal tried his best to calm the situation down. In London recuperating from major heart surgery, the Turkish leader unwittingly found himself caught in a situation whereby his country looked set to fight a neighbour and ally. Taking matters into his own hands, Özal called journalists to his hotel room in order to clarify that the ship would not undertake any exploratory activity outside of Turkish territorial waters and that Turkey would not act against any Greek vessels unless directly provoked.[54] It was therefore with baited breath that the world watched the next morning, 28 March, as the ship left its homeport in Turkey to begin its exploratory mission, accompanied by a number of warships of the Turkish Navy. The first signs were positive. The supporting naval vessels were soon called back and the ship continued its work alone. More importantly, it stuck to Turkish waters. A few days later the two countries reached an agreement whereby Turkey agreed not to explore for oil in return for a Greek promise to halt exploration or drilling in disputed areas. Even though the agreement was subject to a Greek proviso that it maintained the right to restart such activities at any time of its choosing in the future, it nevertheless amounted to an acceptable face-saving mechanism for both countries. The crisis was at an end.

The Davos Process

The events had nevertheless proven to be a 'sobering experience' for both countries and underscored the need for regular and continuous dialogue and the creation of a number of confidence building measures to create a climate for resolving the differences.[55] Soon after the crisis the two Prime Ministers initiated a system of communication between themselves in the hope that further crises could be avoided early on. At the same time Papandreou announced that his government was attempting to find a formula by which the dispute over the continental shelf could be taken to the ICJ. Over the rest of the year contacts continued. Although this certainly produced a less hostile climate between the two countries, little of substance was achieved on the main issues of difference. However, in January the following year, 1988, Özal and Papandreou met with one another at the World Economic Forum in Davos, Switzerland.

Despite the fact that most observers expected little of substance from the meeting, the two prime ministers showed a genuine desire to try to engage in dialogue and find common ground over a range of issues affecting bilateral relations, not least of all over the continental shelf issue. Following two days of talks they announced their decision to form two committees. One would address bilateral differences, while the other would cover joint business and economic concerns. Cyprus would not feature at this stage. This was a major breakthrough. Ankara had long wanted to keep Cyprus off the bilateral agenda.[56] Meanwhile, Papandreou hoped that an improvement in Greek-Turkish relations would eventually lead Turkey to put pressure on the Turkish Cypriot leadership.[57] However, this benefit was balanced by the fact that the Greek Government made clear that it would only agree to discuss the continental shelf. This fell short of the wishes of the Turkish Government, which had hoped for a dialogue that would address the other problems that it perceived to exist, such as the question of the delimitation of Greek territorial waters and airspace. Despite this, the fact that the two countries had managed to construct a means by which to engage in direct dialogue was considered to be a significant achievement in itself.

Over the next year or so, the Davos spirit took hold in Greek-Turkish relations and there was a new stability between the two countries. In late-May, the two foreign ministers, Mesut Yılmaz and Karolos Papoulias, met and signed a Memorandum of Understanding. This agreement sought to put in place a number of basic guidelines regulating the way in which they would approach their respective differences. In September, Yılmaz and Papoulias met once again to sign an agreement on a series of measures to prevent accidental conflicts and incidents in the high seas and airspace around their countries. Furthermore, Greece also lifted her objections to the reactivation of the Association Agreement between Turkey and the European Union, which had been put on hold following the Turkish military coup in 1980.[58] But the most symbolically step was Özal's official visit to Athens, the first such visit in forty six years.

Meanwhile, behind the scenes, Papandreou and Özal were searching for ways in which to address the main questions, and in spite of his comments that he would only talk about Cyprus and the continental shelf, Papandreou even discussed the other issues of contention. However, there were already signs of strain. In Greece the leader of the opposition New Democracy Party, Constantine Mitsotakis, accused the PASOK Government of neglecting the Cyprus issue.[59] However, while the Cypriot Government was certainly a little anxious about developments, it was also cautiously optimistic about the way in which things were progressing.[60] In Turkey, on the other hand, there was a view in a number of quarters that Papandreou was simply engaging in talks with Ankara in order to force concessions out of the Turkish Government on the issue of the continental shelf.[61]

Given the internal opposition to the talks from New Democracy, it came as little surprise when the talks were halted by Constantine Mitsotakis when he became prime minister following PASOK's defeat in the June 1989 general election. Rather than concentrate on trying to use the process as a means by which to address the continental shelf, Mitsotakis now reoriented Greek foreign policy in such a way as to make Cyprus the key issue of Greek-Turkish difference, stressing that no progress could be made on the wider issues without tackling Cyprus.[62] Despite this change in orientation, Mitsotakis sought to continue efforts to improve relations with Turkey. In February 1992, he met with Demirel in Davos. There the two leaders agreed to prepare a treaty of friendship and good neighbourliness. The aim would be for the finished agreement to be signed by the Greek prime minister during a trip to Ankara. Once more there was hope that the Davos spririt could be renewed. However, the idea fell through and no visit took place.[63]

Meanwhile, the following year Andreas Papandreou returned to power. But this produced little impetus for a meaningful change in bilateral relations. Özal had died earlier that year and Papandreou was in failing health. Matters were further complicated in November 1993 when the Greek Government concluded a joint defence pact with Cyprus that was designed to, 'coordinate military strategy, exercises and equipment'.[64] The agreement immediately led to increased tensions with Turkey, which announced that it would offer the same level of support to the Turkish Cypriots. This led to fears of an arms race in the Eastern Mediterranean.

All the while, the atmosphere was further poisoned by disagreements over Turkey's relations with the European Union. The relationship between Turkey and the EU stretched back thirty years to an association agreement signed in 1963. The agreement was seen by Turkish decision makers as the first step to full membership of the EU and in the years that followed a number of financial protocols were signed between the two sides. In 1987 Ankara submitted its application for full membership. Two years later, the Commission endorsed the application but deferred any moves to start talks, arguing that, 'it would not be useful to start progress talks with Turkey straight away'.[65] Nevertheless, a package of proposals put forward by the Commission to strengthen ties between the EU and Turkey. However, these were blocked by the Council. Similarly, Greece also refused to lift its veto over the Fourth Financial Protocol.[66]

All this led to considerable resentment in Turkey, where the general view was that Greece, contrary to a commitment it was supposed to have made with the EEC when in joined in 1981, was deliberately interfering in Turkish-EU relations in order to further its own agenda.[67] This was seen not just in terms of differences over the Aegean, but also in relation to Cyprus, which was pronounced eligible for EU membership at the Corfu European Council in June 1994. In December that year, relations between the EU and Turkey were further damaged when Greece blocked the final implementation of a customs union.

But the resulting compromise between Greece and the EU, announced on 6 March 1995, only served to make matters worse. In return for dropping its opposition to the customs union and the implementation of the Fourth Financial Protocol, Athens had secured a commitment from its EU partners that full membership talks would start with Cyprus six months after the completion of the Intergovernmental Conference (IGC), which was due to start in July 1996.[68] Finally, Cyprus had a clear way forward. Ankara, however, rejected the decision out of hand. Just hours after the announcement the Turkish Government warned that the decision to open the way for Cypriot membership could lead to the permanent division of the island. It also announced that any integration between the EU and the Greek Cypriots would be matched by Turkey and the TRNC.[69]

Meanwhile, tensions were increased even further when, on 21 July 1995, the Greek Parliament ratified the UN Convention on the Law of the Sea, which confirmed its right to extend its territorial waters to twelve nautical miles. In response, the Turkish Grand National Assembly passed a resolution granting the government the right to take all measures necessary, including military action, to counter any attempt by Greece to extend its territorial waters. This caused uproar in Greece, which argued that the declaration was contrary to the UN Charter and amounted to an illegal infringement of the country's sovereign rights under the Convention of the Law of the Sea.[70] Just a few months later, the two countries came to the brink of military confrontation in the Aegean for the third time since 1974. However, this time the crisis was sparked by an entirely new issue.

The Imia-Kardak Crisis

By the start of 1996, Papandreou's health had deteriorated so badly that he was forced to step down from office. On January 18 1996, Constantine Simitis, the modernising industry minister, took his place as premier. However, almost immediately after assuming office, Simitis was confronted with the most serious crisis in Greek-Turkish relations for almost a decade. The crisis was sparked by an incident that had taken place almost a month earlier. On 26 December 2005, the captain of a Turkish ship that had ran aground on one of two small uninhabited 12-acre islets in the eastern Aegean – known as Imia in Greek and Kardak in Turkish – refused help from the Greek authorities, arguing that the islets were in fact Turkish.[71] Although the ship was eventually released by Greek ships and towed to a Turkish port, the Turkish Foreign Ministry submitted a memorandum to the Greek Ambassador stating the islets were in fact Turkish sovereign territory.[72]

Wary of the implications of the message, the Greek Defence Ministry decided to increase naval patrols around the islet. Turkey then announced that it intended to map the Aegean islands and use its findings as the basis for further negotiation. At this point, the Greek Government considered the matter closed.[73] However, on 20 January, the incident was leaked to a Greek newspaper and soon afterwards the ship's captain repeated his claim during an interview on Greek television. In the days that followed several groups of Greek and Turkish journalists landed on the islet to plant their respective national flags.[74] In the end, the Greek Defence Ministry ordered a small contingent of soldiers to the rock.

On Monday 29 January the Turkish Government summoned the Greek Ambassador and presented him with a memorandum asserting Turkey's sovereignty over the islet and demanding that the Greek flag be removed and the troops recalled.[75] Soon afterwards, Tansu Çiller, the caretaker Turkish prime minister, announced that she had ordered two frigates of the Turkish Navy to patrol the waters around the islet and appeared to be readying Turkish forces for a full-scale confrontation with Greece.[76] Even if the move amounted to little more than a dangerous political stunt by Çiller to strengthen her position in the wake of inconclusive parliamentary elections the previous month,[77] the fact remained that this was the first time since 1923 that Turkey had laid claim on Greek territory in the Aegean.

In response, Simitis announced that he did not recognise the Turkish claim and that any attempt by Turkey to take Greek territory would be resisted. Meanwhile, other members of the government made it clear that they saw this as a Turkish ploy to open up a wider discussion on the Aegean issues but that Greece would not negotiate away its sovereignty. Across Greece, military forces were now put on full alert.

By 31 January a military confrontation appeared to be more and more likely. Both countries had sent a number of warships to the vicinity, with more on the way. At the same time the two air forces had engaged in a number of mock dogfights over the Aegean. On the political front Greece had produced a 1954 Turkish map that clearly indicated the islet of Imia to be outside of Turkish territorial waters. Nevertheless, Çiller remained adamant that the islet was Turkish and that the Greek flag should be taken down and Greek forces be withdrawn. By this point, there was growing international concern about the situation and appeals for calm were issued by the Secretaries-General of NATO and the UN.[78] However, the main diplomatic work was done by the United States. As well as calling on the two sides to withdraw their forces, senior members of the Administration, right up to President Clinton, called their counterparts to try to ease tensions and secure an agreement. None of it seemed to do any good.

At around one thirty in the morning three dinghies landed at the smaller of the two islets and a number of Turkish commandos went ashore. In Greece, the government convened the parliamentary Council on Foreign and Defence Affairs (Kysea) and mobilised the Greek war fleet. The United States now pulled out all the stops to avert a conflict. After frantic phone calls to the two governments, Richard Holbrooke, the US Assistant Secretary of State for European and Canadian Affairs, announced that the two sides had agreed to disengage.[79] Starting at six o'clock in the morning local time (0400 GMT) on 1 February, Greece would remove both its flag and troops from the islet. In return, Turkey would pull back from the immediate vicinity of the islet. The withdrawal took just a few hours and was supervised by the US.[80] The crisis was now at an end.[81]

Although it had ended peacefully, the incident had nevertheless raised yet another area of Greek-Turkish contention, the so-called 'grey zones' issue.

In essence, the Turkish government argued that the islets were not necessarily Turkish, but, equally, they could not be definitively referred to as being Greek. No matter what the reason for the incident, it had served to put the relationship between Greece and Turkey under the international spotlight once more. Meanwhile, in Greece, there was a deep sense of scepticism that good relations between Greece and Turkey could ever be achieved. As Theodore Pangalos, the Greek Foreign Minister, stated, 'friendly relations are impossible'.[82] In response to the crisis, Greece blocked the meeting of the Turkish-EU Association Council and also backtracked on its commitment to lift its veto of the Fourth Financial Protocol, which would otherwise have released 600 million euros of aid to the country.[83]

Prelude to rapprochement

Six months after the Imia-Kardak crisis, a new threat to stability emerged. This time the source of tension was Cyprus. That summer a large scale protest against the Turkish occupation was organised by a group of motorcyclists. Their aim was to push past UN peacekeepers and into the areas under Turkish Cypriot control. Once in the UN buffer zone, however, they clashed with Turkish Cypriot youths and members of the Grey Wolves, an extreme Turkish nationalist group that had come to the island in order to prevent the bikers from crossing the line. In the ensuing fight a young Greek Cypriot was beaten to death.

The next day, immediately after his funeral, another demonstration was held. This time several Greek Cypriots made it past the buffer zone and into the Turkish Cypriot controlled area. There one of the protesters was shot dead as he attempted to climb a flag pole and pull down a Turkish flag. There was now a real sense that any further demonstrations could lead to clashes as the Greek Cypriot National Guard stood at heightened alert. In an attempt to prevent more bloodshed, the Church agreed to bend its rules and bury the second victim after dark and thus prevent a further demonstration. At the same time political leaders appealed to the motorcyclists to stop any further protests. The pressure worked. No further demonstrations took place.

Just six months later another, and potentially more serious, crisis arose on the island. As a part of the joint defence agreement signed between Greece and Cyprus in 1993, the Greek Cypriots had decided to construct a new airbase near the western coastal town of Paphos. The aim was to enable Greek fighter aircraft to land in Cyprus to refuel and rearm. As a part of the defences for this base, the Cypriot Government announced on 4 January 1997 that it intended to purchase a sophisticated air defence system, the S-300 missile system, from Russia.[84] But the decision was only in part based on strategic priorities. In reality it was driven more by political than military factors. By this point Greek Cypriots were becoming increasingly frustrated at the intransigence of the Turkish Cypriot leader, Rauf Denktaş, who appeared to have little interest in pursuing reunification talks.[85] The hope was that the prospect of the missiles arriving on the island would encourage Turkey to push him back to the table. If nothing else, it might also force the international community to take a greater interest in the Cyprus issue.

On the first count, the move was a spectacular miscalculation. The Turkish Government quickly made it clear that it would not respond to such threats and that if the Greek Cypriots insisted on bringing the missiles to the island, it would reserve the right to take any necessary measures to deal with the problem. In the minds of most, Turkey would no hesitate to carry out a military strike against the missiles.[86] Naturally, if Turkey took action, Greece would in all likelihood be forced to respond. The possibility of a major Greek-Turkish conflict in the Eastern Mediterranean had once again become a distinct possibility. All this produced an unwelcome effect as regards the second aim. Instead of creating the impetus for a resumption of peace talks, as they had hoped, the Greek Cypriots had in fact forced the international community to devote its efforts to trying to defuse a potential crisis in the Eastern Mediterranean.

In was against this backdrop of growing tensions that President Demirel and Prime Minister Simitis met on the sidelines of a NATO meeting in Madrid on 8 July 1997. At the end of the meeting they announced that a joint declaration had been signed that enshrined six basic principles that would shape their bilateral relations in future: a mutual commitment to peace, security and the continuing development of good neighbourly relations; respect for each other's sovereignty; respect for the principles of international law and international agreements; respect for each other's legitimate, vital interests and concerns in the Aegean which are of great importance for their security and national sovereignty; a commitment to refrain from unilateral acts on the basis of mutual respect and willingness to avoid conflicts arising from misunderstanding; and a commitment to settle disputes by peaceful means based on mutual consent and without the use of force or threat of force. The initiative, which was praised by the US and by the EU, was heralded by many as a new start in Greek-Turkish relations.[87] It was seen to offer the chance for a step-by-step process of rapprochement.[88]

Similarly, hopes for a new opportunity for a settlement of the Cyprus problem grew with the announcement of meetings between the two Cypriot leaders in New York and Switzerland. However, once again, the optimism proved to be very short-lived. In response to an announcement that the EU hoped to open membership talks with Cyprus and five other states the following year, on 6 August Turkey announced that it had reached an agreement on closer integration between itself and the TRNC.[89]

Greece viewed this as a direct violation of the Madrid Declaration.[90] Meanwhile, in September a further crisis of confidence erupted when Pangalos stated that Greece would not negotiate with, 'murderers, rapists and thieves'.[91]

But the final blow to any hopes of détente came just a few months later, in December 1997. Following the entry into force of the customs union, Ankara had been hoping that the time had now come for it to be officially recognised as a candidate for EU membership. However, at the European Council, held in Luxembourg on 12–13 December, the EU stopped short of accepting Turkish candidacy on the grounds of its human rights record, its relations with Greece and its stance on the Cyprus issue.[92] Instead it simply reconfirmed Turkey's eligibility for membership.[93]

Ankara was furious at the result, which it largely blamed on Greece. The situation had been made even worse by the fact that the EU member states had also used the summit to confirm their commitment to Cypriot EU accession.[94] The Turkish Government therefore announced that it would now suspend political contacts with the European Union, and would no longer discuss Greek-Turkish relations, Cyprus or human rights.[95] In an attempt to assuage Turkish anger, the EU called another pan-European meeting in London in March 1998. However, Turkey refused to attend. Meanwhile, Greece was still insisting that it would not lift its veto over the Financial Protocol. At the same time, any hopes of a breakthrough on Cyprus had all but disappeared following the Luxembourg decision. Indeed, Denktaş was now insisting that he would henceforth only discuss a solution based on a confederation, rather than a federation, even though this was in contravention of the High Level Agreements signed in 1977 and 1979.[96]

As a result of these various developments, it now appeared as if all hopes of an improvement in Greek-Turkish relations had by now disappeared. Instead, international attention was now focused on limiting the damage in Turkish-EU relations and trying to prevent any further shocks or crises in the Eastern Mediterranean. In this regard, 1998 nevertheless ended on a positive note when the Greek Cypriots announced that they had reached an agreement with the Greek Government over the S-300 missiles. Rather than being brought to Cyprus, the missiles would instead be installed in Crete. Although the Cypriot Government tried to put a positive spin on the announcement, there was no escaping the fact that Nicosia had been forced into an embarrassing climb down over the issue. However, in Greece there was a clear sense of relief at the move. No one had been in much doubt that if the missiles had been installed there was a strong likelihood, if not a strong probability, that Turkey would have taken some form of military action. As the year ended there was a strong sense that a major crisis in Greek-Turkish relations had been averted. However, just weeks later, a new source of tension emerged between the two countries.

2

BILATERAL AND REGIONAL CRISES

The decision to station the S-300 missiles on Crete marked a welcome end to 1998. But as 1999 started Turkey's attention was already firmly focused elsewhere. For the past three months, the country had been transfixed by the hunt for Abdullah Öcalan, the leader of the Kurdish Worker's Party (PKK). Since 1984 Turkey had been fighting a difficult and bloody guerrilla war against separatist PKK fighters in the South East provinces of the country. The costs, both financial and in terms of lives, were severe. Over the previous fifteen years or so 30,000 people had lost their lives. Additionally, many thousands had been forced from their mountain villages and into the cities of the region. Many more had moved into slum dwellings on the outskirts of the country's other main conurbations. This had opened up a new front in the conflict, as terrorist attacks began to occur in Istanbul and other major towns. At the same time, the PKK started to attack tourist resorts, which not only damaged Turkey's foreign exchange earnings but also damaged its reputation internationally.

As a result of all of this, Öcalan had become Turkey's most despised, and most wanted, man. But what was particularly galling for Ankara that he was not living a shadowy existence in some mountain hideout in Turkey or northern Iraq. Instead, he was living openly in neighbouring Syria, which had established itself as the PKK's 'primary supporter'.[1] By late-1998 the Turkish Government had run out of patience and decided to act. In October, Turkey began to increase the number of troops close to the border in preparation for what was officially described as a major military exercise. In reality, many felt that Turkey was preparing for a full scale invasion of Syria. In the face of this threat, the Syrian Government was forced to reach an agreement with Ankara. On 20 October, the two countries signed an accord in Adana. Damascus agreed to recognise the PKK as a terrorist movement and expel Öcalan from its territory.

While Syria's capitulation was certainly welcome, and shut down a key element of support for the Kurdish organisation, Ankara was nevertheless determined to capture the PKK leader. It therefore decided to pursue him.

Soon a number of rumours began to emerge as to his new whereabouts. Some suggested that he had gone into hiding in the Bekaa Valley in Lebanon, where the PKK had once had training camps. Others suggested that he had gone to ground in the mountains that straddled Turkey and Iraq. But within days it was revealed that he had in fact taken refuge in Moscow. Immediately the Turkish Government began to put pressure on the Russian Government to hand him over. Within weeks Moscow had also decided that harbouring Öcalan was too costly, both politically and economically. Once again, Öcalan was forced to find a new shelter.

On 12 November the PKK leader arrived in Italy, where he was arrested and placed in jail. Turkey at once made a formal request for his extradition. But to Ankara's fury, the Italian authorities refused to hand him over. Instead, they agreed to consider his application for political asylum. Across Turkey there were mass demonstrations protesting the decision. Evidently aware of the potentially disastrous consequences for relations with Turkey if they were to provide sanctuary for the Kurdish leader, in January 1999 Rome rejected his claim for asylum and he was told he had to leave Italy. In the days that followed numerous rumours circulated as to his destination. However, after leaving Italy the trail appeared to go cold.[2]

In fact, Öcalan was now in Greek hands. Following Rome's decision to expel him, he had made contact with a retired Greek naval commander. With the support of a group of other nationalists, and acting with the assistance of some members in the Greek security services, they had managed to transport him from Italy to the Greek island of Corfu. Soon after his arrival the Greek Government became aware of his presence. Realising the danger this had created, around 3 February it had flown him to Kenya. There he was installed in the Greek Embassy compound without the knowledge or authorisation of the Kenyan Government. The Greek authorities hoped that they would be able to find an African country that would be prepared to take him in. However, it soon became obvious that finding him a new place of refuge would not be easy. After having witnessed how Turkey had reacted to Syria, Russia and Italy, few countries were prepared to take the risk of providing him with a safe refuge. Indeed, the first three countries Greece approached all turned the chance down. It was at this point that Öcalan decided to take matters into his own hands. He decided to leave the compound and conduct negotiations on his own.[3] What he could not know was that by this point Turkey had discovered his whereabouts. Planned under conditions of the utmost secrecy, with only ten officials included in the decision-making process, a team of Turkish intelligence officers and commandos were already on their way to Kenya to capture him as he left the Greek embassy.[4]

The consequences of Öcalan's arrest

On the morning of 15 February 1999, the world woke up to news that Abdullah Öcalan had finally been arrested. Within hours pictures were released showing the Kurdish leader bound and gagged on his way back to Turkey. Across most of Turkey, news of the arrest was greeted with jubilation. After almost twenty years on the run the country's most wanted man was now in custody and would soon be facing justice. Huge crowds soon took to the streets to celebrate the arrest. However, elsewhere in the country the scenes were very different. In the predominantly Kurdish south eastern provinces the news was met with anger and violence. Over the next few days 350 protestors were detained.

However, Kurdish protests were not just limited to Turkey. Across the world there were numerous demonstrations against the arrest of the Kurdish leader. Some of the most vocal protests took place in Europe. Ironically, it appeared as if anger was being directed as much towards Greece as towards Turkey. This was no doubt a result of widespread belief that Öcalan must have been betrayed by the Greek Government. Kurdish protestors therefore stormed and occupied a number of Greek embassies, including the one in London. However, their anger was also directed towards other targets. For example, the UN information centre in Vienna was overrun as well. Similarly, an attempt was made to occupy the Israeli consulate in Berlin, no doubt as a result of the widespread belief that Israel, which had excellent relations with the Turkish Government, must have played a part in Öcalan's capture.[5]

In Greece the news led to a major crisis. Prime Minister Costas Simitis suddenly found himself facing a number of problems. For a start, how could he explain the Kurdish leader's presence? While the government had not sanctioned his arrival, it was clear that he had received support from certain elements of the administration. This raised questions about his control over the government and highlighted concerns about the presence of extreme nationalists within the state.[6] Secondly, there were going to be questions at home as to how, once the Greek Government had decided to protect him, Öcalan had been allowed to fall into Turkish hands. While there may not have been an official policy in place to support the Kurds, the PKK nevertheless attracted a considerable following in many Greek public and political circles. After having managed to evade Turkey's reach in Syria, Russia and Italy, the fact that he was arrested after having been under Greek protection was a major source of embarrassment in its own right. Another extremely damaging aspect to the affair was the way in which the Greek embassies had been so easily stormed and was facing threats of further reprisals from Kurdish groups.[7] However, perhaps most significantly, it was clear that the incident would inevitably lead to a crisis with Turkey. In all senses, the incident had become Greece's, 'most humiliating postwar diplomatic fiasco'.[8]

Unsurprisingly, Simitis now came under intense pressure to resign. In an attempt to keep on to his job, the Greek prime minister instead dismissed a number of those most closely linked to the debacle. The first to go were Philipos Petsalnikos and Alekos Papadopoulos, the ministers for public order and justice. The next day, it was the turn of Charalambos Stavrakakis, the chief of the Greek Intelligence Service (EYP). However, the most significant departure was that of Theodore Pangalos, the foreign minister. Despite initial assurances from the government spokesman that he would not step down,[9] in the face of mounting pressure from within PASOK and from the opposition, Simitis was forced to demand his resignation.

In place of Pangalos, Simitis decided to elevate George Papandreou from his post as alternate foreign minister. In the eyes of many it was in some ways a risky choice. For a start, he was seen to be too soft, regarded by many as too 'ineffectual' a character for such an important post.[10] However, balanced against this, his appointment held several key advantages for the prime minister. Perhaps most importantly, Papandreou was known to be a fellow moderniser. In this regard, he was widely viewed as a close ally of the premier. And yet, significantly, as the son of the late Andreas Papandreou, he was simultaneously seen to be insulated against the more nationalist elements of the party. Secondly, he was also a moderate in terms of relations with Turkey and had a track record of trying to foster improved relations across the Aegean. For example, during his tenure as Education Minister, he had won the prestigious İpekçi Award – which is presented to those who make an important contribution to the improvement in Greek-Turkish relations – for his efforts to bring about a better climate between the two countries.[11]

At the same time, Papandreou would also be an undoubted asset on the wider international stage, especially with regard to relations with Europe and the United States. Educated in the US, Britain and Sweden, he also had a native command of English by virtue of his American mother. Moreover, unlike Pangalos who was known for his diplomatic outbursts, Papandreou's quiet manner was widely seen to be far more suitable at this stage. In any case, within days of taking up his appointment, Papandreou was already at work trying to smooth the waters. In addition to insisting that Greece had never provided support to PKK, he also stressed that the Greek Government had been acting on purely humanitarian grounds when it had agreed to shelter Öcalan.[12]

The Turkish Government was unmoved by such claims. It certainly had no sympathy for the difficulties faced by Simitis. In an interview with the BBC, Ecevit stated that Greece was simply paying the price for its support for terrorism.[13] Beyond the statements of condemnation from Turkey, there even appeared to be the possibility that it might lead to armed conflict. On 22 February, a week after Öcalan's arrest, President Demirel launched a scathing attack on Greece, calling it an outlaw state and demanding that it be added to a list of state sponsors of terrorism.[14] Ominously, he also insisted that Turkey retained a right to self-defence against Greece. In response, Greek units along the border in Thrace and in the Aegean were put on their highest state of alert.

It was certainly conceivable that Turkey might seek to take reprisals against Greece. Unlike previous incidents in the Aegean, which had been focused on specific sovereignty issues, the Öcalan affair was centred on what many saw a long-standing and sustained effort on the part of the Greek state to weaken Turkey. It had therefore led to a deep and widespread sense of anger in Turkey. Consequently, there was a degree of popular pressure on the Turkish Government to be seen to be doing something concrete in retaliation. Matters were not made any easier for the Turkish Government when, less than ten days after Öcalan's arrest, it was revealed that three of Öcalan's associates had arrived in Greece from Kenya and had been granted political asylum. This seemed to confirm Demirel's statement a few days earlier that Greece had shown no remorse for its actions.[15]

Meanwhile, a new crisis appeared to be emerging with the news that Öcalan, who had by this stage been formally charged with treason, was now providing Turkish authorities with a full catalogue of Greek support for his movement. In addition to providing training facilities at a refugee camp in Lavrion, he also claimed that Athens had supplied the PKK with arms and rockets and that the PKK had received funds from the Greek Orthodox Church.[16] All this served to confirm the widespread Turkish beliefs about the pernicious influence of the Church on Greek-Turkish relations. Naturally, these latter allegations raised the prospect of attacks on the Patriarchate in Istanbul.

On top of all this, it was also revealed that Öcalan had been travelling on a passport that belonged to a Greek Cypriot journalist. In the minds of most Turks, Greece and the Greek Cypriots were virtually indistinguishable. In Ankara's view the case against Athens was unassailable and it now mounted a sustained international campaign against Greece. For years the Turkish authorities had argued that Greece had supported PKK terrorism and had insisted that Greek officials had met with PKK members.[17] Here was the proof, or so Turkey believed, of Greece's nefarious involvement in a campaign that had sought nothing less then the dismemberment of the Turkish state.[18]

However, the case was not so strong in the view of outsiders. While it was certainly clear that a good deal of sympathy for the Kurdish cause existed in both Greece and Cyprus, few believed that Greece had seriously engaged in a campaign to finance, arm and train the PKK. It seemed highly unlikely that Athens would want to create yet another area of difference with Turkey in addition to the Aegean and Cyprus. Nevertheless, there was simply no denying that Greece had provided refuge for the leader of the PKK – even if Greece had removed him from the country as soon as it had found out about his arrival on Greek soil.[19]

In the face of this simple fact, it did not matter if the other allegations levelled against Greece were not true. The mere fact that they had provided him with a place to hide, knowing full well that Turkey was after him, had the powerful effect of confirming the widespread Turkish belief that Greece was providing active support for Kurdish separatism. This impression not only harmed bilateral relations at the inter-governmental level, it also had a profound effect on contacts between the two countries at a popular level. In the weeks that followed the arrest almost all the groups that had been working on promoting and developing Greek-Turkish co-operation ceased contact.[20]

As a result, a month after Öcalan's arrest tensions between Greece and Turkey remained extremely high. While the immediate threat of conflict may have receded, most observers believed that relations between the two countries would be severely strained for years to come. For many in Turkey, Greece's behaviour had been unacceptable. Indeed, supporting the PKK was viewed by most as nothing less than an act of aggression. Under these circumstances, the potential for reconciliation appeared almost non-existent. The cold war that had developed over the previous few years looked likely to continue for the foreseeable future. This would necessarily mean that the chance of further crises in the Aegean or over Cyprus would remain high. At the same time, it was also likely that Greece would continue to block Turkey's EU candidacy, which in turn would serve to increase tensions. All-in-all, the situation appeared fairly bleak. However, and contrary to all expectations, an improvement in relations was just about to start. A new crisis elsewhere in south east Europe was about to lay the foundations for Greek-Turkish rapprochement.

Greek-Turkish relations and the Kosovo Crisis

While Greece and Turkey had been caught up in the fallout from the arrest of Abdullah Öcalan, international attention had been fixed on Yugoslavia and the events unfolding in Serbia's south western province of Kosovo. For the previous few years, fighting had been escalating in the region and by 1998 it was clear that an all-out conflict was looming. In early 1999, a peace conference was convened in the French town of Rambouillet to try to broker an agreement between the Serbian Government and the leaders of the Kosovo Albanian community. However, this broke down after the Serbian Government refused to accept a deal that would have granted the region NATO-guaranteed autonomy. As a result, on 24 March, the first strikes were launched against Yugoslavia in an aerial bombardment campaign that would eventually last until the start of June.

For Greece and Turkey, the events taking place just a few hundred kilometres away had the potential to become another major source of antagonism. Over the previous decade, Greece had often sided with Serbia and the NATO campaign was met with a chorus of popular disapproval. Within days regular mass demonstrations against the bombing were taking place on the streets of Athens and the country's other major cities. An opinion poll showed that 96 per cent of Greeks supported Serbia and a full sixty per cent directly supported Milosevic. However, as popular opinion was pulling the government in one direction, the United States and the rest of the alliance expected Greece to provide its full support and assistance to the campaign. The bombing therefore came to be seen as a serious test of Greece's commitment to NATO.[21]

Meanwhile, the issue was also stirring up passions in Turkey. At a press conference held to mark the start of the bombing campaign, İsmail Cem noted the ties of history and culture between the Turks and the people of Kosovo. He stressed that Turkey was not prepared to let it become a new Bosnia. Naturally, therefore, many observers wondered whether, given their competing regional loyalties, the crisis over Kosovo could lead to a conflict between Greece and Turkey.[22] However, the two countries soon made it clear that such a prospect was extremely unlikely. For example, when asked about the danger of fighting between Greece and Turkey over the issue, Cem stated that in his view war between the two countries would only be possible in the event that Greece decided to leave NATO to fight alongside the Serbs, which he could not see happening.[23]

In more realistic terms, the conflict quickly proved to be a far greater source of mutual concern than of bilateral tension. Although the two countries may have had their respective sympathies for the Serbs and Albanians, they soon realised that the conflict posed an extremely serious security threat to them both. Within days of the start of the NATO air campaign, tens of thousands of Kosovo Albanians began to stream across the province's southern borders with Albania and Macedonia. Within two weeks, it was clear that the region was facing a massive humanitarian crisis. At the same time, there were growing fears about the impact that such large numbers of Albanians would have on the delicate state of interethnic relations in Macedonia.

On 4 April Cem and Papandreou spoke to each other by phone. Increasingly worried about the effects of the mass exodus of refugees from Kosovo, they agreed to make a joint representation to NATO. They would argue to their partners that the alliance members share the financial burden of housing the displaced and that each member should agree to take in a proportional number of the displaced. At the same time, the two ministers agreed to remain in contact with one another over the coordination and provision of humanitarian assistance. Furthermore, in a show of goodwill, it was revealed that the Greek Government had granted permission to three Turkish military transport planes to cross Greek airspace in order to deliver aid supplies to Tirana and Skopje.[24]

As a result of this co-operation, there appeared to be a sense that relations between the two countries were already improving. In a speech delivered to a conference on EU-Turkish relations at a university in Izmir, the British Ambassador to Turkey, David Logan, welcomed the way in which the two countries had worked together during the Kosovo crisis and stressed that even in times of tension Athens and Ankara should keep the channels of communication open.[25] In Athens, there were some who felt that the Kosovo crisis, and the problems it had generated, had opened the way for a reappraisal of bilateral relations. While there were certainly areas of extreme difference between the two countries, recent events had also highlighted the degree to which Greece and Turkey had to confront a range of issues where their joint interests were far stronger than the respective differences. Already, some believed that there was an opportunity to start the process of trying to improve relations. Indeed, it was noted that the process was already underway. Reports emerged that Simitis and Demirel would meet on the sidelines of the NATO 50th anniversary summit, which would be held in Washington on 23–25 April, to discuss ways to initiate a process of dialogue on a broad range of bilateral issues.[26]

However, there nevertheless appeared to be a certain degree of concern about rushing into any process without having had the opportunity to discuss matters with Washington. For this reason, it was suggested that Papandreou intended to sound out the US administration in advance of the meeting during a working breakfast with US secretary of State Madeleine Albright on the morning of 23 April.[27] But while Greece clearly hoped to improve relations with Ankara on the back of the tentative dialogue that had been established, a major obstacle now presented itself.

Turkish general elections

On 18 April, Turkey went to the polls for a general election. As had been expected, the main winner was Ecevit's Democratic Left Party (DSP), which took 22 per cent of the vote and 136 seats in the 550-seat Grand National Assembly. However, the second largest party was the right-wing National Action Party (MHP), with 18 per cent of the vote and 129 seats.[28] In the aftermath of the arrest of Öcalan, and following the country's rejection by Europe eighteen months earlier, Turkey had quite clearly become more nationalist. But nobody had foreseen just how well the MHP would do in the vote.[29] Although the party's leader, Devlet Bahçeli, had pulled the party into the fringes of the mainstream since taking the helm several years earlier, the MHP had only just acquired the veneer of any sort of respectability. Indeed, under its founder, Alparlan Türkeş, whom Bahçeli had succeeded, it had been a quasi-fascist in outlook. There was also concern about the lingering ties between the party and the Grey Wolves, which for a long time had been the party's paramilitary wing, and which had been at the forefront of the fighting in the buffer zone in Cyprus that had threatened to lead to a major conflict almost three years earlier.

In Athens the news of the results of the election clearly gave cause for concern. For instance, Aris Spiliotopoulos, the spokesman for the main opposition party, New Democracy, remarked that the rise of Ecevit and the 'Grey Wolves' clearly indicated a, 'rise of nationalism in Turkey.'[30] Others appeared to be more sanguine about the whole thing. As one columnist put it, a coalition between DSP, MHP and ANAP would probably be more aggressive than previous administrations, but it would probably make no difference in terms of substance. None of the governments over the previous few years had shown any willingness to abandon the claims in the Aegean or solve Cyprus.[31]

Despite this, the Greek Government decided to put a brave face on developments and wait to see what kind of coalition would eventually be formed. It was by no means certain that the MHP would be in the new government. The results had certainly created a very complicated political situation and there were a wide range of coalition possibilities. In the meantime, Yiannos Kranidiotis, Alternate Minister for Foreign Affairs, held out an olive branch to the new administration. He promised that if Turkey's perspective was the same as the European Union's perspective, and that if Turkey accepted the norms and values of the EU, then Greece would be prepared to offer its assistance to promote Turkey's EU aspirations: 'We hope that Turkey will be able to form a normal political chart and that a strong government will be formed able to function within the framework of the international community, with respect to the rules and the principles governing both the international community and the European family.'[32]

Similarly, Papandreou insisted that he would continue to try to improve ties between Greece and Turkey,[33] and stressed the positive developments that had taken place in Greek-Turkish relations. Speaking to journalists in Washington, just prior to the opening of the Washington Summit, he gave the following appraisal of events:

> The crisis in Kosovo has paved the way for an unprecedented cooperation and solidarity among the countries of the region. The multisided solidarity has allowed Greece and Turkey to establish a healthy cooperation. The two countries have now been cooperating in a very positive way on matters related to humanitarian aid. However,

that does not mean that the problems between them have been solved. The crisis in Kosovo removed the absence of contacts and the chilled atmosphere between the two sides. I hold talks with my colleague, Foreign Minister Ismail Cem, to exchange views at every opportunity. I hope that the new government that will be established in Turkey will take daring steps for cooperation in a similar spirit, regardless of which political party or parties will establish it. I also hope that it will have the necessary political will to take measures to contribute towards the solution of the disputes between the countries in goodwill.[34]

A few days later, during his trip to the United States, Papandreou was faced with claims that Greece was only entering into talks with Turkey because it was forced to do so or because it was in a position of weakness. He soon rebutted these allegations. Speaking at a conference on 'NATO and South Eastern Europe', held at Tufts University, and which was also attended by Pangalos, he stressed that Greece was extending its hand of friendship to Turkey not out of weakness but as a result of the strength of its position and its belief in the benefits to both countries from bilateral cooperation. Yet again he stressed his hope that the two countries would continue to co-operate in the way that they had during the Kosovo crisis.[35]

Meanwhile, the long-awaited meeting between Simitis and Demirel had produced little of value. Although seen as a generally positive development in its own right, Demirel had nevertheless made it clear that no new contacts or initiatives would be possible until a new Turkish government had been formed.[36]

3

THE START OF RAPPROCHEMENT

Despite hopes that the two countries had put the acrimony caused by the Öcalan affair behind them, it already appeared that the co-operative spirit generated at the time of Kosovo was fading rapidly. Quite apart from the fact that Turkey was facing the formation of what would be its most nationalist government since the return to democracy in 1983, behind the scenes the Turkish military appeared to be in no mood for reconciliation. In the days following the general election, the Greek Government noted a significant rise in the number of airspace violations occurring in the Aegean. In response, the Greek Government Spokesman, Dimitri Reppas, called on Turkey to desist and argued that such incidents did little to help the overall situation between the two countries. Indeed, as he put it, 'it reveals the face of a troublemaker.'[1]

Meanwhile, on 5 May, it was claimed that Turkish aircraft had violated Cypriot airspace in order to register disapproval of a joint exercise that was taking place between Cyprus and Greece.[2] Indeed, the following day, at a press briefing at the Turkish Foreign Ministry, Sermet Atacanlı, the Foreign Ministry's Spokesman, rebuffed Greek criticisms, and argued that it was in fact Athens that was increasing tensions as two Greek fighters had recently tried to land at the air base near Paphos, in the west of Cyprus.[3]

That very same day, in a more serious turn of events, the Turkish Foreign Ministry announced the publication of a third volume of material outlining the contribution Greece had made to the PKK's operations. This was sent to all the foreign mission in Ankara and distributed to Turkish Embassies world wide. If there had been any lingering doubts that the spirit of Kosovo had overcome the tensions caused by the arrest of Öcalan, this new booklet laid them to rest. As the introduction stated, 'while international attention is for the time being focused on the crisis in Kosovo, Greek involvement with terrorism can neither be forgotten nor forgiven. And the disturbing question remains yet to be answered: What happens when a [NATO] member country betrays another allied country?'[4]

Matters became worse a week later when a Greek television channel announced that a Greek couple were planning to marry and settle on Plati, another of the 'grey zone' islets. On 14 May, the Greek Charge d'Affaires in Ankara, Michael Christides, was summoned to the Foreign Ministry. There he was asked about Greek 'initiatives' in the region and reminded about Turkey's position on issue of the islets.[5] Later that day, Ecevit, who was still serving as prime minister until the formation of a new administration, announced that any move to reopen the issue of the islets was unacceptable.[6]

General Hüseyin Kıvrıkoğlu, the Chief of the General Staff, went even further. When questioned on the matter by a journalist, he warned Greece against reopening the matter by allowing any settlements to be established on currently uninhabited islets in the eastern Aegean. But if Greece did decide to establish any settlements, Turkey would take all necessary actions in order to prevent a recurrence of what was termed, 'the Kardak situation'. He also insisted that any attempt by Greece to drive a wedge between Turkey and its allies over the issue could not work. Finally, and in marked contrast to the position taken by the Turkish Government, which claimed that the ownership of the islets were unclear, the general insisted that the islets were in fact Turkish.

In response, Greece played down the report. During a press conference, Reppas explained that the Greek Government did not believe that a wedding could constitute serious grounds for a political discussion, let alone provide a pretext for a crisis.[7] He also noted, in response to a request by New Democracy that the government take all necessary measures to protect Greek interests, that the government would adopt a calm and proportionate view of the matter. Importantly, there appeared to be at least one Turkish politician who agreed. When asked about the matter, Cem said that the marriage on the island was simply for 'show' and was 'not important'.[8]

Cem writes to Papandreou

In retrospect, Cem's determination to pay down the incident may have been deliberately designed to avoid creating any further tension just at the moment when he was planning a new diplomatic initiative towards Greece. Just ten days later, on 24 May, he wrote a letter to Papandreou. The stated purpose of the message was to share some views on ways in which to 'ameliorate' bilateral relations. As Cem saw it, the first step must be to address the Turkish perception of links between Greece and terrorist organisations. In Turkey's view, this was, 'a matter of crucial importance'.

> I, therefore, suggest that Turkey and Greece conclude an agreement to combat terrorism. Resolution of this issue would permit us to

approach our known differences with greater confidence. The substance of this agreement may be inspired by accords we have already signed with some of our other neighbors, but is should also be specific to the nature of the problem as it affects our relations. We have some further ideas in this respect which we are ready to share with you.

In parallel with an agreement on terrorism, Cem also proposed developing a plan for reconciliation between the two countries and suggested that, if Papandreou believed that it was worth pursuing both ideas, high officials from the two governments could meet and discuss these issues in privacy.

Soon after receiving the letter, Papandreou called Cem. The first order of business was to congratulate him on his reappointment as foreign minister. By now a new government had been formed. As had been widely expected, it was a coalition between the DSP, MHP and ANAP, with the parties holding 13, 12 and 10 cabinet seats respectively. Importantly, Ecevit, who would continue as prime minister, had managed to keep the external affairs portfolio in DSP hands. This was certainly a welcome relief, even if there was concern at the decision to place the defence ministry in the hands of the MHP. Turning to the letter, Papandreou explained that he would need some time to study it fully before replying officially, but assured him that a response would be forthcoming.[9]

By now the Greek press had heard about the letter and also wanted to know if and when Papandreou would reply. The acting Government Spokesman, Yiannis Nicolaou, announced that the Greek Government would not reply for the time being, but that it would 'in time'. As for the suggestion of new talks on the Aegean, Nicolaou stressed that, 'there are many things that need to be discussed before such an issue can be a topic for dialogue'. In his view, the likelihood of new talks appeared to be, 'a fair distance away'.[10]

As the letter from Cem indicated, the question of terrorism and allegations of Greek support for the PKK still featured highly among Turkish concerns. Although four months had passed since the arrest of Öcalan, Turkey was still keen to discuss the issue. This was further encouraged when the PKK leader, who was now on trial, placed Greece on a list of countries that had aided the PKK. The importance of Cem's letter to Papandreou became clear. By having written to his counterpart, he was able to play down the significance of Öcalan's statements. He could effectively treat the claims as old news. As Cem pointed out, 'for a long time, we've been saying that terrorism is the main issue of our policy towards Greece and that it is an issue which should be solved.'[11]

Just as in Greece, the Turkish media was also interested in the communications between the two foreign ministers and wanted to know more about the conversations between Cem and Papandreou over previous weeks. Cem stressed that these had been entirely about the Kosovo issue, and had not touched upon bilateral issues. Indeed, he warned against reading anything into the conversations as regards any other matters.[12] Perhaps sensing a degree of unease about the discussions, he replied to a question on the recent increase in tensions in the Aegean by announcing that he believed that the islets were Turkish, having been passed on from the Ottoman Empire.

Notwithstanding the public statements, behind the scenes it was clear that Cem and others within the Turkish foreign ministry were increasingly in favour of pursuing rapprochement with Greece. The Ministry viewed Papandreou as someone with whom they could work. This was in marked contrast to their views on Pangalos, who was seen to be irreconcilably opposed to any improvement in Greek-Turkish relations. And although Cem had denied it, it was revealed that he had in fact spoken to Papandreou about the islet and that this had helped to diffuse tensions. Similarly, over in Greece, there also appeared to be a growing sense that a new era in relations could be about to start. It was even being reported that Papandreou had informed his advisors that he intended to visit Turkey in the near future.[13] However, just as things appeared to be improving, another perennial issue of contention again emerged: the question of Turkey's relationship with the European Union.

The Cologne European Union Council

As the European Union prepared for its latest Council meeting in Cologne, on 3–4 June, it once again appeared likely that Turkey's candidacy for EU membership would once again be on the agenda. Eighteen months had now passed since the 1997 Luxembourg decision, and it had been a year since the botched attempt to patch things up in London. Within many quarters, there was a growing sense that now might be the time to reverse the earlier decisions and open the way for eventual membership talks with Ankara. Again, all eyes were on Greece. In light of recent developments many wondered whether Greece would be prepared to drop its veto as a sign of goodwill or as an act of contrition after the Öcalan fiasco.

Athens made it clear that it was not ready to change its position. At a meeting of foreign ministers, held a few days before the main meeting of the heads of government, Papandreou noted that although Turkey had opened the way for bilateral talks, as yet it had not mentioned that it was prepared to refer the question of the continental shelf to The Hague. This remained a basic Greek condition for accepting Turkish candidacy. Under these circumstances, Greece could not at that stage reverse its position. This was confirmed a few days later at the Council. The member states therefore decided to review the situation again at the next Council, which would take place in Helsinki in December.

Explaining his decision, Simitis made it clear that Greece was not opposed to Turkey's European vocation, but that it must meet the same conditions applied to all other candidates, without exception.[14] Responding to the accusation that his position had once again marked Greece out as the *'enfant terrible'* of Europe, he stated that Greece was simply determined to protect its interests, 'using all means possible.' As for a possible backlash from Turkey, Simitis seemed unconcerned by that prospect. As he pointed out, any negative response from Ankara would be contrary to Turkey's own best interests.[15]

Nevertheless, in an attempt to avert any crisis from developing, Papandreou asked Ioannis Korantis, the newly-arrived ambassador in Ankara, to visit the Turkish Foreign Ministry and explain the Greek position. There he emphasised that while Greece certainly harboured deep concerns about a range of bilateral matters, it was not opposed in principle to Turkey's membership of the EU. He also noted that other member states who were opposed to Turkish membership were hiding behind the Greek position.[16] Before leaving, Korantis also explained that he hoped to be able to visit the Turkish Foreign Ministry regularly to discuss questions relating to Turkey's bid for EU candidacy.[17]

Ecevit was sceptical about the ambassador's claims. When questioned about the way in which EU members used Greece to hide their own prejudices he stated that, 'the EU is a big organisation, but it looks like it submitted to Greece. Do some EU countries use Greece or does Greece use the EU against Turkey? This question needs to be evaluated.'[18] But even if the Turkish Government appeared unwilling to take the Greek explanation at face value, it was nevertheless significant that the decision taken at Cologne did not spark another crisis between the two countries.

Tensions and detente

Although Turkey has appeared to take the recent EU decision calmly, relations were again coming under strain over Öcalan. Despite his view that relations with Greece could be improved, over the previous few weeks Cem had made a number of statements drawing attention to Greek links with PKK terrorism. While this may well have been a sop to nationalists in the government, or in order to assuage wider public concerns that the Turkish Government was not doing enough to tackle the issue, the repeated references to the matter were causing unease within the Greek Government. The Foreign Ministry was particularly concerned about the allegations made by Cem and the Foreign Ministry about Greece's involvement in training PKK members, an allegation that had been consistently denied by the Greek Government. On 12 June, Reppas asked

Cem to be 'more' careful in his statements. He also called on the Turkish foreign minister to avoid provocations and, 'to work effectively and contribute by its actions to stability in the region.'[19]

In the meantime, an interview with Ecevit shown on Mega Channel, one of the country's main private television stations, was the subject of widespread attention in Greece. Having ordered the invasion of Cyprus in 1974, Ecevit always aroused a lot of interest amongst the Greek public. This time, the interview attracted a larger audience than usual as it was the first time that he had spoken to Greek journalists since the arrest of Öcalan. Naturally, the arrest and trial of the PKK leader featured prominently in the discussion. Ecevit observed that as long as Greece supported terrorism there could be no moves towards an improvement in relations between the two countries. On the key areas of difference he revealed that his opinions had not changed. When questioned about Cyprus he repeated his long standing position that the issue had been solved in 1974 and that the international community must recognise that two separate states existed on the island.[20] As far as the Aegean was concerned, he again stressed that the best means of addressing the problems was through direct bilateral negotiations.

Most Greek observers felt that Ecevit had not offered anything new. Instead, he had simply repeated his long-standing, and intransigent, views on key questions. There was also a sense that the participation of the MHP in the government had made Turkey even more nationalistic, and that Ankara was apparently hardening its stance, just at the moment when Papandreou was preparing to open a new initiative. One leading newspaper aligned with the government saw the interview as evidence that the Turkish Government was essentially unwilling to engage in substantive dialogue, despite the contrary indications coming from Cem.[21]

Undeterred by the statements of the Turkish prime minister, the first indications that Greece was starting to alter its policies towards Turkey now emerged. In an interview with Reuters, Kranidiotis announced that Greece might be willing to reverse its longstanding position that the Aegean issues had to be referred to the ICJ before it would lift the veto on Turkish candidacy. While he maintained that it would be preferable for Turkey to meet the conditions laid down by EU leaders if it wanted to be considered as a candidate, Greece would be prepared to lift its current objections if it received two major declarations from the European Union. First of all, it wanted confirmation that Cyprus would be eligible for EU membership, even if a settlement had not been achieved. Secondly, it sought a statement of solidarity from the European Union over the Aegean.[22]

Although the comments were not widely noted at the time, they represented a sea-change in Greek thinking. It was the first real indication that the Greek Government was moving away from its traditional policy of using the prospect of EU candidacy as a form of leverage over Turkey. Instead, Greece would use the European Union itself as a mechanism for exerting pressure on Ankara. But while the ideas were certainly radical, implementing them would be difficult. For a start, there was still a great deal of concern within many European quarters about the prospect of accepting a divided Cyprus as a member. Moreover, it was doubtful that member states would be willing to take such a clear stand on the Aegean. Despite Greek claims to the contrary, it was clear that certain legal ambiguities existed. It was unlikely that the EU member states would want to prejudge and subsequent court case. Notwithstanding these obvious difficulties, the first signs of a major change in Greek thinking had apparently emerged. Importantly, the Cypriot Government endorsed the ideas.[23]

Papandreou replies to Cem

On 25 June, just over a month after having received the letter from Cem, Papandreou finally sent a formal reply to his counterpart. It quickly became clear why it had been subject to such a long delay. Rather than focus on terrorism and bilateral relations, Papandreou took the opportunity to outline a far more ambitious programme of discussions. In what proved to be a relatively lengthy response, Papandreou invited his counterpart to engage in substantive dialogue on a wide range of topics of mutual interest, including tourism, the environment, culture, organised crime, trade and regional issues. He also made direct contact between the two of them a central feature of the process. As he explained:

> The possibility of concluding bilateral, or even multilateral agreements, in the above mentioned fields could also be envisaged in the light of the progress of our cooperation.
>
> In this context we could meet when the opportunity arises in order to have a sincere and constructive exchange of views. I have always been of the view that personal contacts between us can in many ways be productive. They particularly can be useful if we are to define common approaches, ways and means to address outstanding bilateral issues and enhance mutual confidence.

Things now moved very quickly. Within hours, the news came from the Turkish Foreign Ministry that the two foreign ministers had already arranged to meet five days later in New York, where they would be attending a meeting convened by the UN Secretary-General to discuss Kosovo. They were evidently pleased at the response from Papandreou. Announcing the meeting between Cem and Papandreou, the ministry stressed that the Greek Government had responded positively to its proposal for a discussion on terrorism. It also revealed that it intended to propose that a meeting be arranged between high-level officials of the two countries to discuss this matter, as well as a range of other issues.[24] This extended agenda for dialogue was confirmed on 30 June, when the two ministers met at the UN headquarters. There they formally declared that a working group made up of senior officials from the two foreign ministries would be established to examine a wide range of practical measures to promote greater bilateral co-operation in non-contentious areas.

The emergence of spoiling tactics

The decision to open talks was certainly a major step forward. However, over the next couple of weeks several incidents occurred that highlighted the mistrust and tension that still existed between the two countries. The most important of these actually occurred on the day of the meeting between the two foreign ministers. On 30 June, a Turkish court pronounced Öcalan guilty and had sentenced the PKK leader to death.[25] Although the result had been widely expected, and was warmly welcomed by many in Turkey, it nonetheless sparked a new round of recriminations.

The sentence was immediately condemned by the Greek Government. Speaking from a meeting of EU-Latin American leaders in Rio de Janeiro, Simitis stated in particularly blunt terms that the trial had been political: 'The decision is a political decision and serves political expediencies. The death sentence does not resolve any problem, it merely complicates it. We hope that Turkey will realise at last that one solution exists: Implementation of human and minority rights.'[26] This view was echoed across the rest of the Greek political spectrum. But Greece was certainly not isolated in its views. Across Europe the verdict was criticised and, almost at once, the Turkish Government came under significant pressure to prevent the sentence from being carried out.[27] Once again, there were further demonstrations by Kurdish communities across Europe. Many of these focused their anger on Greece, which was blamed for the fate of the Kurdish leader. This time, however, the protests remained mostly peaceful. For instance, a small demonstration held by 60 protestors in Athens was broken up without trouble.

In addition to the old wounds that appeared ready to be reopened by the Öcalan verdict, it appeared as if tensions were again about to surface in the Aegean. At the start of June the Greek Defence Ministry had sent a message to the Turkish Government announcing that it intended to hold a sea and air exercise in the Aegean. To this end, it requested that specific areas be put aside for this purpose. The problem was that the planned date of the exercise fell within the period of the summer moratorium. For a number of years, the moratorium had been seen as an important confidence building measure, designed to prevent serious crises from emerging during the height of the lucrative tourist season. If the manoeuvres went ahead, it would mark a break with standard practice. In response to the notice, the Turkish Foreign Ministry therefore lodged an official complaint to the Greek Government. Soon afterwards, it also put in a request for areas to be set aside for military exercises. But even though this request was quite clearly a tit-for-tat response to an initial Greek move, the Turkish decision to stage exercises was roundly condemned by Athens. Indeed, the Greek Government cited it as further evidence that Ankara was unable to make any contribution to the ironing out of Greek-Turkish differences.[28]

Soon afterwards, several Turkish Air Force F-16s harassed a jet carrying the Greek Minister of Transport as it flew in international airspace on its way to Cyprus, where the minister was due to take part in commemorations marking the events of July 1974. The incident was roundly condemned by the Government and the opposition parties alike. Akis Tzohadzopoulos, the Defence Minister, called Turkey, 'an international troublemaker',[29] and Ambassador Korantis went to the Turkish Ministry of Foreign Affairs to deliver a demarche.[30] However, Turkish officials played down the incident. Faruk Loğoğlu, the deputy undersecretary, who had been appointed head of the Turkish delegation for the forthcoming talks with Greek officials, insisted that there had been no hostile intent behind the move. Instead, the Turkish aircraft had simply sought to identify an aircraft flying close to the Turkish coast. He emphasised that the two countries should not allow these types of incidents to spoil efforts to improve relations, nor should they, 'become victims of the mass media or some circles that want to cut the ongoing efforts.'[31] He also asked Korantis to convey to Minister Papandreou that the Turkish team was preparing for what they hoped would be smooth and substantive talks in Ankara and Athens between the two governments.

All-in-all, a mixed picture seemed to be emerging. Papandreou therefore telephoned Cem to speak with him personally about the situation. On the one hand, he noted that he was receiving positive messages from his counterpart. And yet the actions of the Turkish Government appeared to tell a different story. In response, the Turkish Minister agreed that the recent incidents had not improved the climate, but stressed that neither of them should let these interfere or affect the process that was developing.[32] At the end of the conversation, the two decided to meet again on the sidelines of the Stability Summit Meeting, which would take place in Sarajevo just over a week later, on 30 July.

The Greek Government defends bilateral discussions

By this point there was a growing scepticism in Greece about the government's policies towards Turkey. The incident with the aircraft had been seen by many as further proof that Turkey was not interested in improving relations. Meanwhile, others were wary about the exact content of the talks. In response, the Foreign Ministry went on the offensive. In a long interview given to a Greek newspaper, Kranidiotis, who was one of the key supporters of the dialogue, outlined the reasons why the talks had been initiated and explained his views of the future path between Greece and Turkey. First of all, he stressed that this process was not in fact new. It had been suggested several years earlier by himself and Christos Rozakis, who had been the deputy Foreign Minister at the time, and was now serving as a judge at the European Court of Human Rights.[33] However, the initiative was rejected at that point on the grounds that the time was not right for such a move. As for the rationale behind the process, Kranidiotis explained it as follows:

> The initiative for a Greek-Turkish dialogue of issues of 'low political significance' is designed to discuss specific issues in sectors that are basic for cooperation between two neighbouring nations that lack a fundamental framework…the sectors that have been chosen for a dialogue are being offered because both sides can benefit from them and they do not involve a concept of winners and losers. This initiative also aims to improve the climate in bilateral relations. This could contribute to the settlement of other issues, such as Greek-Turkish affairs and Cyprus. Thus, having a discussion and cooperating on issues of 'low political significance' can help to solve problems of 'high political significance' according to the new view on how international relations should function, which was explained by Jean Monnet. It was this view that led to the formation of the EU.[34]

The interview also provided Kranidiotis with a chance to ease concerns that Greece was about to make a major concession on bilateral issues. He was adamant that the dialogue would not touch upon the question of the Aegean. Greece would continue to insist that the dispute over the continental shelf must be dealt with by the International Court of Justice. Similarly, efforts to resolve the Cyprus problem would continue to remain under the auspices of the United Nations. He also rejected claims that Turkey could use the talks to promote its EU candidacy by claiming that it was now discussing substantive matters with Greece. As he noted, the conditions for Turkey's candidacy had been established at Luxembourg. These would not change as a result of the talks. On top of this, he made it clear that Greece would continue to seek an assurance from its EU partners that Cypriot accession to the EU could not be conditional upon a solution and that the Greek position on the Aegean was supported.

Although the talks would not touch on the key issues of difference, he explained that the matters of 'low significance' to be addressed were still highly important issues affecting bilateral relations. In this sense, the discussions would have real value. Turning to the structure of the talks, he noted that Greece had not agreed to a Turkish proposal to form a number of committees. Instead, both countries would have a single team. He also explained that the two ministers would meet again in September, at the UN General Assembly, in order to review progress.[35]

The following day, Kranidiotis followed up the interview by publishing a commentary article in one of Greece's leading Sunday newspapers. Explaining that the Kosovo crisis had highlighted the 'interdependence of regional relations', he again stressed that the talks would not be focused, 'on all issues'. They would certainly not touch upon the core issues relating to the Aegean or Cyprus. Instead, they were designed to investigate the possibility for high-level co-operation on what he termed as 'second category' issues at the low political level. These issues included tourism, trade, crime, the environment and culture. 'Sovereignty issues are non-negotiable', he wrote.[36]

The first round of talks begin

The first round of bilateral talks took place in Ankara on 26–27 July. As expected the Greek delegation was led by Anastasios Skopelitis, the Foreign Ministry Political Director. On the Turkish side the delegation was led by Mithat Balkan, the Deputy Undersecretary for Economic affairs. The first item on the agenda was tourism. This was followed, after lunch, by a discussion on the environment.[37] However, in Turkey as much as in Greece, it was clear that there were many who were deeply unhappy at the start of talks between the two countries. That evening the Greek Orthodox cemetery in Istanbul was attacked and a number of gravestones were desecrated. While such incidents had occurred many times before, the timing of this attack was clearly linked to the talks. And while on previous occasions these incidents had produced little more than token condemnation from the Turkish Government, on this occasion the Turkish Foreign Ministry issued a strongly worded statement in which it apologised for the incident and said that the Turkish Government would capture the assailants. It also announced that all measures would be taken to prevent similar incidents from occurring again.[38]

The next morning the two delegations met again, this time to discuss commercial and economic relations. And although little was revealed about the actual substance of the talks, in the days that followed both the Greek and Turkish foreign ministries noted that the first round had gone very well.[39] The talks were also endorsed by Ecevit. At a meeting of the ruling DSP he noted his pleasure at the way in which Greece had sought a dialogue and announced that he expected the process to, 'yield positive results soon.'[40] It was against this backdrop that the second round of discussions began in Athens on 29 July. This time the core subjects for discussion were terrorism, organised crime and illegal immigration.[41]

However, the talks in Athens were also mired in controversy following an interview given by Papandreou to a Greek magazine.[42] Defending his policy of dialogue, he stated that, 'when we go down to the root of the problem we may see that the solution is not as hard as we feared.' He also played down claims about recent provocations from Turkey, hinting that the events had been blown out of proportion by those who wanted to see the talks fail and that he would not become, 'a hostage to provocations and to those who are trying to block it.' However, it was when he was questioned about the question of the Muslim minority in Thrace that Papandreou sparked a firestorm. Concerning his role in securing quotas for the minority at Greek universities during his time as Education Minister, he was asked to comment on the fact that while the Greek Government refers to them as Moslem, many of them refer to themselves as Turks. In reply, he stated that they had adopted a Turkish identity because they were Turkish, just as others claim that they are Gypsies or Pomaks (Bulgarian Moslems). Brushing these points aside, he stated that the, 'important thing is for these people to see themselves as Greek citizens before anything else.' He was then asked about whether the term had been avoided by the Greek Government because of the territorial implications of admitting that Greece had a 'Turkish' minority. In reply, Papandreou broke new ground:

> If a Greek citizen feels that he belongs to some ethnic group, international treaties allow this. And Greece is a country that respects international agreements. (...) No one challenges the fact that there are [in Greece] many Muslims of Turkish origin. Of course, the [Lausanne] treaties refer to Muslims. If the borders are not challenged, it concerns me little if someone calls himself a Turk, a Bulgarian or a Pomak. (...) Whoever feels he has such a [Macedonian] origin, Greece has nothing to fear from it and I want to stress this is not just my thought. It is a well-established practice that allows the integration of minorities throughout Europe, as well as in other countries like Canada, Australia, and the USA. Such an attitude defuses whatever problems might have existed, allows the real blossoming of democratic institutions, as well as gives these people the feeling that they too are citizens of this country.[43]

In Turkey, his comments were warmly received. A glowing article appeared in Hürriyet, which praised the minister and showed the extent to which Papandreou had started to show a far more positive position on Greek-

Turkish relations. Meanwhile, another paper ran with the headline: 'Bravo, George'. But in Greece there was uproar from across the political spectrum, with calls for him to step down or be sacked.[44]

In order to respond the heavy criticism he faced, Papandreou gave another interview a few days later.[45] Regarding the calls for his resignation, he emphasised that he would only do so if asked to do so by Prime Minister Simitis. He was also unrepentant about his general approach towards bilateral relations with Turkey, insisting that he would continue on a path of dialogue that was essentially no different from the discussions established with Romania and Bulgaria. As far as the 'Bravo, Georgia' headline was concerned, he noted that it could simply have been the result of a well-intentioned journalist, or else might have been deliberately done in order to smear him in the eyes of the Greek public. In any case, the 'bravos' should be reserved for such time as the two countries had managed to solve their bilateral disputes, which he stated would only happen when Turkey abandoned, 'its goals against our country in the Aegean', and contributed to a Cyprus solution. Again, he stressed that the only bilateral issue recognised by Athens was the continental shelf. In conclusion, he made it clear that he viewed the controversy over his statement as having been stirred up deliberately by nationalists and by the media, and warned against allowing either to determine Greek foreign policy, pointing out that the Imia crisis had been largely caused by television channels.

Despite this defence, it was clear that Papandreou had made a serious miscalculation with his comments about the minority. Thanks in part to the over exuberance of the Turkish press, which, on balance, had probably meant well by its comment, the nationalists in Greece were now strengthened in their opposition to the talks. Over the next few weeks a number of editorials emerged strongly criticising the talks and suggesting that the ultimate aim of the discussions was to undermine the Greek position. Indeed allegations were now published that used his comments on the minority to argue that the whole dialogue was little more than a step to allow Turkey to gain what it wanted from Greece. For example, one nationalist newspaper even tried to equate the talks on tourism, discussed at the first meeting of the teams from the Foreign Ministries, with a Greek retreat on the Aegean issues as a whole, claiming that joint advertising would be used by Turkey to designate the Aegean, 'as a territory ruled jointly by Greece and Turkey'.[46]

As the traditional August holidays started in the region, the process of rapprochement was coming under increasing fire, especially from the Greek nationalists. Likewise, while many people in Greece saw the talks as presenting a good opportunity for the two countries to improve their bilateral relations, the majority of Greeks nevertheless remained extremely sceptical about the process. However, all this was about to change.

4

DISASTER DIPLOMACY

At around three o'clock in the morning on 17 August a major earthquake measuring 7.5 on the Richter Scale struck the industrial city of Izmit in north-western Turkey. Soon afterwards the Greek Embassy in Ankara received a call from the Turkish Foreign Ministry explaining what had happened and requesting Greek assistance. Ambassador Korantis immediately sent a message to Athens.

Less than an hour after the quake Papandreou was on the phone to Cem asking for a full run down of any immediate needs and offering whatever assistance was necessary. It was the first call the Turkish Government received from any country.[1] Cem explained that the first priority was for rescue specialists. Given its own experiences of earthquakes, the Greeks had established an emergency rescue team, EMAK, and within hours it had been assembled and was ready to depart for Turkey under the leadership of the Civilian Protection Secretary General, Dimitris Katrivanos.

In addition to a twenty-five strong team of EMAK rescue workers, fully equipped and complete with sniffer dogs specially trained to locate people trapped in debris and wreckage, a group of Greek seismologists had also been put together. They would assist their Turkish counterparts ascertain the possible extent and whereabouts of aftershocks. At the same time two mobile hospital units were made available with a team of eleven doctors. Later that afternoon the group was flown to Istanbul on three C-130 transport planes of the Greek Air Force. Shortly afterwards a number of other teams left for Turkey, including a delegation of fifteen Greek nurses and, following a decision taken by the Parliament, a six-member delegation of Greek MPs with medical training. Athens also sent two fire fighting planes to Izmit to help the local authorities put out a major blaze at one of Turkey's largest oil refineries.[2]

By now the full extent of the disaster had become apparent. The scale of destruction was far larger than at first realised. Across the city and the wider region whole apartment blocks had collapsed and it was obvious that the death toll would be measured in the thousands.[3] The Greek Government informed Ankara that all the relevant ministries in Athens were on full alert and were ready to send further aid and assistance whenever requested. That same day, the Turkish Ambassador in Athens, Ali Tuygan, met with Kranidiotis, during which the Greek minister once again reaffirmed Greece's readiness to help in whatever way possible.

Indeed, offers of assistance were by this stage being made from all quarters of the Greek Government. The Greek Defence Minister, Akis Tzohadzopoulos, wrote to his Turkish counterpart, Sabahattin Çakmakoğlu, stressing that Greece was ready to offer any assistance required.[4] A few days later he followed this up with a call to Çakmakoğlu in which he volunteered the help of the Greek military in the rescue operation and offered to send tents, containers, food, blankets and whatever else might be needed by the Turkish people.[5] At the same time, President Stephanopoulos, Prime Minister Simitis, and the Speaker of the Parliament, Apostolos Kalamanis, all sent messages of support to their counterparts expressing their deepest sorrow about the earthquake.[6] Soon messages of thanks were coming from all sections of the Turkish Government and across the political spectrum. The Speaker of the Grand National Assembly, Yıldırım Akbulut, expressed his gratitude for the rapid Greek response to the disaster and all the assistance it had offered.[7]

Popular Greek reactions

While official assistance continued to flow across the Aegean, the Greek public also started to get to work raising money and collecting food, medicines, and other desperately needed items to help the victims of the quake. In Athens, the Mayor, Dimitri Avramopoulos appealed to all Athenians to give generously to the efforts. At the same time, most of the television channels, which had also taken the lead in promoting nationalist feelings over the years, had sent representatives to the region to cover the unfolding events. Indeed, on most of the major television stations the tragedy of the Turkish earthquakes received round-the-clock coverage. Particular attention was paid to the efforts of EMAK. On particularly poignant image that was aired repeatedly was of a Greek rescue worker lifting a nine-year old survivor from the rubble of a collapsed apartment block.

Donations now started to arrive from across the country and within hours 24 million Drachmas (US$75,000) had been raised by ordinary Greeks. Meanwhile, a number of groups launched appeals of their own. These groups included the Greek Women's Association and the Greek Municipalities Association, which presented a cheque of US$100,000 to Tuygan. There were also a number of major personal donations. For example, Vardis Vardinoyianni, a wealthy Greek ship-owner, contributed US$100,000 to the appeal. Perhaps the most surprising fund raising drive, at least in the view of the Turkish people, was by the Orthodox Church, which had long been seen as a bastion of anti-Turkish sentiment in Greece. In churches across the country it had launched an appeal for funds for Turkey, taking collections after Sunday services. In response, Tuygan sent a message of thanks and appreciation to Archbishop Christodoulos of Athens.[8]

In addition to the assistance from the central government and the people, a number of municipalities also played an active role in the relief efforts. On 24 August, the mayors of five of the largest Greek cities – Dimitri Avramopoulos of Athens, Vassilis Papageorgopoulos of Thessaloniki, Christos Agrapidis of Piraeus, Evangelos Floratos of Patras, and Costas Aslanis of Irakleion, in Crete – met to discuss the best means by which to co-ordinate the distribution of humanitarian aid to Turkey. At a news conference held after the meeting, Avramopoulos announced that the mayors had established a co-ordinating body, entitled 'Operation Solidarity' in Athens. This would oversee the common effort of the five cities to gather and dispatch humanitarian aid, which already amounted to 10 containers worth of material.[9] Meanwhile, each of the mayors also explained some of the specific activities taking place in their city. For example, in Thessaloniki a major blood donation drive was being held. Meanwhile, Patras, which had suffered a major earthquake in the 1980s that had also received widespread international attention, would be holding a fundraising concert attended by Mikis Theodorakis, the eminent Greek composer. It would also be sending a team of civil engineers to Izmit to assist with the damage assessment exercise and help Turkish engineers assess the structural damage to the buildings left standing. All the mayors agreed that efforts to assist the people of Turkey were a 'self-evident duty' of all Greeks. As Agrapidis stated, 'there is no name, no flag, no ideology, nor fixations of mindless leaders. We must leave prejudices aside.'[10]

Soon afterwards, Avramopoulos travelled to Istanbul, where he was met on arrival by the city's mayor, Ali Müfit Gürtuna, as well as the mayor of the Avcilar district and the Greek Consul in Istanbul, Fotis Ksidas. Speaking about the enormous impact that the earthquake had had on Greek public opinion, Avramopoulos expressed his hope that, 'this will be a step to bring together the Greek and Turkish people. The ditches formed by the quake could turn into a passage-way between two nations.'[11] Gürtuna agreed that he hoped that the events could lead to a lasting peace. He also expressed the gratitude of all Turks for the assistance provided by Greece and the Greek people. Meanwhile, they quickly got down to work, discussing the establishment of a settlement of 1000 tents for people made homeless by the tragedy.

As well as the efforts taking place across mainland Greece, a number of initiatives were also taking place in the Aegean, where tensions between the two Governments were often at their highest. For example, on 26 August a humanitarian consignment arrived in Cesme, near Izmir, donated by the people of Chios. Offering the aid, the Mayor of Chios, Petros Panteleras, told the welcoming crowd that the Greek people shared the grief and pain of Turkey and that following the announcement of a drive to collect aid for the country over five hundred packages had been gathered in just four days. 'This shows the Greek people's feelings and sympathy towards the Turkish people. The aid will continue. The Greek people want to be a friend. The people have given a decision. From now on, we will be together and united. The politicians cannot prevent this. Let us sit side by side instead of sitting across from one another.'[12] Thanking Panteleras for the delivery, Faik Tütüncüoğlu, the Mayor of Cesme, explained that there was also willingness for a new spirit of friendship in Turkey and that the aid from Chios would improve relations between their municipalities.

By now, efforts to raise money were taking place across Greece. On 30 August, George Dalaras, one of the most well-known singers in Greece, held a concert in the town of Xanthi, in Thrace. The concert, at which both Greek and Turkish songs were performed, was broadcast simultaneously in both countries.[13] But in addition to the urgent efforts of the Greek government to supply equipment and supplies and the fund raising efforts of the Greek people, the Greek business community was also providing practical support for their Turkish colleagues. Despite the fact that business contacts between the two countries had tailed off in the months since the Öcalan crisis, following the earthquakes the differences were quickly put aside. The chairman of the Greek Businessmen's Association, Panayiotis Koutsikos, announced that he had informed Şarik Tara and Rahmi Koç, two of Turkey's leading business figures, that a number of Greek factory owners had offered to let Turkish producers use their factories for production until the ones destroyed could be rebuilt.[14]

Already Greek efforts to help those stricken by the earthquakes were receiving widespread international attention. Speaking from Thessaloniki, where she was attending a signing ceremony for the 'Social Solidarity' non-governmental organisation, UN High Commissioner Florinda Rojas Rodriquez praised the efforts of the Greek people and Government.[15]

Assistance from Cyprus

But perhaps the most astonishing aspect of the tragedy was the effect it had in Cyprus. Despite the long-standing hostility towards Turkey caused by the 1974 invasion and occupation of the island, the Cypriot Government and many Greek Cypriots, stepped in to offer aid and assistance. Despite the fact that no diplomatic relations existed between the two countries, the day following the earthquake the Cypriot President, Glafkos Clerides, sent a telegram to his Turkish counterpart:

> It is with deep sorrow that the Cypriot people and myself were informed of the grievous news about the catastrophic earthquake which has struck your country with so much loss of life and material damage…I wish to express our deep sympathy over this terrible catastrophe and convey to the families of the victims our sincere condolences.[16]

Clerides also noted that his government had informed the Red Cross that it was prepared to send medical assistance in the form of medicines and other suggested items to the disaster areas.[17] Meanwhile, the Greek Cypriots were following the example set by Greece and had started to raise funds for Turkey. In all the Greek Cypriot areas accounts were opened to receive donations and fund-raising drives were launched on several of the local radio stations. At the same time, following a suggestion from the Ministry of Health, the Government of Cyprus offered to send CY£100,000 (US$200,000) of assistance to Turkey. Speaking of the decision, Ioannis Cassoulides, the Cypriot Minister of Foreign Affairs, stated that the amount would be sent via the UN in Geneva in the form of 'aid, medicines or other items considered necessary.' Furthermore the Minister announced that just two days after the earthquake notes were sent to the Turkish Government and the relevant United Nations' agency informing them that a forensic expert, two general surgeons, two nurses and a civil engineer were willing to go to Turkey to help. However, no reply had been received.[18]

Nevertheless, within 48 hours of the earthquake, a three-member team – two doctors and a nurse – from the Cyprus branch of *Médecins du Monde* had gone to Turkey. Despite the fact that they had chosen to fly to Turkey on a Greek Air Force transport plane, to get there more quickly, one of the doctors revealed that the Turkish Ambassador in Greece had actually offered the group free tickets to Istanbul with Turkish Airlines. Moreover, in news reports sent back to the island they noted that they had been greeted very warmly by the people of Turkey, many of whom had expressed surprise that a team of Greek Cypriots had volunteered to come to the region. When the time came to leave Turkey, all the members of the team made it clear that they would be ready to return to Turkey if needed and that their organisation would continue to send medicine to the victims of the disaster.[19]

The response from Turkey

The effect of all of this on Turkey was profound. To a country that had long believed that Greece and the Greeks sought to destabilise the Turkish state, the pictures of massive amounts of aid now being collected for their benefit at a time of weakness proved to be a watershed in their perceptions of their neighbours. While one might have assumed that there may have been a tendency to regard such moves with suspicion, this reaction could not have been further from the minds of the people of Turkey. Instead, most people welcomed the help with open arms and praised the Greek people for the generosity at such a time. Nowhere was this feeling of gratitude more pronounced that in the Turkish media, which, like their counterparts in Greece, had for so long been the vanguards of nationalism in the country. It was not long before the newspapers took to proclaiming the ever-lasting gratitude of all Turks to the Greek 'brethren'. In the days that followed the significant changes that had occurred in relations became even more pronounced as the Greek SKAI television station teamed up with TGRT, a Turkish television channel, to conduct joint live broadcasts.

Yet perhaps the most surprising demonstration of Turkish gratitude was shown at a ceremony marking the retirement of Admiral Selim Dervişoğlu, the commander of the Turkish Navy, just ten days after the earthquake. For the first time since 1974, the commander of Greek Naval Forces, Admiral Georgios Ioannides, was invited to the event, which was also attended by the Turkish Prime Minister, the Speaker of the Grand National Assembly, and most of the high-ranking commanders of the Turkish military. Upon his arrival, Ioannides was greeted with an honour guard and there was loud applause when the Greek admiral presented his counterpart with the shield of the Greek Navy.[20] In response, Dervişoğlu thanked Ioannides, referring to the Greek Admiral as 'my friend'. But what many of the observers did not realise was that the words were more than a gesture. It was a sincere statement of fact. The two men knew each other well. Over the previous year and half they had met eight times.[21] Moreover, the Turkish Admiral spoke some Greek from his youth, when he grew up amongst Greeks in Halki. Importantly, the first major signs of the effect of the earthquakes on bilateral relations were now being seen. The sight of a Greek military commander attending such an important function for the first time in twenty five years seemed to mark the first real proof of a significant change in relations between the two countries.[22]

However, the developments that were taking place did not meet with universal approval. In both countries there were those who appeared to disapprove of the growing spirit of solidarity between Greeks and Turks. For example, in Turkey, the Minister of Health, Osman Durmuş, a member of the nationalist MHP, was reported to have said that neither Greek nor Armenian assistance was required or wanted. Furthermore, the Minister informed a US hospital ship, which had arrived to provide medical assistance, that it was not required, as there was no one to transfer to it. The comments provoked a major outcry in Turkey, and were soon being reported internationally. Throughout the following days, the offices of *Hürriyet* were inundated with faxes and calls from readers appalled at the comments and calling for the resignation of the minister. Another Turkish newspaper led with the headline: 'Enough. Shut up and Go'.[23]

Within the Turkish Government there was also sever consternation about the comment, so much so that the matter was reportedly discussed within the Council of Ministers. Ecevit was even reported to have gone as far as to rebuke the minister in front of his colleagues; asking Durmuş to 'please remain silent from now on. The Foreign Ministry is responsible for our links with foreign countries. It informs them on what we need and thanks them for their aid in a diplomatic way.'[24] At the same time, ANAP, the minority partner of the coalition government, called an extraordinary meeting of its Parliamentary Group and the Chairman of the Grand National Assembly's Commission on Foreign Affairs asked, 'can a minister inform a US hospital ship, which arrived to help earthquake victims, that we do not have any sick people to transfer to it? Under the present conditions, there must be a least one sick person.' Going further, another MP called for the Durmuş's resignation on the grounds that 'a minister who rejects foreign aid for the earthquake victims cannot maintain his position in the Government...I urge the partners in the Government to adopt a conscientious approach to the matter.'[25]

Such was the backlash that the minister was forced to apologise, saying that he had been misquoted and that all help was welcome from whatever sources. This was followed up a few weeks later when Durmuş gave an interview to Thanasis Tsitsas, of the Greek newspaper *Kyriatiki Eleftherotypia*, in which he responded to the allegations made against him.[26] Concerning the accusations that he had refused help from Greece and Armenia, he explained that this had not been the case. Instead he insisted that he had taken on board the advice from the World Health Organisation (WHO) at the time of the major earthquake in Armenia that no medicines, clothes personnel of mobile hospitals should be sent without first asking the country concerned what it needed. As he was in the affected area he did not know where the offers of assistance had come from. He accepted what was needed and turned away what he felt was not, regardless of the origins of the assistance.

As for the claims about rejecting Greek blood, Durmuş stated that such allegations made no sense and that the accusations had been put around by 'Marxists'. As a doctor he knew about blood groups. As everywhere else, people in Greece and Turkey people were A, B and O and that if he was in an accident he would take any blood. Moreover, he announced that he was prepared to visit Greece and meet with his counterpart, 'to see if there is a possibility of cooperation in the health sector. I will become the bridge of cooperation between the two people to dissolve the misunderstandings over blood.' Finally, he explained that contrary to any impression that might exist he too shared a sincere desire to see peace develop between Turkey and Greece.[27]

But the scepticism was not just limited to Turkey.[28] In Greece there were also those who dissented to the new feelings being expressed between the two countries. Just days after the earthquake, several articles appeared in the newspaper *Eleftheros Typos* criticising Greek assistance on the grounds that the Turks were enemies who had sought to destroy Greece, and therefore should not be helped. For example, in an article published under the title, 'Do not extend a helping hand to blood-stained Attila, Georgie', one columnist asked whether the, 'polite, sensitive, benevolent, and unbelievably civilized' people of Greece were so willing to forgive Turkey for Cyprus. 'Are we going to extend a sweaty and scared hand to Demirel, Ecevit, and the crafty Ismail Cem for 'Hurriyet' again to shout aloud: 'Bravo, Georgie'?…Perhaps this is the opportunity for an opposition movement to rise up in that country too, which would bring about changes. And only then would a rapprochement between the two peoples be welcome, beneficial and useful.'[29] However, it was clear that the voices of the nationalists were in the minority. For the vast majority of Greeks and Turks the earthquakes had brought about a feeling of solidarity and goodwill.

The question of EU reconstruction funds

One area that did directly affect the official relations between the two countries was the question of Greece's continued veto over funds from the EU to Turkey, under the terms of the 1985 Fourth Financial Protocol. This issue had been a major source of contention between the two countries. Indeed, in his interview, Durmuş had stated that he hoped that Greece would lift its veto over the EU funds in order to help pay for reconstruction,[30] which preliminary estimates suggested would cost in the region of US$7–8 billion.[31] Many now saw a perfect opportunity for Greece to lift its objections on humanitarian grounds. Within days of the earthquakes many prominent newspapers such as *To Vima* and *Kathimerini* called on the Greek Government to reconsider the use of the veto, citing that should it wish to lift its blockade on the funding now would be a perfect opportunity to do so as the opposition would not have the courage to counter such a move.[32]

Yet such calls were opposed by others who called upon the Government to leave aside sentiment and ensure that no hasty moves were made to give ground on the question of the veto. In their view, the veto remained a strong bargaining chip for Greece to try to lever Turkey into taking significant steps to resolve some of the major outstanding issues. Other conservatries commentators were even more scathing. For example, another editorial in *Eleftheros Typos*, argued that Simitis and Papandreou were using the recent earthquake as, 'an alibi for yet another national retreat'.[33] Meanwhile, a few days later another columnist in the paper wrote an article entitled 'Blank Cheque from Athens', in which he declared that the Greek efforts would simply be used by the European Commission to send whatever sum it liked to Turkey under the guise of humanitarian assistance. This 'back door policy' was both known and supported by Papandreou.[34] The paper also drew attention to comments by the Minister for the Aegean, Stavros Benos, who had reportedly stated that the lifting of the veto should be welcomed as a means by which Greece could get 'rid of the label of being small and insecure.'[35]

Apart from the growing speculation about whether Greece would lift its veto on the funds, more and more observers were starting to ask whether the earthquakes had created the conditions for a major reorientation in Greek-Turkish relations. The cooperation shown between Athens and Ankara had shown that an entirely new type of interaction between the two countries was possible. This could produce benefits in a range of areas, not least of all in the economic sphere. Rodoula Zisi, the Greek Deputy Minister for National Economy, called upon the Greek and Turkish business communities to resume their cooperation and for the reactivation of the Greek-Turkish Business Council, which had ceased contact in the aftermath of the Öcalan arrest.[36]

Another suggestion, this time made in *Milliyet* by Takis Berberakis, a Turkish journalist of Greek descent, was that the two Governments might be able to come to an agreement concerning joint exploitation of the Aegean oil fields. This might also allow Turkey to shelve plans to construct a highly controversial – especially in the aftermath of the earthquakes – nuclear reactor at Akuyu, on Turkey's Mediterranean coast.[37] Others looked beyond Greece and Turkey and examined the possibilities of regional economic and commercial cooperation. Writing in *Eleftherotypia*, George Pandayias, a close advisor to Simitis, suggested that, 'Turkey and Greece could together share out an important part of the economic investment opportunities planned for Kosovo and other countries in the region.'[38]

Nevertheless, many still took a sceptical, if not hostile, view of what was happening and questioned whether the earthquakes really could constitute a meaningful basis for rapprochement between the two countries.[39] Rumours also started to circulate the Greek Government was on the verge of initiating a secret dialogue with Turkey on the key issues of Cyprus and the Aegean. In a report appearing in *To Vima*, just a few days after the earthquake, it was reported that the Greek and Turkish Permanent Representatives to the European Union, Loucas Tsilas and Nihat Akyol, had already held preliminary discussions along these lines. Indeed, another newspaper even claimed that Tsilas had stated in a report back to Athens that, 'regarding the Aegean, Ankara believes that there is great potential for reaching a settlement that will fully satisfy Greece. However, on Cyprus, the ability of the two sides to change the status quo substantially is extremely limited.'[40] However, these reports were quickly and firmly denied by both the Greek and Turkish Foreign Ministries. In a written statement the Turkish MFA said that the reports in the Greek papers were little more than works of imagination, as were any reports on Turkish positions. It stressed that the only talks taking place were under the terms of the 30 June agreement, covering matters such as crime, the environment and culture.[41]

Meanwhile, on the matter of the financial aid, it was now being reported that Papandreou had already formulated a new financial package to put to other EU foreign ministers at a meeting due to take place in Finland on 4 September. The proposal would draw together the three existing EU regulations for financial assistance to Turkey into a new package, which would also include financial assistance for the disaster. Importantly, the reports noted that he had already discussed the idea with Cem and with the Finnish Foreign Minister, Tarja Halonen.[42] This created a potential problem for the government. If the Government went ahead and released the funds without consulting the opposition then it would inevitably find itself open to criticism in the future that it had used a moment of impetuousness to give away one of its key cards in its relations with Turkey. Papandreou therefore announced that before any decision was taken on the issue he would consult with the other party leaders and try to reach a consensus view on the best course of action.

These consultations began on 30 August with a visit to two elder statesmen of PASOK, Karolos Papoulias and Ioannis Haralambopoulos, who had served as foreign ministers.[43] Both advised caution. In particular, they noted that funding for humanitarian assistance should be seen as separate from structural funds that Greece had vetoed.[44] Meanwhile, although not consulted directly, Theodore Pangalos had by this point presented his opinion on the matter. In an article published the day before in *Ta Nea*, he clarified that Greece did not exercise a veto on the question of the funds. Instead, it simply did not adopt the wishes of the majority. While he actively supported the release of humanitarian funds for Turkey, this was nevertheless 'as far as [Greece] should go.' In fact he argued that anyone calling for the lifting of the veto was, 'ignorant of history'.[45]

The article was naturally seen as a direct attack on Papandreou, in particular, and the process of rapprochement in general.[46] However, this was denied by Dimitri Reppas, the Government Spokesman. In a briefing to journalists, he stressed that Pangalos was actually fully supportive of Papandreou's efforts.[47] He also explained that the Government's proposal on the funds certainly did not amount to a blank cheque to Turkey.[48] Soon afterwards, Papandreou met with Constantine Mitsotakis, the honorary president of New Democracy, Dimitris Tsovolas, the leader of the

Democratic Social Movement (DIKKI), and Antonis Samaras, a former foreign minister and leader of the right-wing Political Spring, in order to inform them about developments.[49]

While trying to build consensus in this way may have been seen as a responsible course of action, many were concerned about what would happen if the opposition objected. This would put the government in a difficult position. For this reason, it was asked whether it would not be better to press on with releasing the funds and use this as a springboard for improving relations rather than give in to the opposition and squander a chance to make a real political gain.[50] Others believed that while the consultation was important, the Government should not be prevented from doing what it believed to be right by the opposition. As one commentator noted, the question of the veto was not the central issue. The main question facing the government was whether it wanted better relations with Turkey. If so, then Athens should take advantage of the atmosphere that had developed since the earthquake. Lifting the veto would not be a short-term measure of goodwill or appeasement, but instead represented a chance to change the entire the shape of relations with Ankara. Public opinion showed that the people wanted a new direction.[51]

This was echoed in another commentary article by George Pandayias in which he argued that the earthquake had presented a possible unique opportunity to change relations. Specifically, he argued that the Greek Government should not be bound by the principal of reciprocity. The creation of a good climate between the two countries would have a deeper and more significant long-term benefit on bilateral relations than the continuation of a policy that viewed all actions as an exchange.[52] However, in Turkey there were those who did feel that Ankara should offer some gestures to Greece in return for its generosity over the previous two weeks. As one writer argued, it was time for Ankara to put aside its pride, show its emotions, and make an urgently needed gesture to Greece.[53] But none of the arguments about the need to redefine relations appeared to have much of an effect on New Democracy, which announced that it was opposed to the lifting of the veto on structural funds and that this would be made clear to Papandreou during his forthcoming meeting with Costas Karamanlis, the party leader.[54]

Meanwhile, Greek efforts to support Turkey were continuing throughout the country. By now numerous meetings were taking place between local officials coordinating micro humanitarian efforts. At the same time, more and more officials from the central government were lining up to support the rapprochement that was taking place. For example, in an television interview given TRT in Turkey, Vasso Papandreou, the Greek Interior Minister (and no relation to George Papandreou), noted that the governments and the peoples on both sides of the Aegean wanted to improve relations and were not enemies. The earthquakes had shown this again. Explaining that there were of course problems between the two countries, she emphasised that there was a sincere desire to solve these issues in accordance with international law. In the meantime, and in view of the widespread nature of the disaster, the Greek Government would continue to send relief to Turkey.[55]

In Turkey, there was an overwhelming sense of gratitude at what Greece had done. For example, on 7 September, the Greek Ambassador in Ankara, Ioannis Korantis, received a delegation from the Women's Commission of the True Path Party (DYP), which had come to thank him for Greek support over the previous weeks. Speaking to the group, he made what were to be prophetic comments:

> Many people wonder what happened to the Greek people in the earthquake. The answer is so simple. Greece is in the same seismic zone and faced serious quakes in the past. Some cities were levelled. The earthquake in our neighbourood was perceived as a disaster in Greece…the earthquake has destroyed our taboos. From now on, we will follow the path of peace and co-operation.[56]

An earthquake strikes Athens

At three o'clock in the afternoon on 7 September a ten second tremor registering 5.6 on the Richter scale was recorded about 27 kilometres northwest of Athens. Although a lot smaller than the quake that had hit Turkey, initial reports nevertheless suggested that a number of buildings had collapsed and that almost thirty people had been killed.[57] Within minutes of the news being received, a member of the AKUT search and rescue team called Korantis to inform the ambassador that they were ready to offer any assistance necessary. Keeping him on the line, Korantis called Athens. The offer was accepted and within two hours the team was ready to depart.[58] It was the first time the team had been sent to a foreign country.

Soon afterwards, Korantis received a call from Ecevit's foreign policy advisor explaining that the prime minister had tried to call Simitis but that all the lines had been busy. He asked the ambassador to convey the prime minister's best wishes to the Greek Government.[59] Meanwhile, President Demirel and Speaker Akbulut had also met with the same problem when they had tried to telephone their counterparts to wish Greece well.[60] However, Demirel did manage to send a telegram to President Stephanopoulos:

> We feel and share your sorrow due to the deaths and losses that the quake that hit your country today caused because we have experienced

a similar disaster a short time ago. I would like to convey a 'get well soon' and condolence messages for the survivors on behalf of the Turkish nation and myself and would like to express that we are in solidarity with the Greek nation at this hard time. I would like you to be sure that Turkey will not abstain from any support and aid to your country and nation against this disaster.[61]

However, Cem was able to get through to Papandreou, who was away from Greece at the time, to offer support and assistance. While the scale of the earthquake in Greece was far smaller than the one in Turkey and eventually resulted in around 140 deaths, as opposed to the 15,000 in Turkey, the offer of support was received with gratitude in Greece. Speaking on the Turkish support for Greece, Prime Minister Ecevit noted that the news of the disaster in Greece had met with immediate reaction in Turkey, and the government had worked round the clock to co-ordinate its efforts to assist Greece. Explaining the reasons for such swift action, Ecevit stated that just as the people of Greece had shared in the grief and suffering caused by the earthquakes in Turkey, the people of the Turkey shared the suffering of the Greek people and that they would do anything they could to relieve their pain. 'The earthquakes that rocked the two countries have forced the two neighbours to remember again that they have a common fate.'[62]

In the end, little assistance was needed. The number of causalities and the extent of the damage were relatively small. However, this did not diminish the significant psychological benefits. The immediacy of the Turkish response and the overwhelming number of goodwill messages from ordinary Turkish citizens – the Greek Consulate in Istanbul reported that its switchboard was being overwhelmed by calls from well-wishers calling to wish Greece a speedy recovery and offer help in whatever way they could – were seen to be a strong indication that the people of Turkey also wanted to build a new relationship.[63] Moreover, as had been the case with EMAK in Turkey, the presence of AKUT in Greece became an important symbol of the new found desire for greater co-operation and proof of a change that was taking place between the two countries. Upon his return to Istanbul, on 9 September, Nasuh Mahruki, the head of the AKUT team, noted that he had been pleased to be able to fulfil his duty in Athens and that they had worked non-stop for two days. Another member of the team insisted that they had put just as much effort in their operation to help the Greeks as the team had exerted helping their own people just a couple of weeks earlier.[64]

By this stage it appeared as if only the most hard-line of nationalists were prepared to cast a shadow over the growing spirit of goodwill that was developing between the two countries. Even those who had traditionally taken an extremely sceptical line on the possibilities for peace between

Greece and Turkey now began to accept that the earthquakes had brought about an opportunity for a new relationship between Athens and Ankara, even if they had not quite become used to the change in language that this new relationship required. For example, İsmail Köse, the MHP parliamentary whip, stated:

> There has been hostility between Turkey and Greece because of the latter's attitude dating back to the Ottoman period, an attitude that was recently manifested by Greece's support for the PKK, which engages in activities against Turkey...However, the aid extended by Greece after the earthquake in the Marmara region and Turkey's attitude regarding the quake experienced in Greece some time after that brought about a rapprochement between the two nations. This is a historic opportunity. This opportunity must be well utilised and the problems between the two countries must be resolved.[65]

In Ankara, the Greek Ambassador, Ioannis Korantis, gave an interview to *Milliyet* in which he thanked all the Turkish people and the Turkish Government for all that they had done for his country since the Athens earthquake. He recalled that over the previous week he had received hundreds of calls from people offering words of sympathy for Greece, and that the Embassy had received gifts of flowers, and offers to donate blood, money and other necessary items. He even referred to one caller who had offered to donate a kidney to a victim in Greece after remembering that a Greek had made a similar offer. When asked about whether or not the feelings of good will that had been generated would last, Korantis replied that the two sides wanted to improve their relations before the earthquakes occurred. In fact, he noted that they had taken positive initiatives for that purpose even before the disasters. The significance of the earthquakes was that they had strengthened the positions of the two governments with regard to the dialogue as the people and the media are now watching the behaviour of the two governments. He hoped that there would not be a return to the previous state of bilateral relations and that, if there was such an adverse change, it would be difficult to explain to the people why it had happened.[66]

Indeed, it was the way in which the disasters had led to a transformation of popular attitudes that made them so important. This spirit of the people was caught well in an editorial, appearing in *Eleftherotypia* on 14 September in which the paper stressed the extent to which the earthquakes had managed to bring the people together and had served to break down prejudices between the two nations. Calling on the political leaders of both countries to respond to this new atmosphere the paper called for a non-aggression pact to be signed, without the use of a mediator, between

Greece and Turkey. As the paper noted, such an agreement would not only carry great symbolic significance, it would have tremendous practical value, especially if it were to be combined with a separate treaty that would reduce defence spending by both countries.[67] 'It is time they built mutual cooperation on the foundations of the solidarity built by the two peoples when shedding tears in amongst the ruins of the earthquakes, when counting the dead and estimating the damage.'[68]

Proliferation of bilateral contacts

By this point the old contacts that had been broken at the time of the Öcalan arrest were being repaired. Many of the groups that had broken off ties just six months earlier were now re-establishing contact. Meanwhile, many new ones were being created. Day-by-day the number and range of new relationships across the Aegean grew as political parties, companies, non-governmental organisations and associations, and even individuals, started to make contact with one another.[69] For example, on September 9, a delegation from the centre-left Republican Peoples Party (CHP) met with representatives from PASOK, led by Kranidiotis, in Brussels. There they discussed how they could work more closely together within international organisations. At the end of the meeting CHP accepted an offer to visit Athens.[70] Soon after this Nikos Konstantopoulos, the leader of Synaspismos visited Turkey.

In addition to the growing ties between politicians at a national level, there was also a proliferation of contacts at the local government level. Leading the way were Athens and Istanbul. On 19 September, Ali Müfit Gürtuna, the Mayor of Istanbul, paid a visit to Athens to see his counterpart, Dimitri Avramopoulos. As he left for Greece, Gürtuna told waiting reporters that he was going to Greece to express his good wishes to his Greek counterpart following the Athens earthquake and to find out what assistance the Istanbul municipality could give to the city. Welcoming him at the airport, Avramopoulos joined with the Turkish mayor to stress once again the importance of the ties that were developing between the two peoples and emphasised that a historical process had started that politicians had a responsibility to respond.[71] Following their talks, Avramopoulos announced that Athens would set up a further tent camp in Istanbul for eight to ten thousand people and that another aid convoy would reach Turkey in 2–3 weeks. The two mayors also announced that they had agreed to initiate contact in sports, tourism, technical, business, and cultural fields. They also announced their intention to work with one another to preserve historic sites in the two cities and that they would build a 'Friendship and Solidarity Monument'.[72]

Elsewhere similar examples of contacts between municipalities could be found. Even relatively small towns and cities started to make contact with one another. For instance, a delegation of Turkish MPs and Mayors visited the northern Greek town of Sapes, at the invitation of the Mayor.[73] This was seen as especially significant as the Rodopi prefecture, in which the town is located, is the home to many of Greece's Muslim minority. Twinning of towns also became highly popular. In Antalya, the Mayor, Bekin Kumbul, announced that he was launching an initiative to declare Antalya and Athens as sister cities. Citing the match between the football teams Antalyaspor and Ialyos as an example of Greek-Turkish co-operation the mayor noted that ties between the two towns was a natural step.[74]

Meanwhile, the growing rapprochement was having an effect in other ways. For instance, in Izmir, the usual celebration staged on September 9 to mark the liberation of the city by Atatürk's Turkish Nationalist forces in 1922 were stripped of all the traditional anti-Greek sentiment. Usually the event was marked by a recreation of the Nationalists' entrance into the city. This would involve lowering the Greek flag from Government House and throwing it into the sea as a Turkish flag was hoisted in its place. This time the ceremony was replaced with a subdued commemoration devoid of pageantry. The Turkish flag was raised alongside the Greek flag.[75]

Yet by far the most important effect of the earthquakes was the degree to which they had prompted individual citizens and non-governmental organisations to initiate contacts with one another. In the first instance, these efforts concentrated on fund raising for the victims of the disasters. Throughout Greece and Turkey great efforts had been made to try to collect money, but now the efforts combined as football matches and concerts were arranged. The regular supply of aid continued to flow from Greece to Turkey was soon matched by a massive growth in other contacts between the two countries. Whereas in previous times those Greeks and Turks who had tried to promote greater understanding and communication between their two countries had needed to keep a fairly low profile, in the months following the disaster there was a proliferation of groups established that sought to bring together the two peoples.[76] The previous taboos concerning contacts between the two countries had been broken. In the new political environment there was no stigma or suspicion attached to those who wanted to take practical steps to build upon the goodwill that developed in the aftermath of the earthquakes. This was important insofar as it not only legitimised the process of talks that had started between the governments in July, it also led to a popular desire in both countries to see it succeed and bring about tangible results.

5

NEXT STEPS

The earthquakes had radically transformed the atmosphere between Greece and Turkey when, on the 12 September, Cem and Papandreou met in Brussels on the eve of an EU meeting of foreign ministers. Following the meeting they announced that they were both extremely pleased with the progress that had been made in the talks thus far and that they had decided that the subjects under discussion should be expanded to cover a range of technical issues, such as the energy transfer lines. Cem also noted that security matters had also been touched upon briefly, but did not elaborate any further, stating that they would be returned to at another meeting. Papandreou, in his statement to the press, reiterated that a positive atmosphere existed between the two people. However, aware of the sensitivities that still existed about the possibility that there was a hidden agenda behind the talks, he emphasised that as far as Cem's comment on security issues was concerned, neither Cyprus nor other similar matters were raised in their discussions.[1]

By this stage it was known that the two foreign ministers were speaking to one another by telephone on a regular basis. However, their face-to-face discussions were an important part of the process, not least of all because of the symbolism of having the two ministers meeting so often. For this reason, it was made clear that they would continue to talk on a regular basis, mainly on the sidelines of international meetings. For example, it was announced that the two would see each other again less than two weeks later, at the opening of the United Nations General Assembly in New York. They would then meet again in Brussels in mid-October. This time the meeting would be on the margins of an EU summit, where it was expected that Union would confirm that it would give a substantial aid package for post-earthquake reconstruction in Turkey. Meanwhile, speculation was growing that it was only a matter of time before the two prime ministers would meet. In the minds of most observers the best opportunity would come at the OSCE summit, which was due to be held in Istanbul in November.[2]

In the meantime, the level of contacts between the two governments continued to rise. A ceremony held in Bulgaria to mark the opening of the headquarters for the South East Europe Peacekeeping Brigade (SEEBRIG) – a joint initiative of Greece, Turkey, Bulgaria, Romania, Albania, FYROM and Italy[3] – provided a historic opportunity for the Greek and Turkish Defence Ministers, Akis Tzohadzopoulos and Sabahattin Çakmakoğlu, to meet with one another. While they had spoken on the telephone a few weeks earlier, when Tzohadzopoulos offered Greek military assistance to Turkey, this was the first time the two men had met face-to-face.

The media hailed the meeting as a particularly important indication of the new spirit of co-operation between the two countries. Both Tzohadzopoulos and Çakmakoğlu were generally considered to represent the nationalist camps in their respective governments. For his part, Çakmakoğlu noted that the earthquakes had shown the peoples of both countries how much they needed each other and that, through dialogue, the Turkish government felt that the two countries would be able to resolve their differences. In response, Tzohadzopoulos stressed that the co-operation shown during the earthquakes would continue between the two countries. Going further still, the Greek Minister noted that such co-operation should be extended to cover the civil defence field and proposed the establishment of a joint rescue team to tackle emergencies that may arise in future.[4]

Elsewhere, there were other signs of the way in which the earthquakes had transformed the perceptions of the two governments towards bilateral relations. In Turkey the National Education Minister, Metin Bostancıoğlu, marked the start of the new school year by noting that the friendship that had developed between the two countries would be reinforced through education. Such efforts would include reviewing the Turkish textbooks to purge them of 'unfriendly sections', a suggestion that had been at the forefront of efforts to promote better bilateral relations for some time, and through exchange visits between the two ministries that would include the two ministers.[5]

It was against this backdrop of growing optimism that the news emerged in the early hours of 15 September that Yiannos Kranidiotis, the alternate foreign minister, and one of the key architects of the rapprochement process, had been killed when the plane he was travelling suddenly lost altitude on the way to a meeting of regional foreign ministers in Romania.[6] In Athens there was deep shock at the news. Expressing the feeling within the Government, Prime Minister Simitis stated that the death had shaken everybody and that Kranidiotis had, 'represented Greece with knowledge, skill and determination.'[7] Similar sentiments were echoed by Papandreou. In a more personal message, he stated: 'We are shaken, the whole government, the whole ministry. I cannot believe it. We lost people who gave the battle for peace in the Balkans. Peace lost a friend, I lost a friend, the most capable colleague in the ministry. Greece and Cyprus lost a tireless worker for their national interests.'[8] Tributes were also paid by all the opposition parties.

But the impact of Kranidiotis's death was felt beyond Greece. It was a particular shock for the Cypriot Government. As a Greek Cypriot by origin, Kranidiotis was held in high standing on the island. In fact, there had even been frequent speculation that he may one day have run for the presidency of the island.[9] In the meantime, as a senior member of the Greek government, he had been seen as a vital link between Nicosia and Athens and was trusted by the Greek Cypriot people to represent their interests. President Clerides, speaking from London on his way to New York for the opening of the UN General Assembly, paid tribute to the minister, stating that he had dedicated time and effort to 'protect and promote' the interests of Greece and 'his homeland' and that his death had left a void.[10] In tribute, the Cypriot Government declared three days of national mourning.[11]

It was a measure of his esteem that his death was also mourned in Turkey. Although a Cypriot by birth, and a staunch supporter of the Greek Cypriot cause, the Minister had nevertheless won a lot of respect and praise in Ankara for his clear thinking and constructive approach over the course of the previous months. President Demirel sent a letter to his Greek counterpart in which he offered his deepest condolences to Greece on the death of, 'a distinguished diplomat and politician who will be remembered for his valuable works for his country', and noted that Turkey shared the grief of the Greek people.[12]

Few doubted the role Kranidiotis had played in the process of rapprochement so far and most knew that it would be difficult, if not impossible, to replace him. Nevertheless, a successor was needed and five days later Simitis named Christos Rokofyllos to the post. Rokofyllos was seen to be a safe pair of hands. A former Greek Ambassador to France and deputy Industry Ministry, he had also been the head of the Greek parliament's delegation to NATO and was also the chairman of the PASOK's foreign affairs and defence committee.[13]

The second round of talks

On 15 September, the delegations gathered again in Ankara for the second round of direct talks. Despite the news about Kranidiotis, the two governments agreed that the talks should take place as scheduled. As previously agreed, the first half of the day was devoted to cultural matters. Following a lunch hosted by the Greek Embassy, the discussions turned to issues relating to regional integration. Notwithstanding the fact that the death of the Greek minister was dominating news coverage, there was nevertheless considerable interest in both countries about the outcome of the talks. However, it was clear that neither country wanted to conduct negotiations under the glare of media attention. In response to the state of play following the end of the first day of talks, Ambassador Korantis explained that that if a press release was to be issued, it would only happen at the end of the talks the next day.[14]

The next morning the discussions turned to the thorniest issue to date: terrorism. Despite the fact that the teams did not issue a statement to the press following the meeting, in a report produced by the *Anadolu Agency* afterwards it was noted that the teams met for nearly three and half hours and had a constructive exchange of views on the question of combating terrorism and dealing with organised crime.[15] A communiqué issued after the meeting confirmed that the discussions had focused on tourism, environment, economic and commercial relations, culture, cooperation in the multilateral regional field and combating organized crime, illegal immigration, drug trafficking and terrorism, and that the atmosphere was friendly and businesslike and confirmed that a third round of talks would take place in late-October.[16] Later on, it was announced that the first round would take place on 21–22 October in Ankara, with a second phase in Athens, on 25–26 October.

Although the official announcements about the talks were framed in rather cautious language, the two ministers' could barely hide the degree to which they were delighted with the new relationship that seemed to be developing between their countries. Papandreou was now speaking more openly about his contacts with Cem and was actively promoting the benefits from increased contact between the two countries. And although the exact details of the discussions had not been revealed, it was reported that a large number of specific ideas had now been put on the table by the two delegations.[17]

For example, there was talk about the reactivation of the Joint Transportation Committee. This would examine how to develop a high-speed rail link between Thessaloniki and Istanbul. Others suggested that there were discussions about the ways in which to modernise the customs procedures between the two countries. Another area of interest was tourism. It was reported that the Turkish delegation had suggested could this topic could form the subject of a forum in October drawing together the public and private sectors from the two countries. Other areas of focus included co-operation in the energy sector, such as technology exchanges and the inter-connection of circuit systems, and education, although questions of minority education were not included. Indeed, it was also claimed that any points of the difference between the two countries were, at this stage, being 'religiously' avoided. For instance, in their discussions on the environment the Greek team also avoided the sensitive subject of the proposed nuclear power plant in Akkuyu in order to prevent embarrassment to the Turkish group.[18] Similarly, it was reported that Turkey apparently avoided direct mention of the PKK in the joint discussions on terrorism for the same reason. It was also noted that in the talks about the environment questions of a sensitive territorial nature, such as 'coastal zones', were also kept to one side.[19]

Cem and Papandreou meet at the United Nations

Cem and Papandreou met again in New York at the start of the last week of September for the opening of the UN General Assembly. By now the first tangible results of the discussions were emerging. The two countries had drawn up an agreement to establish a joint rescue team, comprised of participants from the governmental and non-governmental sectors, to tackle future disasters. In a highly symbolic move, this proposal was submitted to the United Nations for consideration by the Secretary-General as a part of the wider international contribution to the UN's efforts to deal with natural disasters. However, the meeting in New York also allowed for the two ministers to discuss future steps to broaden and strengthen the level of co-operation between Greece and Turkey. Following a working lunch, it was announced that the two foreign ministries had decided to establish a political consultation mechanism that would be managed by the political directors of the two ministries.

It was also decided that further steps would be taken to bolster the work being done by the delegations in the direct talks. For example, the two ministers agreed to establish an energy subcommittee that would examine the opportunities for both co-operation and the transfer of technologies. It was also decided that attention should be given to the possibilities for improving bilateral relations in the context of regional and multilateral initiatives. Also, in what appeared to be the first tentative step towards an examination of some of the key issues of difference, the possibility of establishing a think tank composed of selected members of the two foreign ministries and including representatives from academia and the media was discussed.[20] In an interview given to the Athens News Agency following the meeting, Papandreou noted that the process was necessarily going to be a long-term project, but that it had made satisfactory progress so far.[21]

Despite the progress that had been made in bilateral relations over the previous few months, and especially in the aftermath of the earthquakes, the current focus on low-level issues did little to mask the deeper problems that existed between the two countries. As ever, Cyprus was a key sticking point. On 23 September, just the day before he met with Papandreou, Cem had stood before the General Assembly and spoken about the Cyprus issue in hard line terms. Making it clear that Turkey believed that it was not possible for the Turkish Cypriots to return to the situation prior to 1974, he reiterated that any settlement should necessarily take into account the current political realities of the situation. There were now two people and two states on the island. While he agreed on the need for confidence building measures, he nevertheless called for the lifting of the 'unfair' embargo that had been placed on the Turkish Cypriots.[22]

Cem's comments caused consternation in Greece. To all intents and purposes the view he expressed were fully in line with the position adopted by Ecevit and by the Turkish Cypriot leader, Rauf Denktaş, that the Cyprus problem had been solved in 1974 and that if any reunification was to take place it should be done on the basis of a loose confederation made up of two sovereign states. This call for a confederation stood in marked contrast to the internationally agreed basis for a settlement based on the formation of a bi-zonal and bi-communal federation.

When questioned about his counterpart's comments, Papandreou responded by drawing attention to the most recent statement by the five permanent members of the UN Security Council describing the situation on the island as unacceptable.[23] The Greek Government supported this view. As for what Greece would do if Turkey did not change its positions, he explained that the recent improvement in relations would allow for a step-by-step approach to a solution of the Cyprus problem on the basis that a solution would, 'add substance to Turkey's European orientation.'[24]

The message was clear on two levels. First of all, it again emphasised the degree to which Athens regarded a settlement of the Cyprus issue as being intimately and inextricably linked to Turkey's hopes to join the European Union. Secondly, the comment was significant insofar as Papandreou had again highlighted that the talks should not be dependent upon moves to resolve the key issues. Instead, and more importantly, the aim was to create the conditions that would eventually make substantive discussions more likely. Significantly, Papandreou had just created a powerful defence against those who would inevitably call for an end to low-level bilateral talks if no results were achieved on the core issues dividing the two countries.

Opening the debate on Turkey's EU candidacy

By this point feelings in Greece towards Turkey had improved significantly. A poll published in a leading Greek newspaper showed that 74 per cent of Greeks supported the direct discussions with Turkey. Meanwhile, popular attitudes towards Turks had also improved. They now received an average sympathy score of 4.4 on a scale of one to ten. This put them ahead of Slav-Macedonians (4.3) and Albanians (2.8); the other two neighbouring peoples that were traditionally demonised in popular Greek thinking.[25]

But in spite of everything that had taken place over the previous six weeks, it was nevertheless clear that there were those on both sides of the Aegean who remained opposed to the process of rapprochement. On 28

September, arsonists attacked the Gökçepinar Mosque in the Xanthi region of Thrace. Although only minor damage was caused, the Greek Government immediately released a statement in which it condemned the attack and promised to bring the perpetrators to justice. The Turkish Foreign Ministry responded to the news by issuing its own press release in which it condemned the attack and stated that it expected the, 'Greek Government to identify and bring the assailants of that arson attack, which targeted spiritual values, to justice, and take the measures that will prevent the reoccurrence of such attacks.[26]

Notwithstanding such incidents, the transformation that had taken place in Greek-Turkish relations was such that attention inevitably turned to the question of Greece's position on Turkish candidacy of the European Union. In just over two months the leaders of the European Union would meet at the European Council in Helsinki. As had been agreed at the previous meeting in Cologne, in June, the subject of Turkey would be on the agenda. At that time Simitis had made it clear that Turkey would be expected to conform to certain principles before it could be accepted. The question was whether Greece would continue to maintain this view in light of recent events. If it did, it would run the risk that Turkey would not take the steps required and the process of rapprochement would suffer. Alternatively, Greece could drop its opposition in the hope of receiving some sort of measure in return at a later stage. However, this might prove to be unpopular back in Greece.

But, as had been shown by the statements by Kranidiotis earlier in the summer, and more recently by Papandreou, within the Greek foreign ministry there was a growing sense that EU candidacy should not be used as leverage against Turkey. Instead, it would be far better to open the way for membership. This would encourage long-term reform and create both the incentives and the conditions to resolve the main points of difference. In the meantime, drawing Turkey closer to Europe would hopefully defuse the current tensions between Athens and Ankara. Significantly, it would also have a third benefit. Rather than try to continue to manage things at a bilateral level, the issues of difference between Greece and Turkey would henceforth be incorporated within the wider questions of Turkey's relations with the EU.

This philosophy came out clearly during an interview Papandreou gave to a Greek newspaper at the end of September.[27] Regarding the issue of Cyprus, Papandreou stressed that this problem, along with questions relating to bilateral Greek-Turkish relations, fell within the 'broader framework of Turkish-EU relations'. However, it appeared that the idea of exacting some concessions out of Turkey in advance of the EU summit was still expected, and that Turkey's candidacy could well be judged on this basis. When questioned about the specific steps that could be taken by

Ankara, he avoided giving any specifics: 'any substantive Turkish move that will contribute in defusing Greek-Turkish tension and help our relations operate within the framework of international law and the international treaties that are the basic principles for an honest and constructive relationship.'

But, in a significant new move, he also outlined the idea of creating a 'road map' for Turkish EU candidacy. Under this model, 'Turkey will be called upon to respond to the contents of the road map starting from the day it receives the candidate status until substantive accession negotiations begin.' Nevertheless, the interviewer pushed Papandreou for more concrete examples of steps. In response he sought to focus on the recent positive developments, such as the discussions on low-level issues and the recent statement made by Ecevit that Turkey had no territorial designs on Greek territory: 'If these statements are consolidated into a new practice of relations this could improve the climate greatly and the bilateral relations substantially.'

The apparent change in thinking that was taking place within the Greek Government appeared to be confirmed a few days later by Loucas Tsilas, the Greek Permanent Representative to the European Union. When asked to comment on the prospect of opening the way for Turkey's EU accession, Tsilas explained that this was the 'EU's problem'. It was not simply a Greek issue. As he explained, many 'high-ranking people' in Greece now recognised Turkey's European orientation and saw Turkish candidacy as a benefit to Greece:

> Greece [has] started to be constructive, and will continue to be so. Scandinavian countries are making efforts for the candidacy of Latvia and Lithuania, and Germany is making efforts for Poland's candidacy. Greece's interest is to support Turkey's candidacy and set up solidarity with Ankara.[28]

The interview by Papandreou and the comments by Tsilas were the first serious indications that a thorough rethinking of Greek policy towards Turkish membership of the European Union had taken place within the Greek Government. The question at this stage was whether Simitis would be willing or able to reorient Greek foreign policy so radically in the weeks left before the Helsinki summit. Despite recent events, it was obvious that a move to accept Turkish candidacy without conditions and without a gesture would be extremely difficult, if not impossible, for many Greeks to accept.

Papandreou visits Turkey

Meanwhile, on 3 October, Papandreou arrived in Turkey to deliver a lecture at the University of Istanbul. Although the trip was not official, in was nevertheless highly symbolic both in historical terms and in view of the developing rapprochement. For many people in Turkey the visit was seen as an opportunity to thank the minister for all that Greece had done and he was met at the airport by the Mayor of Istanbul, Ali Müfit Gürtuna, as well as by the Governor of Istanbul, Erol Çakir, and the Istanbul representative of the Turkish Foreign Ministry, Acar Germen. After leaving the airport his first appointment was to inspect a prefabricated school that had been set-up to replace the Greek elementary school in the city, which had been destroyed in the earthquake. There he received a briefing from the leader of the Greek community in the area, Costas Ioannis, and promised that Greece would do everything possible to ensure that the school was rebuilt.

Next he visited the Greek Orthodox Church of St Stephen, which had also be damaged, and after that he went to the Derince district to see a project to construct a complex of one hundred and fifty prefabricated homes that had been supplied by the Greek Government. This project, which cost of 500 million drachmas, (US$1.6 million), was due to be completed by 18 November and would be opened by Prime Minister Simitis, who would be in Istanbul for the OSCE summit. His final meeting was with a survivor of the earthquakes who had been rescued by EMAK, the Greek rescue team, after 108 hours buried under rubble.[29]

That evening Papandreou delivered his speech on 'Greek-Turkish Relations' before a packed house at the Marmara Hotel. Rather than deliver a bland statement of goodwill, he instead made an important statement regarding Greek policy in which he directly addressed many of the important points affecting bilateral relations. For example, he noted the very positive statement made by Ecevit a few days earlier, in which he stated that Turkey has no territorial ambition with regard to Greece. If true, then relations between the two countries would 'soon blossom.' However, if Turkey did in fact harbour desires to change the borders between the two countries then it should understand that this is not in its short- or long-term interest. Both countries should realise the enormous costs, both economic and political, of their continued conflict. A new peace process would, he argued, allow for a reduction in defence expenditure, which would, in turn, allow for greater development spending and lead to increased prosperity and investment. Yet for this to happen there must be the necessary level of political will. Extremist voices should not be allowed to separate the two nations. As members of the wider European family, both countries had a duty to resolve their differences without resorting to force.

But he also used the speech to caution against expecting too much too soon. He stressed that the dialogue process initiated by himself and Cem was necessarily a long process and that in the process there was a need for 'balanced and active' participation by international actors. While there had been progress on a number of areas, the reduction of mutual suspicions would take time and that the current lack of information in both countries about each other was a significant problem that would need to be solved. On the question of regional issues he asserted that the two countries must refrain from adopting contrary positions and should work together to address problems in Kosovo, the Caucasus and the Middle East. In conclusion, the Minister noted that, 'We need more communication.'[30]

The next day the comments on the speech were generally positive. In Greece there was a feeling that Papandreou had proven that he was not a soft touch and that he had not chosen to disregard the major issues of difference existing between the two countries. In Turkey, there was warm praise for the way in which he was able to approach the issues of conflict in a way that escaped from the antagonistic language that had, in their view, been the hallmark of Greek politicians in the past. That day, Papandreou met with Cem for a working lunch at the OSCE building. However, while it was reported that the two spoke positively about the developing dialogue, and had once again agreed that there was an opportunity to go even further, Cem was reportedly concerned about the reference to Turkey having to rethink its positions in light of its European aspirations. Avoiding any reference to these concerns, after the meeting, Cem simply stated that the two had, 'had some talks, mainly fact finding. I believe that we understand one another much better.' When asked about whether Cyprus had been mentioned in their talk, Papandreou replied that he had had the opportunity to raise the issue.'[31]

Differences between Athens and Nicosia

No matter how much Turkey may have wished to keep Cyprus out of the bilateral relationship, Greece could not overlook the issue. On the one hand, the recent improvement in relations between Greece and Turkey had also seen a reduction in tensions in Cyprus. For example, at the start of October, Greece and Cyprus held their annual joint military exercise. Although this was described by Turkish officials as worrying,[32] senior Greek officers noted that the traditional increase in Turkish military activity in the region had been milder than usual. The number of Turkish aircraft entering the Greek and Cypriot flight information region (FIR) was only twenty-eight. This was far lower than expected. Furthermore, as none of the aircraft was deemed by Greece to have invaded its territorial airspace,[33] no Greek aircraft challenged the Turkish planes.[34]

However, balanced against this, the Greek Cypriots were growing increasingly concerned about the implications of the rapprochement process on efforts to reunite the island. This had become particularly noticeable since the death of Kranidiotis, who had played an important role as a bridge between Nicosia and Athens. In the minds of many Greek

Cypriots, Papandreou seemed too keen to reach an accommodation with Turkey. Many felt that he, and by extension Simitis, who was also regarded as untrustworthy by many Cypriots, were now on the verge of discarding Cyprus in order to cement better bilateral relations with Turkey. Some commentators even argued that Cyprus was going to have to once again put aside its own best interests in favour of a decision taken by Athens, as they had done with the S-300 missiles a year earlier.[35]

The prospect of the Greek Government accepting Turkish candidacy without specific movement on Cyprus was regarded by many in Cyprus, as well as nationalists in Greece, as completely unacceptable. The leaders of all the main Greek Cypriot parties openly expressed the view that there could be no Turkish candidacy of the European Union without movement on Cyprus. However, in public Nicosia appeared to want to keep rumours of a split to a minimum. On 4 October, the Cypriot Government Spokesman, Michael Papapetrou, responded to journalists' questions on the matter of a possible divergence of views between the two capitals by stating that the Cypriot Government fully agreed with the Greek Government's policy and that, 'even if Turkey acquires the status of candidate for accession it will have specific obligations to meet throughout its course.'[36]

Meanwhile, in Athens, there was a growing perception that Nicosia was seeking to 'entrap' the Greek Government and hold the process of rapprochement hostage to movement on Cyprus. Many felt that the Cypriot Government wanted, 'to impose its own policy on [Greece]'.[37] Matters were not made any easier by the fact that Athens made it clear that it was not going to publicly divulge its policies simply in order to assuage Cypriot concerns. This was made clear by Christos Rokofyllos, the new alternate minister of foreign affairs, during an interview televised on a Greek Cypriot channel.[38] When warned of growing dissatisfaction in Cyprus about the perceived changes, the minister refused to divulge exactly what, if anything, Greece would seek from Ankara. All he would say was that the intention of the Greek Government was, 'to help Cyprus as much as possible.' However, he sought to play down growing rumours that the Greek government had already made its decision regarding Turkey's candidacy. When asked when a final decision would be made, and if the decision would follow the visit to the region of President Clinton, he explained that, 'the decision will be made after assessing all the factors and all the developments right up until the last minute, that is, 12 December, in Helsinki.' The next day, Papandreou sought to ease Cypriot concerns following a meeting with Ioannis Cassoulides, the Cypriot foreign minister, by publicly reaffirming that Cyprus remained a touchstone of Greek-Turkish relations.[39]

Setting the conditions for Turkish candidacy

On 16 October, Simitis travelled to Tampere for a meeting with other European leaders to discuss the forthcoming European Council in Helsinki in December. There he made it clear that Turkey's candidacy must be real and not fictitious and that Ankara must abide by the Copenhagen political criteria and accept the conclusions of EU summits – a position accepted by the other leaders.[40] It was the highest level indication to date that the Greek Government was actively considering a change to its position, by that this would require some very clear commitments on the part of the Turkish Government and by the European Union.

Meanwhile, Papandreou now embarked on a tour of a number of European capitals. Following the EU meeting in Finland, over the course of the following month he would visit Britain, Spain, France, Italy, Germany and the Netherlands.[41] The purpose of the tour was to explain the current Greek perspectives on the question of Turkey's EU candidacy and outline the conditions the Greek Government wanted met before lifting its current objections. Specifically, it was reported that, following a conversation with Prime Minister Simitis, Papandreou was asking Greece's EU partners that specific reference be made within the conclusions of the Helsinki summit to the need for all countries seeking EU membership to recognise the role of the International Court of Justice as a condition for membership.[42] On top of this, Athens would be looking to ensure that Cyprus remained firmly on track for membership.

Papandreou's first stop was in London, where he met with the British Foreign Secretary, Robin Cook. Cook restated Britain's full support for Cypriot membership of the EU and Turkish candidacy, but no mention was made about the ICJ.[43] In Rome, however, Papandreou seemed to receive the assurances he was after. Following a meeting with Lamberto Dini, the Italian Foreign Minister, Papandreou announced that the positions of the two countries were close and that Greece could expect Italian support for its positions in Helsinki.[44] However, a problem arose during his visit to Paris. As the French Government saw it, the fact that it did not recognise the compulsory jurisdiction of the Court made it unfair to demand that prospective candidates for EU membership did so. This appeared to make any definitive European stand on the principle unlikely.

Although there was a body of opinion within the foreign ministry that sought to downplay the need for a specific gesture from Turkey, preferring to push the matter firmly into the realm of Turkish-EU relations, many in the government still believed that Turkey should take some sort of step to show its goodwill and commitment to the process. Included in this camp was Prime Minister Simitis. Importantly, and with less than eight weeks to go before the Helsinki summit, he wrote to Ecevit highlighting the importance of a gesture.[45] While the Government spokesman sought to downplay the importance of the letter, perhaps realising that if an open demand was made and left unrealised it would create more problems, rumours nevertheless persisted that Simitis was now waiting to see if Turkey would take some sort of concrete step, such as the re-opening of the theological school at Halki.[46]

Indeed, soon afterwards, Simitis made it clear that he was now waiting for a gesture. This was made clear in a letter sent by the Greek prime minister to Ekrem Demirtaş, the President of Izmir's Chamber of Commerce. Demirtaş had originally written to the Greek Prime Minister to stress the desire of many in Turkey to improve relations with Greece and open up trade between the two countries. In response Simitis noted that, 'Greece shows sincere and particular willingness to improve relations with Turkey, expressing specifically support for your country's European vocations. It is only natural for us to expect the Turkish Government to respond positively with specific acts to our moves.[47]

In large part Simitis appeared to be responding to widespread concern in Greece about the implications of giving up the veto in expectation of a later Turkish move. Many wanted action first. An opinion poll published days after Simitis had sent his letter showed that more than fifty percent of the Greek population believed that Turkey should make a significant gesture to Greece before the Greek Government accepted Turkish candidacy. More importantly, the respondents also made clear that such a move should be judged totally independently of any EU gestures to Greece. No matter what the EU offered, Greece should expect a significant move from Turkey. Moreover, the general view was that a gesture such as the reopening of the School of Theology would not be enough. If Turkey wanted candidacy then it would have to make a serious gesture, such as lifting the Casus Belli resolution in the Turkish Grand National Assembly.[48]

This presented Papandreou with several problems. For a start, there was a growing belief in Greece that Turkey should offer some gesture before being accepted. Under these circumstances, even a gesture from the EU might be insufficient to placate Greek public opinion. Moreover, in the event that Turkey did not make a move and he nevertheless continued to support its candidacy, then it would be claimed by the opposition that he had obviously given in to foreign influence, for example from the United States – a criticism that held particular weight given that he was half-American and had spent many years living in the US. Matters were made all the more difficult for Papandreou following a report on CNN-Turk announcing that he had stated during a meeting with one of its correspondents that Greece would be prepared to drop its veto without a gesture from Turkey. In Turkey the news was greeted with delight and Cem issued a statement welcoming the Greek position. The trouble was that Papandreou had said nothing of the sort. In the face of uproar in Greece, the Greek Foreign Ministry was forced to issue a formal denial that there had been a change in policy.[49]

The third round of talks

As the Greek Government pondered its position, and Papandreou sought support from Greece's EU partners, the third round of talks between the two governments got underway, in Ankara on 21 October. This time the focus was firmly on tourism, which had been the subject of a conference organised by the two foreign ministries in Bodrum just a few days earlier.[50] The aim of this round of talks was to come up with a final set of proposals to enhance cooperation in this field. At the end of the meeting, Sermet Atacanlı, the Turkish Foreign Ministry's Spokesman noted that there had been a number of positive results achieved during the talks. Specifically he noted the friendly atmosphere and the fact that two teams had decided to establish a number of working groups, involving officials from other ministries but headed by ambassadors from the two countries, which would discuss proposals in greater detail and would then pass their findings to the two Foreign Ministers. Summing up the process so far, Atacanlı said that the developments were positive but that everyone should wait for the results of the meetings.[51]

That same day, Cem and Papandreou met in Thessalonica on the fringes of a meeting of the Black Sea Economic Cooperation Foreign Ministers' Council. In the course of discussions lasting more than one hour, it was reported that the two men had discussed the significant progress that had taken place between the committees and the fact that an interim report on the progress made by the working groups had now been prepared. Nevertheless, in a press conference following their meeting, Cem sounded a familiar note of caution. Although he emphasised that the recent events had led to greater mutual confidence, had lowered tensions and increased the level of contact between the peoples, the achievements to date should not be exaggerated. As he put it, 'the problems between Turkey and Greece could not be solved in a short period. The process is moving positively and much more quickly than I had anticipated. But we should be prudent.' At the same time, Papandreou agreed that the results thus far had been good. But that he also hoped to see much more progress in the future.[52]

A few days later, on 25 October, the delegations met again in Athens for the second half of the third round of discussion. This time the main focus of attention was once again terrorism and organised crime. Importantly, at the end of the discussion it was revealed that a working party had been established to review the texts of a number of agreements that had been developed as a result of the talks. It was also announced that the fourth round of talks would take place in December.[53]

Growing discord in Athens

But although there was a growing confidence about the dialogue and that the Greek Government appeared to be making progress towards securing the concessions it required from its EU partners, if not the Turkish Government, there was a growing sense of dissatisfaction within certain quarters in Athens about the willingness of the Government to give in to Turkey. While Simitis was in Finland he was forced to issue a strongly worded statement rejecting a call by New Democracy's for Papandreou's resignation on the ground that he was surrendering Greek sovereign rights.[54]

However, there appeared to be a wider rebellion brewing against the foreign minister, even from within his own party. On 1 November, Theodore Pangalos, the former Foreign Minister, in an interview broadcast on Cyprus television, accused his successor of giving in to US pressure regarding Turkish EU candidacy without gaining anything in return on the core issues of the Aegean or Cyprus. He also highlighted the fact that many people were increasingly concerned that Papandreou was not doing enough to keep the Greek people fully informed about the nature and extent of his contacts with Cem.

A few days later Papandreou faced similar charges from the Foreign Affairs Committee in the Greek Parliament.[55] As Yiannis Kapsis, a PASOK MP, and former deputy foreign minister, stated, 'We cannot be receiving information from the Turkish Foreign Minister on developments in our foreign policy – accurate or distorted. If Mr Cem's statement that Greece will raise no obstacles to Turkey's being characterised as a candidate country by the EU is correct, this is a matter for discussion.' Constantine Mitsotakis, the former prime minister, put it more bluntly: 'the lack of information in the current phase never existed in recent years. During Pangalos' ministry we were informed but now we don't even have briefings for party leaders.'[56] Although the allegations that the ministry was not keeping the parliament and the people informed about developments were denied by Rokofyllos,[57] it was clear that concerns existed across various parts of the political spectrum about the way in which Greek foreign policy towards Turkey was being made.

Concerns were not just centred on the way in which the process of rapprochement was being managed, there were also growing doubts about whether the process was even bringing results. Although a new era in relations was meant to have come about between Athens and Ankara, the Turkish Government appeared to maintain a hawkish line on key issues. Attention fell on two statements by senior Turkish officials. The first of these was a comment by Ecevit that Greece had forfeited its right to be a Guarantor Power in Cyprus by virtue of the fact that it had been Athens that had launched a coup on the island in 1974 that had deposed

Archbishop Makarios and led to Turkish intervention. In Greece there was a furious reaction to this statement. Responding to these charges, Dimitri Reppas, the Government Spokesman, stressed that Greece had 'both nominally and practically, fulfilled its obligations as a Guarantor, under the terms of the 1960 Treaty of Guarantee', and retorted that it had been Turkey that had not met the conditions of the Treaty.[58]

The second comment came from Sabahattin Çakmakoğlu, the Turkish Defence Minister, who appeared to reopen the question of the 'Grey Zones' when he rejected claims that Turkey was following an expansionist policy against Greece: 'Among the 1,753 islands in the Aegean there are islets, rocks and a large number of geographic formations which have not been assigned Greek sovereignty by agreements.' Reacting to the comments, Akis Tzohadzopoulos, the Greek Defence Minister, stressed that Greek sovereignty over all these territories was not negotiable. More importantly, Greece could not improve its relations with Ankara as long as the latter made, 'continual, relentless, unilateral and illegal demands.'[59]

6

THE PATH TO EUROPE

By this point the main issue attracting attention was the forthcoming OSCE Summit meeting in Istanbul, during which it was expected that Ecevit and Simitis would meet with one another. But the summit was also significant insofar as President Clinton would be visiting Greece and Turkey. The arrival of a US President had always been seen as being a major event in the region, and this trip was no exception. Many naturally assumed that Clinton would use his presence in the region to reinforce the current détente and press for a resolution of outstanding differences between the two countries.

However, hopes that this might even lead to a yet another initiative on Cyprus appeared to be dashed by Nicholas Burns, the US ambassador in Athens, who stated that Cyprus, 'would not be at the heart of the visit to Athens.' The Greek Cypriots reacted with fury to this. Even if Clinton did not wish to make it a central point of discussions, it was nonetheless incumbent upon the Greek Government to give the matter the highest attention. A few days after Burns' comments Michael Papapetrou, the Cypriot Spokesman, noted that the Cypriot Government had received a promise that it would be at the top of the agenda.[1]

It was against this backdrop that Clinton arrived in Turkey on 12 November at the start of what was due to be a five day visit to the country. He quickly ingratiated himself to his hosts. Travelling around the country, he received warm praise from Turkish commentators. The high point of the trip came when he gave a speech before the Grand National Assembly in which he congratulated Turkey for all the advances it had made and appeared to show a genuine interest in Turkish history and culture. As one MP said, 'you could feel the spirit of friendship towards Turkey.'[2]

But behind the scenes Clinton took every opportunity to reinforce the importance the US attached to the process of rapprochement. In addition he also made it clear that the Turkish Government needed to offer some gesture of goodwill to the Greek Government before the Helsinki summit. As he explained to Turkish officials, Simitis had taken a great political risk in promoting Greek-Turkish rapprochement and that he was now under a great deal of pressure at home to show firm results if he was to consider lifting the veto of Turkey's EU candidacy in Helsinki. For example, he suggested to President Demirel that the Turkish Government might consider re-opening of the Halki School of Theology – an idea that was also put to Cem by Madeleine Albright, the US Secretary of State. Demirel assured Clinton that the Turkish Government was already examining how this might be done in accordance with Turkish law, a message that Clinton later passed on to Patriarch Bartholomew when he went to see him in Istanbul.[3]

Clinton also highlighted the need for a gesture when he met with Ecevit, just prior to the start of the summit. This time, however, he used stronger tactic. In addition to emphasising that such a move would not only help Greece to lift its veto, it would also allow him to make the case for Turkish candidacy when he visited Athens on the next leg of his regional tour. It would also enable his administration to build up an argument for Turkish candidacy with European leaders. In addition to the Halki seminary issue, this time he also suggested rescinding of the Casus Belli resolution of the Grand National Assembly, which threatened war with Greece if Athens extended its territorial waters to 12 nautical miles. However, Turkish officials referred to this suggestion as being 'unrealistic'.[4] However, while direct bilateral moves may have seemed unlikely, there was nevertheless some news relating to Cyprus. On 13 November it was announced that after a two year hiatus the two sides in Cyprus had accepted an invitation from the Secretary General to resume proximity talks. These would take in place in New York, starting on 3 December.[5]

Ecevit and Simitis meet in Istanbul

This provided a positive backdrop for the long awaited meeting between the two prime ministers, which took place five days later, on 18 November. Although their discussion was seen by many to be relatively short, lasting less than an hour, it was reported that the atmosphere between Simitis and Ecevit was friendly and relaxed.[6] Opening the talks, Ecevit praised his counterpart for promoting cooperation on the basis of honesty and integrity and explained that he too was keen to promote a spirit of friendship and greater contact between the two countries. Turning to the main issue of discussion, Simitis stressed that his government believed in Turkish candidacy of the EU in principle, but that there were lingering concerns that if it were to receive the green light in Finland it would quickly return to its previous disruptive policies. He also emphasised the degree to which a decision to go before the ICJ could prevent the possibility of conflict, briefly outlining the working of the Court for the Turkish prime minister. Ecevit responded that Turkey held no territorial ambitions against Greece, before highlighting the benefits that EU candidacy would bring to his country. As far as bilateral differences were concerned, the Turkish Premier called for a framework of bilateral negotiations to be established on the question of the Aegean. Importantly, he stated that should this process fail then matters could be taken to the ICJ, however he took pains to point out, according to long held Turkish views, that bilateral discussions should be the starting point.

Simitis then raised the Greek concern that such talks could simply be a process without end, and that nothing concrete would be achieved, to which Ecevit countered that a time limit could be set in place to cover this problem. On the question of Cyprus, it was rumoured that Ecevit did not take his traditional line that the problem had been solved, but instead referred to the fact that the forthcoming proximity talks under the aegis of the UN was the natural home for such discussions. To the Greeks this was an important statement as it was evidence that the Turkish Government, and Ecevit in particular, recognised that a problem still existed.[7] At the end of the meeting the two refrained from issuing a joint communiqué, instead making their own individual statements. However, Simitis was able to make clear to the Turkish people his views on the rapprochement and the outstanding points of difference between the two countries during an interview he gave to the Anatolian Agency on the sidelines of the conference. This was the first such interview given by a Greek Prime Minister to the Turkish press for a number of years.

Clinton arrives in Greece

On the evening of 19 November, President Clinton arrived in Greece. The visit had originally been scheduled to take place earlier, just prior to the OSCE summit, but had been changed so as not to clash with the commemoration of the 17 November crushing of a student uprising by the US backed military dictatorship in power in Greece at the time. Nevertheless, serious security concerns remained in a country that had a strong history of anti-American sentiment. Numerous groups, including the Greek Communist Party (KKE), had made it clear that they intended to use the visit to protest against US policy in general and the NATO bombing of Kosovo earlier in the year in particular. Others intended to send the message that US interference in Greek-Turkish relations was unwanted, especially given the prevailing view that Washington favoured Ankara over Athens. As a result of concerns over the safety of the President, US officials shortened the trip from two and half days, as originally planned, to just 24 hours.[8] At the same time, Greek police took stringent security measures. In marked contrast to the large number of cheering well-wishers who had turned out to greet him on his arrival in Turkey, the streets of Athens had been cordoned off, and a heavy police presence put in place, to prevent violent demonstrations.

Nevertheless, despite the precautions, fierce protests erupted as Air Force One touched down.[9] However, political tensions soon emerged. The first official engagement was a dinner hosted by President Stephanopoulos, which sparked controversy on two counts. First of all, during his speech Stephanopoulos, although referring to the positive developments taking place between Greece and Turkey, used the occasion to stress the importance of an improvement to Turkey's human rights record. This statement was condemned by Turkish officials.[10] Secondly, in his address Clinton also claimed that he had asked Demirel for a gesture on Cyprus. However, this claim was strongly denied later by the Turkish President, who insisted that no such request had been made.[11]

The following morning Clinton had a meeting with Stephanopoulos, before seeing Simitis and Papandreou. In the previous days, Greek officials had stressed that the Prime Minister would use the opportunity to express their view that the responsibility for any improvement in bilateral relations between Greece and Turkey was with Ankara. Simitis would also ask that the US should take into account Greek positions of the questions separating the two countries.[12] This move was no doubt inspired, in part, by calls from the leader of the opposition, Costas Karamanlis, for the US President to be told in no uncertain terms that in the view of Greece, the US policy of equidistance on Greek-Turkish relation simply encouraged, 'Turkish aggressiveness and provocativeness'.[13]

A little later on, Karamanlis had the opportunity to put this message to Clinton directly when they met for discussions. At the end of their meeting, both refrained from making comments. However, a few hours later, Karamanlis held a press conference at which he explained to reporters that he had had a 'sincere' and 'substantive' discussion during which he had told the President that matters of national interest were above party politics and that his party rejected the notion of making unilateral concessions towards improving Greek-Turkish relations and that Cypriot EU accession should be separated from efforts to find a solution.[14]

Clinton's last appointment before leaving was an address at the Forum Intercontinental in Athens. To many observers, the speech marked the highlight of the visit. Clinton used the occasion to welcome the resumption of talks between the Cypriot leaders and press home the need for movement on both Cyprus and the Aegean and to the applause of those, he stressed that, 'Turkey cannot be fully integrated successfully into Europe without solving its difficulties with Greece.'[15] But others were more cynical, arguing that Clinton had just said what he thought Greeks wanted to hear. Moreover, he had simply confirmed what Greeks had said for decades, but successive US administration had consistently denied, namely that, 'responsibility for many of modern Greece's problems rests with Washington.'[16] Soon afterwards, he departed.

Despite the fact that there had been demonstrations, the prevailing view was that the trip had been a lot more successful than many had dared hope. The US President had managed to win a lot of support in Greece during his short stay and many felt that Clinton had shown a deep understanding of Greece's position. However, as officials noted, the visit would only prove to be a real success if it resulted in positive developments.[17] Such optimism, however, was not reflected in all quarters. The leader of the Left Coalition, Nikos Konstantopoulos, who had boycotted the dinner welcoming Clinton's arrival in protest at violence used to break up the anti-Clinton demonstrations, was more scathing. He accused the US president of simply staging a public relations exercise which did not mark any substantive change in American positions.[18] Meanwhile, in Turkey, many thought that Clinton's reception in Greece had been a disgrace compared with the warm welcome he had received in Turkey.[19]

Continued Greek Cypriot concerns about Turkish candidacy

With the Clinton visit now over, attention once again turned to the forthcoming Helsinki summit. While efforts had been made to convince the Greek Cypriots that the Greek intention to use the meeting as an opportunity to separate the question of Cypriot EU accession from the search for a solution, it was clear that Nicosia was still concerned about developments. While Simitis was in Istanbul, Tzohadzopoulos, the Greek defence minister, was in Cyprus for talks with his counterpart, Socrates Hasikos. Although the meeting was meant to focus on bilateral issues within the framework of the joint defence doctrine, Helsinki was the main topic of conversation. In an attempt to allay Cypriot concerns, Tzohadzopoulos made it clear that Greece supported Turkey's EU candidacy in principle but that it would ensure that it received a number of commitments from its partners, including a commitment of Cypriot accession, before allowing any acceptance to go ahead.[20]

Another opportunity to ease fears that Greece was preparing a major policy shift on Cyprus came days later when, on 22 November, Glafkos Clerides, the Cypriot President, visited Athens for discussions with Simitis in advance of the forthcoming proximity talks. However, it appears as if the Greek Government was unable to convince the Cypriot Government. At the end of the talks, which lasted most of the day, the two leaders decided not to hold a joint press conference. Instead they issued a joint communiqué expressing the level of co-operation and support that existed between Greece and Cyprus. Observers read this to mean that problems still existed.

This view was seemingly confirmed when, just three days later, Papandreou paid a high profile visit to the island in order to meet with the political leaders. At the heart of the visit was his desire to sell the formula on Cypriot EU accession to Nicosia in return for Cypriot acquiescence to Turkey's candidacy. Following a meeting with the Cypriot Foreign Minister, Ioannis Cassoulides, the two ministers held a joint press conference.[21] While Cassoulides stressed that they were in full agreement with one another about the Greek course of action, some of the journalists present were sceptical. Papandreou was challenged by one reporter to prove that the decision of the Greek Government at Helsinki would not result in the solution to the Cyprus issue being pushed to one side, either as a priority of Greek foreign policy or as a European Union matter.

In his reply, Papandreou emphasised that this was not the case. He argued that reinforcing Turkey's European course in Helsinki, 'can only contribute to the final Cyprus solution, to a viable solution the way we want it'. Another reporter then asked him about the recent statements made by Prime Minister Ecevit in which he said that Greek-Turkish relations should be kept separate from the Cyprus issue. Giving exactly the type of response the Cypriot Government had hoped for, Papandreou stated that:

> We feel that we cannot have a final rapprochement or a true rapprochement between our two countries unless the Cyprus issue is addressed and resolved. That does not mean that we cannot improve bilateral relations and this is what we are trying to do. However, the Cyprus problem is the heart, we believe, of the differences between Greece and Turkey. It is not a Greek-Turkish problem. It is an international problem. However, it is the heart of the problem, which keeps our two countries from coming closer together.[22]

The Greek Government considers its position

With a little less than two weeks to go before Helsinki the picture became more complicated following an announcement by Ecevit that the Turkish Government would not offer any concessions to Greece on Cyprus or the Aegean prior to Helsinki. In response, Dimitris Reppas, the Greek Government Spokesman, accused Ankara of undermining its own position. However, not wanting to be seen to close down Greece's room for manoeuvre, he nevertheless continued to put Turkey's chances of gaining candidacy at '50-50'.[23]

Behind the scenes the Turkish prime minister's comments raised a number of important questions. Realising that no gesture should be expected, Athens now needed to focus its attention on securing gestures from its EU partners instead. This presented a major difficulty insofar as any attempt to put in place conditions aimed at Turkey must be done in a way that made them appear applicable to all. This was extremely important as any hint that extra conditions were being placed on Turkey that did not apply to other candidates would elicit a backlash from the Turkish

Government. And while Papandreou had seemingly managed to gather support for a clause within the summit's conclusions that would refer to the necessity of candidates' recognising the jurisdiction of the ICJ, this presented a difficulty as it was tantamount to naming Turkey directly. It was therefore unclear how Ankara would respond. The second factor concerned Cyprus. Again, the problem was how to ensure that Cyprus could join without a settlement, but do so in a manner that would not force a crisis with Ankara or lead Denktaş to walk away from the proximity talks.

But there was also a domestic political calculation that needed to be made. While Simitis could probably get away with taking such a major decision in the middle of a parliamentary cycle, in the hope that by the time of elections the matter would have blown over, at this stage he was facing elections within the next nine months. Indeed, it could well be sooner as the question of the re-election of President Stephanopoulos, which was due to be held by the Parliament in March, seemed to be developing into a vote of confidence in his administration. If Simitis could not get the President re-appointed he would have no choice but to go to the polls by April, just five months away.

Public support for his decision was therefore seen as being vital for his party's re-election prospects. But while there would be little problem selling a positive vote if Ankara offered a goodwill gesture, the question was how could the Greek Government sell its acceptance of Turkey's candidacy to the Greek people if, at the time of Helsinki, Ankara still had not offered something. As had been shown in the poll the previous month – when the earthquakes were still very fresh in people minds – the majority of the Greek people felt that some gesture should be made by Turkey in advance of the summit. Such feelings had been strengthened as a result of Clinton's statements during his trip to Greece. It therefore appeared as if exacting promises and securing benefits from the European Union would not be enough to generate public support for Turkish candidacy.

This highlighted the second problem facing the Greek premier. What would happen if he chose to follow the people's wishes and vote against Turkish candidacy? Such a decision would surely be catastrophic for the process of rapprochement. Even in the very best-case scenario, it would halt the process of further discussions. At the opposite end of the spectrum, such a result could well lead to renewed hostility and tensions with Turkey and write off any chance of reconciliation for a number of years. It could also end talks over Cyprus for the foreseeable future. Thus with just a few weeks to go, Simitis was faced with a major decision. If he voted for Turkish candidacy but with onerous conditions that could be interpreted by Ankara as being more than the conditions placed upon other candidates, he would risk Turkish rejection and a possible backlash. But he would also face a similar backlash from Turkey if he decided not to lift the veto. Meanwhile, if he was seen to be too lenient on Turkey, he would come under heavy criticism at home. This could even lead to electoral defeat. It appeared as if, no matter what route he chose to take, he would face an extraordinarily high political cost.[24]

Turkey pushes its case for candidacy

Meanwhile, Cem continued to push the case for Turkish candidacy. In a speech delivered at the opening session of a conference in Istanbul, on 3 December, he noted that Turkish candidacy could have a significant effect in terms of resolving the differences with Greece, 'within the framework of international law and European Union agreements.'[25] Moreover, such a development could also contribute to regional peace, stability and the economy of both countries. While maintaining Turkey's stance on Cyprus and restating Ankara's support for a solution based on confederation, the Minister also seemed to offer a lifeline to Greece concerning any move to separate Cypriot accession to the EU with a solution: 'We told our interlocutors and the EU countries that we are not included in a Cyprus-EU-Turkey balance.'

But perhaps sensing that the Greek Government was still wavering, and might still reject candidacy, Cem appeared to start preparing Turkish public opinion for the worst by emphasising that the Turkish Government would not accept any conditions on its candidacy on top of those imposed on other potential members as this would be nothing more than discrimination. However, in the event that Turkey was rejected, or even if it voluntarily chose to reject an offer of candidacy that came with excessive or unfair conditions, Cem explained that this should not be viewed as a national disaster:

> 'Full membership of the EU is Turkey's target, but it is not her obsession. We, of course, want to become a member of the EU. We have been striving for it for a long time. But Turkey will continue to exist without the EU…We do not need our European identity to be confirmed. Turkey has been part of Europe geographically and historically for 700 years. If Europeanism is a matter of culture and if European culture is regarded as religious culture, then, we are not Europeans. But if the EU attributes importance to main criteria such as democracy, human rights, and pluralism, the Turkish culture is, of course, a part of European culture in spite of some deficiencies.'[26]

Cem's words were given added resonance when, just two days later, a report appeared in *Cumhuriyet*, a leading establishment newspaper, claiming that Athens had decided against lifting its veto and had already informed the Turkish Government of this. The article stated that notwithstanding earlier comments from Ankara that Helsinki would be the final chance for Turkey to open the way to EU membership, it was likely that the decision would be taken at the next summit in June 2000. According to the report, the US and other EU members had already informed Ecevit that this delay would also allow time for the Simitis Government to be re-elected, which meant that the Greek government could take the decision with relatively little political fallout. Importantly, the paper noted that despite this obvious setback the Turkish Government remained committed to the dialogue process and that Cem would invite Papandreou to Ankara soon after the summit.[27]

The report certainly sounded plausible. However, it was wrong. Athens had still not made up its mind. While there had, as yet, been no attempt by Ankara to offer a goodwill measure in advance of Helsinki, as had originally been expected by Greece, there had however been some clearly discernable improvements made in the course of bilateral relations that seemed to be related to the summit. For example, there had been a reduction in the number of Turkish military aircraft flying in contested airspace over the Aegean. Although the commander of the air force, General Ergin Celasin, explained during a press conference that this was in no way related to the forthcoming Helsinki summit, but was a product of the reduction in Greek flights being made in the area,[28] it was nevertheless taken as a sign that the Turkish military was playing its part to try to minimise tensions in the run up to summit.

But more importantly, there was a growing recognition in Athens that regardless of whether Turkey acted or not, by dropping the veto Greece could gain a substantial amount at the summit. Indeed, in the longer term these would certainly outweigh the benefits that would come from any small gesture made at this point. For example, if the EU would accept the separation of Cypriot EU accession from the need for a solution, this would effectively ensure the island's accession within five years. Similarly, the acceptance of the jurisdiction of the ICJ as being a fundamental criterion of EU membership would also force Turkey's hand on the question of the continental shelf. Thus, with days to go, the Greek Government abandoned hope of receiving a gesture from Ankara. Instead, it decided to work on finding a means by which to have Turkey accepted in a manner that would prove to Greece's benefit, rather than cost.

The Helsinki European Council

On 10 December European leaders met in Helsinki. As expected, the main area of discussion was centred on Turkey's candidacy. As expected, Turkey had failed to deliver a gesture. However, Athens had by this stage given up hope that this would be the case. Instead it had decided to focus on the longer-term benefits of having Turkey as a candidate for EU membership.

In this respect, the more important issue was the wording of the Council conclusions. In this regard, Greece was actually helped by the fact that Ankara had refused to offer a sign of goodwill. Not only did Greece appear reasonable in general terms, the other EU leaders were also aware that Simitis was facing a general election and so was taking a particularly big gamble. As a result, the wording of the final document was likely to be far more in line with Greek wishes than might otherwise have been the case. The first major victory focused on the Aegean. Although framed in general language that did not point to any single candidate, paragraph 4 of the conclusions left little doubt as to its origins and purpose:

> The European Council reaffirms the inclusive nature of the accession process, which now comprises 13 candidate States within a single framework. The candidate States are participating in the accession process on an equal footing. They must share the values and objectives of the European Union as set out in the Treaties. In this respect the European Council stresses the principle of peaceful settlement of disputes in accordance with the United Nations Charter and urges candidate States to make every effort to resolve any outstanding border disputes and other related issues. Failing this they should within a reasonable time bring the dispute to the International Court of Justice. The European Council will review the situation relating to any outstanding disputes, in particular concerning the repercussions on the accession process and in order to promote their settlement through the International Court of Justice, at the latest by the end of 2004. Moreover, the European Council recalls that compliance with the political criteria laid down at the Copenhagen European Council is a prerequisite for the opening of accession negotiations and that compliance with all the Copenhagen criteria is the basis for accession to the Union.[29]

This was exactly what Greece had been hoping for. However, this was not all. The Greek Government had also managed to secure a strong statement on Cyprus. While stressing that a settlement would facilitate the island's accession, the Union nevertheless made it clear that the Council's eventual decision on whether to accept the island would be taken on the basis of all relevant factors and that a solution was not a precondition for membership. This was quite clearly a victory for Greece. In particular, it put to rest Greek Cypriot concerns that Athens had in any way overlooked their interests.

Although the decision to accept Turkey as a candidate was a major triumph 36 years after the accession agreement had been signed, Ankara was furious at the outcome. While not naming Turkey specifically, paragraph 4 was quite clearly a reference to the Aegean. Moreover, the option of accepting Cyprus even without a settlement was also seen as completely unacceptable. Therefore, while recognising that improvements needed to be made on key issues such as human rights and democratisation, the Turkish Government steadfastly refused to accept the conditions put down as regards Greece and Cyprus.[30] Indeed, for several hours it even appeared as if Turkey would turn the offer down completely. Faced with a major crisis in EU-Turkish relations, an emergency delegation from the EU – which included Javier Solana the High Representative for Foreign and Security Policy, and Günter Verheugen, the Commissioner for Enlargement – travelled to Ankara to sell the result as a victory for Turkey. They succeeded. Still insisting that Turkey would not be bound by any extra conditions, and maintaining that two states existed in Cyprus, Ecevit agreed to accept the offer. Shortly afterwards, he flew to Finland to attend the final day of the summit.[31]

Reactions in Turkey and Greece

Returning from Helsinki, Ecevit called a meeting of a small group of those most involved with the decision: Ismail Cem and the Ministers for Europe and Cyprus, Mehmet Ali İrtemçelik (ANAP) and Şükrü Sina Gürel (DSP). Speaking before the meeting, Cem told journalists waiting outside the Prime Ministry that the words about the ICJ were in fact good for Turkey. The wording of the text referred to 'problems', rather than a 'problem'. This could therefore be taken to mean that the conclusion recognised the existence of a number of problems, as Ankara had been arguing all along. Furthermore, the conclusion did not state that the matters must be taken to the ICJ before 2004, but instead said that the matter would be reviewed once more at that stage. When asked about whether the decision was in Turkey's favour, Cem was clear that it was. As for Cyprus, although Greece had managed to secure the EU's support for its position that Cypriot accession could not be held up because of a failure to reach a solution, which was certainly not the outcome Ankara had wanted, on a positive note the wording was sufficiently vague as to allow Turkey some 'breathing space'. However, he was also quick to point out that Turkish policy towards the issue would not change. In overall terms the outcome was therefore good for Turkey. As well as putting Turkey on the same footing as the other candidates, it now had a formal voice in the EU:

> The EU has so far listened to Greece and the Greek Cypriots side. They were the only source of information on the problems. But I will also be able to address EU forums from now on. I have never been able to do that in the past. We will be able to defend our policy on

Cyprus inside the EU from now on. They will listen to us as well. That is the important achievement for us.[32]

Meanwhile, the Greek Government found itself strongly praised for its stance. As well as winning plaudits from the Finnish Prime Minister, Paavo Lipponen, Simitis also received a letter from Clinton congratulating him on his stand. However, within Greece the reaction to the conclusion of the Summit was mixed. While the government emphasised that it had met all of its goals in Helsinki, the opposition viewed the outcome as some form of capitulation.[33] Kostas Karamanlis, the leader of the opposition New Democracy party, criticised Simitis for having legitimised unilateral Turkish claims by accepting them as 'Greek-Turkish differences'. Similarly, the Greek Communist Party (KKE) accused the government of having signed away the country's sovereign rights in the Aegean and sold out Cyprus. However, a strong voice from the opposition now came to the aid of the Government. Constantine Mitsotakis, the former Prime Minister, chose to break with his party on the issue and endorsed Simitis' decision. Stressing that Simitis had simply followed a policy towards Turkey that had originally been implemented by his own government from 1990–93, Mitsotakis expressed his belief in the importance of Turkey finding a European orientation. As he explained, 'the fact that the Government followed our policy should not be unpleasant to us in New Democracy.'[34]

The aftermath

Significantly, the outcome of the decision was also lauded by President Demirel of Turkey. In an interview on Turkish television shortly after the summit, he pointed out that Turkey had committed itself to finding peaceful solutions to their differences. The road to better relations has opened', he stated.[35] To be sure, most observers expected that the general atmosphere between the two countries would improve dramatically in the aftermath of Helsinki. However, it was only days before several events proved that relations between the two countries were still prone to problems.

The first issue to arise related to the Muslim minority in Thrace. On 1 December, a Greek Court had once again sentenced Mehmet Emin Aga to six months in jail for illegally calling himself the Mufti of Xanthi. This issue had served to damage relations between the two countries on a number of occasions in the previous years, and this time the Turkish Foreign Ministry once again issued a statement condemning the charges and calling on Greece to adjust its behaviour towards the minority and recognise its international responsibilities.[36] On 14 December, just days after Helsinki, the Turkish position was seemingly vindicated when the European Court of Human Rights in Strasbourg ruled that Greece had violated the rights of

İbrahim Şerif, another of the three muftis of western Thrace, who had been also been accused of offences similar to Mehmet Emin Aga. Stating that the Greek state had violated Article 9 of the European Convention on Human Rights, which governed freedom of religious thought and expression, the Court found that the Greek argument that his actions had represented a public order threat was not justified. Athens was ordered to pay 2.7 million drachmas (US$9000) in compensation.[37]

Two days later, the Turkish Defence Minister called for the Moslem community in the region to be granted dual Greek-Turkish citizenship. Arguing that this would mean that members of the community could feel comfortable remaining in Greece, Çakmakoğlu noted that it would allow a Turkish presence to remain in the region. Furthermore, he hinted that there might be a chance of reopening the Halki School of Theology, but appeared to link it to a change in religious education in Greece, when he stated that, 'the principle of reciprocity should govern [Greek-Turkish] relations. If a Greek Orthodox religious school it to be opened, then we should look into the situation of the Muslim religious affairs directorate and their education facilities.'[38]

Papandreou immediately rejected this link between the issue of Halki and the education of the Muslim minority in Thrace. Meanwhile, the Foreign Ministry in Athens found itself having to answer questions as to why, within days of Helsinki, the number of Turkish aircraft violating the Greek airspace had risen dramatically. The Greek Government had registered a total of seven formations of Turkish jets in the area around the island of Chios, Lesbos and Rhodes, which, it argued, had violated Greek airspace a total of eight times and had violated air traffic control code within the Athens flight information region (FIR) a total of nine times. Seemingly unfazed by these developments, Papandreou stressed the positive aspects of the new post-Helsinki political environment:

> We must view Helsinki as creating a new opportunity, a new dynamic, a new page that allows a long-term strategy of improving the climate, but also of solving important problems. If we focus on isolated incidents...then we can't see the forest for the trees. We didn't open the door to paradise, we opened a door of opportunity.[39]

While it was clear to everyone that building a better relationship would not be easy, as 1999 ended it nevertheless appeared as if relations between Greece and Turkey were now on a new course. As the world celebrated the start of the new millennium, there was a real hope in both countries that an era of peace was beginning across the Aegean.

EPILOGUE

Although this work concentrates on the developments that took place in 1999, the true impact of the events of that year can only be appreciated by reviewing the evolution of rapprochement since then. Perhaps the most important point to emphasise is that, despite the fears that the process would quickly fizzle out, in much the way that the Davos Process had in the late-1980s, the détente has in fact proved to be far more resilient than many observers expected. However, as will be seen, it is far less easy to make a firm judgement on its success, or its future direction.

To many it seemed fitting that the start of a new millennium marked what appeared to be a start of a new era in relations between Greece and Turkey. On 19 January 2000, just over a month after the decision taken in Helsinki, George Papandreou arrived in Turkey for a four day visit. It was a moment laden with symbolism as it marked the first time in 38 years that a Greek foreign minister had visited Ankara officially. A couple of days later, he and Cem signed four bilateral agreements covering tourism, environmental protection, citizens' security and the safeguarding of investments.[1] The following month Cem visited Athens. Again it was a highly significant move. The last visit by a Turkish foreign minister to the city had been in 1960. There a further five agreements were signed. These agreements were centred on education, science and technology, maritime transport, customs cooperation and the creation of a joint economic committee to supervise the development of bilateral economic relations. In total, nine major agreements were signed between the two countries. Hours afterwards the two men were awarded the İpekçi Award, the most important award given to individuals and groups that had worked to improve Greek-Turkish relations.

In the months that followed the contribution they had made to the transformation of relations across the Aegean was recognised elsewhere. Most notably, the two men shared the Statesman of the Year prize by the East-West Institute, a leading US NGO, in April 2000.[2] The Institute also presented representatives of AKUT and EMAK, the two rescue teams that had played such an important part during the earthquakes, with a humanitarian award for the enormous contribution they had also made to improvement of the climate between the two peoples.

Meanwhile, contacts between the two countries continued to grow, both at an official and at an unofficial level. The number of tourists travelling across the Aegean doubled.[3] At the same time, trade between the two countries expanded from $650 million to $1 billion.[4] This strengthening of commercial and economic ties served to underpin the political relationship. It also gave a further impetus to the two governments to continue to build upon the rapprochement. This in many ways proved to be another vindication of the approach adopted by the founders of the European Union, who believed that economic interdependence was the best guarantee against further conflict.

However, the détente also grew from an increase in contacts across a range of other areas. For example, sport played an important role. Quite apart from the apparent reduction in nationalist sentiment expressed at matches between teams from the two countries,[5] it also provided opportunities for firm cooperation. In September 2000 the two foreign ministers even announced a joint bid to host the 2008 European football championships.[6] Although the bid was eventually unsuccessful, having been beaten by Austria and Switzerland, the fact that the bid was put forward was an important symbolic sign of the wish of the two governments to build upon the process established the year earlier.

Cultural contacts between the two countries also flourished. Greek and Turkish musicians and artists regularly performed or exhibited their works in the other country. This was also seen in film and television. For instance, one of the most successful Greek films of recent years, released internationally under the title, 'A Touch of Spice', examined the expulsion of the Greek minority in Istanbul in 1964 from a far more sympathetic and non-confrontational angle than would have been the case in the past.[7] Meanwhile, a Turkish soap opera, 'Love without Borders', about an affair between a Turkish man and a Greek woman, was the most watched television show in Greece in the summer of 2005. At the same time, it was also noticeable that the news media in both countries adopted a more positive outlook towards bilateral relations.[8]

Another area of transformation was in the defence and security sphere. In 2000 Turkey announced a major reduction in its military spending. This was followed, in April 2001, by an announcement from Athens that it was downgrading the threat from Turkey and would launch a major cut back in arms expenditure, totalling US$4.4 billion. It also announced that it would be reducing the personnel in the armed forces from 140,000 to just 90,000. Both announcements contributed to the virtuous circle of détente that was developing.[9] Similarly, an early development that also attracted considerable attention was the decision by the two countries to conduct joint exercises under NATO auspices. In early May 2000 a Turkish military aircraft landed in Greece as part of a joint NATO exercise. This was followed by the sight of Turkish marines coming ashore a Greek island – something that would have been unthinkable just a few years earlier.

But developments were not all positive. In autumn 2000, the Turkish military refused to allow the inclusion of Lemnos in flight plans for a NATO exercise, arguing that the island is demilitarised under the terms of a 1936 treaty. As a result, Athens withdrew its participation in the manoeuvres. At the time this was seen by observers as the most serious setback to the rapprochement process since it had started eighteen months earlier.[10] But the most serious source of tension centred on continuing disputes over airspace. Despite the process of rapprochement, Greece continued to log regular incursions by Turkish military aircraft. For example, in 2002, Athens noted 3,200 violations.[11] And there was a particularly significant rise in the number of cases reported by Greece in the run up to the European Union's decision in December 2004 to set a date for the start of formal accession negotiations with Ankara.[12] However, many observers saw this as being an attempt by the Turkish military to emphasise that Turkey would not give up its declared rights in the Aegean and Cyprus in return for EU membership.[13]

Balanced against this, there have also been major developments in strategic political co-operation. In the Balkans the two countries have recognised a mutual interest in stabilising the region.[14] Energy has been another important area where ties have flourished. One of the most significant announcements was that the two countries had reached an agreement on the construction of a pipeline that would pump Iranian natural gas across Turkey into Greece and from there into Europe. Construction of the pipeline was inaugurated in July 2005.[15] This was a highly symbolic step, which also proved to be geo-politically significant insofar as it was seen as a vital means by which to open up new energy supplies to Europe. It was therefore noteworthy that it was widely seen to be a product of the improving climate that had come about between Athens and Ankara.

Meanwhile, a number of further agreements have since been signed by the two countries. These have included a readmission protocol intended to help combat organised crime, a protocol for the formation of a joint Hellenic-Turkish Disaster Response Unit, an agreement covering plant and veterinary protection, and a memorandum of co-operation between the diplomatic academies of the two countries.[16] Moreover, high level contacts continued to take place between the two governments covering a range of areas. Importantly, these are no longer seen as being unusual or exceptional. Instead they have become normal, if not wholly mundane.

Linked to this has been the establishment by Greece of a task force that aims to provide practical advice and assistance to Turkish officials as Turkey prepares to join the European Union.[17]

However, for all the benefits that the process has undoubtedly brought to both countries, and while there have been no major crises that have brought the process of détente to a halt, the rapprochement has not produced the types of results that many had expected. Or more accurately, it had not produced the results in the time frame that many foresaw. While the benefits of increased co-operation have been felt across a wide range of areas – for example there has been an improvement in the way that the two countries have treated each other's minorities[18] – there has still been little indication that any moves are afoot to solve the main issue of bilateral contention. A first move on the question of the Aegean that was initiated in 2002 has thus far produced no obvious results.[19] Meanwhile, 2004 came and went with no Turkish move to take the question of the continental shelf before the International Court of Justice, as had been laid down in the Helsinki conclusions.

Cyprus peace process, 2002–2004

The one area where the process of rapprochement produced concrete results was on the questions of Cyprus. Although a new Cyprus initiative was launched in December 1999, at the same time as Greece was preparing to lift its veto on Turkey, the initial hopes that this would lead to a major breakthrough and produce a settlement proved to be short lived. By the following summer Rauf Denktaş, the Turkish Cypriot leader, had resorted to his usual intransigence. In the period that followed the Turkish Government repeatedly made it clear that it would not accept Cypriot accession to the European Union and that the island's membership would have dire consequences for peace and security. In November 2001, Prime Minister Ecevit spelled out just what those consequences would be when he announced that Turkey was even willing to consider annexing northern Cyprus if the island acceded to the Union.[20] This was seen as a clear indication that a major crisis was brewing in the Eastern Mediterranean. And yet, just days later, Denktaş surprised international observers by approaching Clerides to ask for a one-on-one meeting to discuss regional developments in the context of the island's accession.[21]

This paved the way for a new peace process, which began in January 2002. But in spite of initial expectations that an agreement could be reached by June, within weeks it was clear that the new process was little more than a stalling tactic designed to derail the island's EU accession hopes. As a result, the talks quickly reached deadlock. Meanwhile, political turmoil in Turkey cast the wider rapprochement process into doubt as Cem announced, in July 2002, that he was quitting the DSP to form his own political party. Since the start of the détente, observers had questioned whether the process would be durable enough to survive the departure of one of the foreign ministers. In the event this questions was given even greater relevance with the announcement that Ecevit had appointed Şükrü Sina Gürel, a noted hard-liner, to replace Cem. In this turmoil, the improving relationship between Greece and Turkey also came to a standstill, although predictions that Gürel would herald a return to the bad old days proved to be wide of the mark. Indeed, Gürel stressed that he wished to continue to see an improvement in bilateral relations. And while there were no positive new developments in this period, it was notable that there was no major downturn in relations either.

In the meantime, attention turned to the outcome of the Turkish general elections, held in November 2002, which had been won by the Justice and Development Party (AKP). Recep Tayyip Erdoğan, the leader of AKP, was a keen supporter of Turkey's accession to the EU and quickly announced that his main foreign policy priorities were to improve bilateral relations with Greece and solve the Cyprus issue.[22] This immediately led to new hopes that the rapprochement process would be revitalised. Less than ten days later, the Secretary-General, Kofi Annan, presented the Cypriot communities with a comprehensive blueprint for reunification. However, Denktaş continued to present an insurmountable obstacle. Despite considerable pressure, he refused to reach an agreement at the Copenhagen European Council, in December 2002. Three months later, in March 2003, he rejected a request by the UN Secretary-General to put the peace plan to a referendum. As a result, the UN called off its peace-making mission.

The situation changed nine months later with the victory of the pro-reunification Republican Turkish Party (CTP) in the December 2003 Turkish Cypriot parliamentary elections. This paved the way for a resumption of peace talks in February 2004. This time a strict timetable was put in place with the aim of securing a final agreement and putting it to a vote prior to 1 May. Following a further month of discussions on the island between the two communities, a second round of talks was convened in late-March in the Swiss mountain resort of Burgenstock. There the two sides were joined by representatives of Britain, Greece and Turkey – the Guarantor Powers. However, these discussions failed to produce a final set of proposals. Therefore, on 31 March, the UN Secretary General filled in the sections of the plan that remained incomplete and presented the two sides with a finalised set of proposals. But while the plan was welcomed by the international community, including the European Commission and EU member states, as well as by Greece, Turkey and the Turkish Cypriots, it was strongly opposed by Tassos Papadopoulos, who had succeeded Clerides as Greek Cypriot leader the year before. On 24 April, the plan went before the two Cypriot communities in simultaneous referendums.

But while two-thirds of the Turkish Cypriots supported the proposals, the Greek Cypriots voted by a margin of three-to-one against the plan.[23]

Rapprochement under Karamanlis

The result of the Cyprus referendum was certainly a blow to those who believed that the island of Cyprus would at long last be reunited, thus solving the most divisive issue in Greek-Turkish relations. However, in the aftermath of the vote, both Athens and Ankara quickly made it clear that the result would not interrupt or otherwise destabilise the process of rapprochement. This was doubly important insofar as by that point a new government was in power in Greece.

On 7 March 2004, New Democracy, the main centre-right opposition party, brought to an end ten years of PASOK rule. This naturally raised questions about the future of the process of rapprochement. Had PASOK won there was little doubt that the process would have continued, especially as George Papandreou had now taken over the leadership of the party from Simitis, who was retiring from politics.[24] Indeed, many felt that it would have been strengthened. However, few could be sure of the direction of the process under the new Prime Minister, Costas Karamanlis. On the one hand, there were grounds for optimism. Karamanlis and Erdoğan knew each other and were known to get on well. Moreover, as leaders of centre-right parties, they held similar political outlooks. However, Karamanlis was relatively inexperienced in matters of foreign policy and few felt that he would be willing to take the sort of risks that Papandreou had done. These concerns increased when he appointed Petros Molyviatis, a known hard-liner who had been an advisor to the late President Karamanlis, as his foreign minister.

But the change of administration did not lead to a fundamental shift away from the policy of rapprochement. Certainly there was a change of style. As a career diplomat, Molyviatis believed that diplomacy was best done by specialists. In a marked break with Papandreou, he significantly reduced the influence of the political advisors and academics that had done so much to reform Greek foreign policy under the previous administration.[25] However, balanced against this, Karamanlis and Erdoğan continued to forge a strong personal relationship. It was particularly notable that just six weeks after Karamanlis took office Erdoğan visited Athens, and in doing so became the first Turkish premier to visit the city since Turgut Özal in the 1980s. Just a few months later, in July 2004, Karamanlis travelled to Istanbul for the wedding of Erdoğan's daughter.[26] A year later, in July 2005, he accepted an invitation to visit Turkey officially, thereby raising the prospect of the becoming the first Greek premier to make such a trip in almost fifty years.[27]

All the while, Karamanlis reaffirmed his belief that Turkey's continued EU accession was Greece's best hope for the eventual normalisation of relations.[28] As he explained in an interview with a US broadcaster:

> We have made a decision to support the Turkish European perspective. I think this is a basic strategic decision founded on a basic premise, which is what does one prefer? A neighbor which is prosperous, democratic, Europeanized, if I may use the word, or a neighbor who is alienated, isolated, feels rejected by the European family? I think the answer is clear. On the other hand, we have a government in Turkey which has given evidence that it is willing to reform; it is willing to put aside the military in its predominant political role of the past, it is willing to take steps in the direction of full democratization, respect for human rights, et cetera…Now, of course, it is eventually for Turkey itself to decide, or its government to decide to fulfill all these prerequisites, which are put by Europe itself. But as a basic choice, I would very strongly argue in favor of the support of this choice they have made.[29]

However, despite continuing to support Turkey's EU accession process, it has been noted by many observers that little substantive improvement has been made in bilateral relations. To be sure, certain areas are less inflammatory than in the past. Most notably, although Cyprus continues to be a major underlying issue in Greek-Turkish relations, Karamanlis has maintained the policy put in place under his predecessor of ensuring that Cyprus does not dominate, let alone determine, the bilateral agenda. For example, it was notable that when the Greek Cypriots decided to ignore international pressure and stage a major military exercise in autumn 2005 – the first time the manoeuvres had been held since 2001 – Greece declined to participate.[30]

It was also telling that the Greek Government sought to distance itself from inflammatory remarks made by the Greek President, Karolos Papoulias, on a visit to Cyprus in the summer of 2005.[31] Similarly, Athens diverged from Nicosia on the wording of an EU response to Turkey's announcement that its decision to extent the customs union to the ten new member states that had joined in May 2004 did not amount to recognition of the Republic of Cyprus.[32] However, there is little else to show for the process of rapprochement in terms of formal results. Almost no appreciable progress has been made on either the key issues of difference in the Aegean or on confidence building measures, despite ongoing high-level talks between the two countries.[33]

All this has naturally had an effect on public opinion. Notwithstanding the significant increase in economic and cultural contacts that has occurred, one cannot ignore the effect that the failure to address the underlying issues is having on bilateral relations. In Greece, the process of rapprochement remains fragile largely as a result of the belief that most of the changes that have taken place have originated Athens.[34] At the same time, support for rapprochement also appears to be in the balance in Turkey. A study published in early 2004 on the subject of Turkish attitudes to détente showed that 41 per cent of Turks continued to believe that Greeks and Turks could never be friends. At the same time, while 1 per cent were willing to see Greece as Turkey's best friend on the world stage, 36 per cent saw Greece as Turkey's 'worst friend' – the highest tally in this category.[35]

Nevertheless, there appears to be little room for doubt that the rapprochement process that came about in 1999 has brought about a range of tangible benefits. To be sure, it has not achieved the type of progress on the core bilateral issues that many had hoped for, if not expected. Nor have the range of direct confidence building measures increased substantially beyond those introduced in the year or so after the start of the process. However, it has nevertheless played a decisive role in reducing tensions between the two countries and fostering a wider atmosphere of economic and cultural co-operation across the Aegean. Moreover, had it not been for the decision taken in December 1999 to open the door for Turkish candidacy of the European Union it is quite possible that the peace talks that took place in Cyprus from 2002–2004 would not have occurred. Indeed, the results of Cypriot membership of the EU in the political atmosphere that had existed prior to rapprochement may well have resulted in a major crisis between Greece and Turkey. Like so many other such crises, this would also have the potential to lead to an armed clash between the two countries. If not this, then a prolonged period of tension may well have occurred, especially if Ankara had followed through on its threats to annex northern Cyprus. In the end, this did not happen. Instead, on 3 October 2005, and with the continued support of Greece, Turkey at long last began formal accession talks with the European Union. Although there may be questions about the success of détente, the decision to admit Turkey proved the durability of the rapprochement process. Whether it will survive the pressures of the accession talks in the years ahead remains to be seen.

CONCLUSION

Despite the fact that the Kingdom of Greece and the Ottoman Empire had been in conflict throughout the nineteenth and early twentieth centuries, the formation of the Republic of Turkey in 1923 marked the start of a new era in Greek-Turkish relations. The Treaty of Lausanne had successfully resolved a number of important legal issues between the two countries. Moreover, the massive population exchange that took place in the aftermath of the treaty, which saw almost a million and half Greeks and Turks uprooted, had seemingly removed the potential for ethnic friction between the two states. In 1952, in what was seen as the clearest example of the degree to which Greece and Turkey had put aside the past enmity, the two countries became members of the North Atlantic Treaty Organisation (NATO).

However, in 1955, after thirty years of relative harmony, the situation began to change as events on the island of Cyprus reawakened tensions. In 1959, as the island hovered on the brink of civil war, Athens and Ankara reached a compromise and, in 1960, Cyprus became an independent state. However, hopes that bilateral relations between Greece and Turkey could now be repaired were short lived. Three years later fighting broke out between the Cypriot communities. Despite the creation of a UN peacekeeping force in 1964, tensions continued for the next ten years until, in 1974, the Greek Junta ordered the overthrow of Archbishop Makarios, the President of Cyprus. In response, Turkey invaded the island. By the time the operation was completed, over one third of the island was under Turkish control and more than 160,000 Greek Cypriots had been displaced. More importantly, Cyprus had now been confirmed as a central issue in Greek-Turkish relations.

Meanwhile, the Aegean had also become a source of fundamental contention between the two countries. In large part the problems that arose were the result of differing interpretations over the rights and consequences of various treaties. For example, although Greece accepted that a case could be made with regard to the extent of the continental shelf, it categorically rejected any attempt by the Turkish Government to open up a discussion on the extension of territorial waters and airspace. Similarly, disputes arose over the militarisation of a number of islands in the eastern Aegean, close to the Turkish coast. While these issues were certainly serious, the poor political climate that had developed over the previous twenty years, and particularly in the aftermath of 1974, nevertheless served to make any effort to address these differences all the more difficult. Indeed, the Cyprus question became central to Greek-Turkish disputes. No matter how much Ankara may have wanted to separate the Cyprus issue from bilateral Greek-Turkish relations, Athens held firm to its position that there could be no improvement in relations without a solution to the island's division.

On top of this, there were also a number of lesser issues that nevertheless served to poison the overall atmosphere still further. These included the treatment of the Muslim minority in Western Thrace and the Greek minority in Istanbul. And while several efforts were made to improve relations, most notably the Davos process launched by Turgut Özal and Andreas Papandreou in 1988, these came to nothing. In large part, these efforts failed because they were consciously trying to resolve the bilateral disputes without any agreement as to what exactly constituted the points of contention. Just as Greece would not recognise Turkish concerns in the Aegean, Turkey was unwilling to make any significant moves towards the reunification of Cyprus.

Matters were also complicated by the fact that both countries were using what they perceived to be their natural strengths to secure their position. For the Turkish Government this was an emphasis of military might. In the case of Greece this meant using its membership of the European Union as a means by which to leverage concessions from Ankara. As a result, the quarter of a century from 1974–99 saw a gradual deterioration of relations and an increase in tensions as Greece felt continually threatened by its eastern neighbour and Turkey felt frustrated that its efforts to draw closer to Europe were being blocked.

It was against this backdrop that three major crises erupted between the two countries. The first two of these crises, those in 1976 and 1987, centred on the question of the continental shelf and the search for oil in the Aegean. However, the 1996 crisis was focused on the sovereignty over a number of small islands in the Aegean Sea. On this last occasion it was only with the timely intervention of the United States that a full-scale military showdown between Greece and Turkey was averted. In the months that followed a number of sources of tension emerged. The most significant in terms of regional security was the decision by the Greek Cypriots to purchase a Russian-made air defence system. This brought about a fierce reaction from Ankara, which threatened to destroy the missiles if they were installed. On top of this, Greek-Turkish relations suffered yet another blow when Turkey found its EU candidacy rejected at the Luxembourg European Council in December 1997.

The arrest of Abdullah Öcalan, in February 1999, brought about yet another major crisis in bilateral relations. The discovery that Greece had harboured the man regarded by most Turks as being ultimately responsible for a fifteen year civil war in their country was considered to be an unforgivable act of hostility. Many in Turkey demanded retribution. Although a direct armed confrontation did not occur, it was widely believed that it would take many years before the two countries could even begin to try to mend their relationship.

Such views proved wildly off the mark. Instead, the first tentative steps towards reconciliation occurred a little over a month later with the start of the Kosovo conflict. Faced with a massive humanitarian crisis as tens of thousands of people fled the province, the two foreign ministers, İsmail Cem and George Papandreou, held a number of conversations to co-ordinate their responses to the situation. This opened the way for a more substantive dialogue. Following the Turkish general election, in late April, Cem sent a letter to his counterpart proposing talks on the issue of terrorism. In response, Papandreou suggested that, in addition to terrorism, the two countries should start a dialogue on a number of other low-level issues. For example, tourism, culture, trade and the environment were all considered to be areas where the two countries had an interest in fostering co-operation.

Following a meeting in New York shortly afterwards, it was agreed that the two ministries would begin talks on a range of matters of mutual interest. While this was undoubtedly a major breakthrough, not least of all because of the climate that had existed just a few months earlier, the news was greeted with a mixture of scepticism and suspicion. This was particularly evident in Greece, where there was concern that the talks might be used by Turkey as a means to open up direct negotiations on the Aegean issues or as a mechanism to by-pass the Greek Cypriots and enter into direct discussions with the Greek Government over the future of Cyprus. Despite the concerns that existed in both countries, the first round of talks was held in July.

In August the political landscape between the two countries changed dramatically. The massive earthquake that struck northwest Turkey, killing over 15,000 people, led to a massive and unprecedented outpouring of goodwill from Greece. In the weeks that followed the disaster, the people of Greece collecting food, shelter and medical equipment to send to the devastated region. This in turn prompted many in Turkey to look at their neighbours in a new light. The developing feelings of mutual solidarity were further strengthened following the earthquake that struck Athens the following month, which brought rapid offers of help from across Turkey. To most observers the symbols of this newfound friendship were the EMAK and AKUT rescue teams that had worked under the most difficult of circumstances, and with little rest, to assist the trapped and injured with little thought for their nationality. They richly deserved the credit they were given for their work.

Meanwhile, the earthquakes opened the way for a massive increase in contacts between the two countries. At all levels and across all fields of activity, it suddenly became not just acceptable but in many cases fashionable to be seen to be crossing the Aegean. The dreadful disasters that had struck the two countries in the space of three weeks appeared to show that a positive relationship could be forged between the two countries if the will was there to do so.

In early September the governmental talks reconvened in a completely new political environment. The previous caution attached to the dialogue in the minds of the public in both countries had been forgotten. Not only was there now broad public support for the talks, the two governments found themselves under significant pressure from the media to achieve concrete results. The process of rapprochement had become fully legitimised in the eyes of the wider Greek and Turkish public. Moreover, those who had been working towards improved relations prior to these events were no longer treated with contempt as traitors or idealistic peaceniks. Instead, they found themselves joined by innumerable other groups that sought to promote better relations between the two countries.[1] This not only opened the way for significant progress to be made on the range of issues that had originally been tabled for discussion between the two governments, it also meant that all sorts of new possibilities for cooperation had become available that might usually have been considered to be off-limits.

Very quickly, however, the focus of attention shifted away from the low-level talks and became fixed on the question of whether Greece would change its long-standing opposition to Turkish EU candidacy. Significantly, by this point there had been a fundamental realignment within the Greek Government. Rather than view candidacy as a tool with which to exact concessions from Turkey, many in Greece saw candidacy as a mechanism for encouraging the development of a less threatening and confrontational neighbour. The trouble was that this could not be easily sold to the Greek public. To this extent, an effort was made to encourage Turkey to offer at least some sort of gesture prior to the European Council in Helsinki. In this endeavour, Greece was supported by its EU partners and by the United States.

All the while, Athens also had to alleviate Greek Cypriot anxiety about the process of détente. Nicosia was concerned that rapprochement, and the possibility of the lifting of the veto on Turkey's candidacy for European

Union membership, signalled a downgrading of the importance of Cyprus in the eyes of Greek decision makers. The Greek Government, which certainly had no intention of downgrading the Cyprus issue, therefore had to ensure that any decision reached in Helsinki protected Greek Cypriot interests and reaffirmed Greece's ongoing commitment to reaching a resolution of the Cyprus issue.

With just weeks to go before the Council, and despite considerable pressure, the Turkish Government made it clear that it would not be offering Greece a gesture prior to the European Council. This put Prime Minister Simitis in a difficult position. If he chose to exercise a veto he would almost certainly bring to an end the developing process of rapprochement. However, if he accepted Turkish candidacy with nothing in return he would be accused of having given away a key Greek bargaining tool for nothing. With elections less than a year away, this view could be disastrous. Faced with such a choice, the Greek Government decided that the longer term interests of encouraging a peaceful and democratic Turkey outweighed the short-term requirement for a gesture. At the same time, the Greek Government was successfully able to lobby its EU partners to produce a form of wording in the final conclusions of the summit that could be sold at home as a Greek victory.

On 11 December, at the European Council in Helsinki, the European Union formally announced that Turkey had been accepted as a candidate for membership. Significantly, the conclusions contained two vital elements for Greece. In the first instance, the statement contained a clear reference to the need to resolve territorial disputes by 2004 and that issues left outstanding by that point should be referred to the International Court of Justice (ICJ) in The Hague. Although this did not explicitly mention Greece, Turkey or the Aegean it was nevertheless clear that this is what the text meant. At the same time, there was also a clear statement that a resolution of the Cyprus problem would not be a precondition for the island's eventual membership of the European Union. This naturally led to anger in Ankara. The statement about the ICJ was viewed as an unfair extra condition placed on Turkey over and above the other members and the decision on Cyprus was seen to be a deliberate provocation. However, the EU was quickly able to defuse the tensions and persuade the Prime Minister Ecevit that, all things considered, the conclusion represented a victory for Turkey.

The decision by the Turkish Government to accept the conclusions marked a suitably dramatic end to a year that had been full of surprises. Regardless of how the process of rapprochement develops in the future, the sheer range of developments that took place in the space of those twelve months will ensure that 1999 will go down in history as one of the most significant years in the modern history of Greek-Turkish relations.

The role of the European Union

The first major question that needs to be addressed relates to the roles of the European Union and the United States in the process of rapprochement. Generally speaking, the EU terms played a decisive part in fostering détente. However, this was not due to the active role of the Union as a peacemaker. Indeed, the EU was noticeably absent for most of the period. Instead, the EU's influence was passive. Its significance was mainly derived from the fact that Greece was a member and Turkey wanted to join. But even in this regard the influence of the EU was rather more different, and certainly more interesting, than might initially be suspected.

Conventional thinking would suggest that Turkey's desire to join the EU would have spurred the process of rapprochement. However, in reality the role played by Turkey proved to be rather minimal. Certainly one cannot ignore the fact that it was Cem that initiated the process when he wrote to Papandreou requesting direct discussions on terrorism. However, from that moment onwards, Greece took the more active role. Indeed, all things considered, Turkey did very little in substantive terms to push the process forward. Most importantly, the Turkish Government refused to offer any gesture to Greece in order to pave the way for Athens to lift its veto over Turkish membership. Certainly, the European Union's 'power of attraction', as the lure of membership is more widely termed, was significant to Turkey. And yet this power of attraction was not so significant that Ankara was willing to make a relatively minor gesture to Greece, thereby overcoming the main obstacle obstructing its EU candidacy. In this regard, one can perhaps argue that the far more interesting and significant effect of the European Union in the course of events was actually on Greece, rather than Turkey.

It was apparent throughout the process that the main impetus came from Greece. This rather goes against what might have been expected. Since joining the European Economic Community in 1981, Greece had seen its membership as a tool of leverage over Turkey.[2] As a result, in the years that followed, Athens became one of the key factors in the development of EC-Turkish relations.[3] And yet the policy of vetoing Turkish candidacy until such time as it changed its positions on key issues singularly failed to bring about any substantive change in Turkish policy, either on the Aegean or on Cyprus. In fact, the decision to block Turkey was in fact a major source of frustration for Ankara, which in turn led to greater tensions. While this in many ways proved the Greek thesis that Turkey was a belligerent neighbour, and therefore had a certain value in terms of proving Greek concerns on the international stage, it did not help to change the situation.

Indeed, it was the realisation that the problem lay more with Turkey's overall approach to foreign policy, rather than its precise positions on specific issues, which drove the change in Greek thinking that took place in

1999. It was realised that EU candidacy, followed eventually by substantive membership negotiations, could in fact be a far better tool for policy change than the lure of candidacy. Once Turkey started talks with Europe, it would not only be expected to change its general approach, the process of accession would fundamentally change the mindset of Turkish decision makers. It was this rationale that prompted the radical transformation in Greek attitudes that was seen in the period leading up to the European Council in Helsinki. EU membership ceased to be a tool of leverage, but instead was seen more as a mechanism for change.

Certainly this change of approach had its critics. On the one hand there were the traditionalists who opposed giving up Greece's trump card for little or no direct and tangible benefit. However, others were able to frame a more sophisticated argument that generating a process of rapprochement on the basis of Turkish membership of the EU was dangerous insofar as it would, 'only encourage Turkey to maintain illusions about an EU membership that it will never, in fact, attain.'[4] In reality, this is a much more convincing argument. However, it is ultimately invalid insofar as Greece had no real choice but to frame rapprochement in terms of Turkish EU accession. Had it rejected Turkey at Helsinki, it would almost certainly have done significant damage to the process, if not killed it off altogether. Meanwhile, Byron Theodoropoulos, one of Greece's most respected diplomats, noted that some critics had offered a third reason why tying rapprochement with EU candidacy was potentially troubling: 'if Turkey is sure of achieving EU membership, it might conclude that it no longer has an interest in giving way to any negotiations.'[5] Nevertheless, he concluded that encouraging Turkey's European Union membership aspirations on the grounds that it would reduce the danger of armed conflict was also a justifiable view.

In any case, the way in which rapprochement was more a product of a change in Greece than in Turkey has profound implications. It suggests that in situations where an EU member is in conflict with a state that desires membership the EU is not simply a tool of leverage. Instead, if the example provided by Greece is anything to go by, it would appear that EU membership has the potential to change the way in which a member state approaches conflict. Rather than encourage 'good behaviour' in return for EU candidacy, it is realised that 'good behaviour' is encouraged by candidacy. In this sense, it could be argued that the EU actually promotes 'good behaviour' in its own members. This is highly significant insofar as it indicates a transformative effect of EU membership. If this is the case, then it naturally has wide reaching consequences. Obvious examples of where this finding could have relevance in the future include Cyprus, which is also locked in confrontation with Turkey, as well as the Western Balkans, where Croatia, Bosnia, Serbia and Macedonia are all in line for EU membership and yet are likely to face outstanding issues with the neighbours. Perhaps even further in the future, it could have significance in the Caucasus. In any case, it is to be hoped that the case study provided in this work will provide those working on the question of the role of the European Union in the management and transformation of conflict with some useful insights into this most interesting and important of subjects.

The impact of the United States

The second related issue concerns the importance of the United States in the process. Since 1947, when Britain handed over responsibility for Greece and Turkey to the United States, Washington has been the most significant external party in the Greek-Turkish relationship. On numerous occasions it had stepped in to defuse tensions between the two countries. Perhaps the most notable occasion was in 1996, when the two countries came close to conflict over the Imia-Kardak issue. And yet the United States appeared to be relatively insignificant throughout the period examined in this work. It appeared to play no discernable role in the process of rapprochement. To be sure, it would have supported the effort from behind the scenes. However, it was not the instigator of the process. In another way, its influence was clearly seen to be rather limited. Although the visit by President Clinton to Turkey and Greece in November 1999 was hailed as a significant development, it failed to achieve its main goal as far as the process of rapprochement was concerned. Despite repeated, and surprisingly public, efforts by Clinton to persuade the Turkish Government to offer a gesture to Greece in advance of the Helsinki European Council, Ecevit made it clear that he would not be willing to do so. In this regard, the actions of the Turkish Government can be read to be as much a snub to the United States as a signal of Turkish defiance towards Greece and the EU.

Whether the relative unimportance of the United States in the events of 1999 can be seen to be evidence of a permanent change in the significance of the US in Greek-Turkish relations is difficult to say. Certainly, there is a good argument to be made that Helsinki has increased the role of the EU in Greek-Turkish relations and, simultaneously, reduced the overall influence of Washington.[6] However, it should not be taken for granted that this marks an irreversible change in the situation. Looking ahead, should Turkey find its path to EU membership blocked, it may well be the case that the US influence will increase once more. However, in terms of the period reviewed here, the process of rapprochement between Greece and Turkey was ultimately shaped more by the passive influence of the European Union than by the active role of the United States.

The significance of 'disaster diplomacy'

Another key question this work sought to address was the degree to which we can ascribe the process of rapprochement to the earthquakes and the phenomenon of 'disaster diplomacy'.[7] The conclusion that emerges is that there has been far too much emphasis on the role of 'disaster diplomacy' in the events of 1999.[8] This is not to say that phenomenon was unimportant in the development of rapprochement between the two countries. In fact, it had an enormous impact. The problem is that, in both Greece and Turkey as much as the outside world, far too much emphasis has been put on the way in which the rapprochement between Greece and Turkey was a product of the earthquakes. Many analysts have erroneously argued that the improvement in relations was actually caused by the disaster.[9] This view is not only factually wrong – as shown in this work the process of rapprochement clearly predated the events of August and September[10] – such a view also undermines the whole process. By according legitimacy to the thesis that the process of rapprochement between the two governments was the result of the earthquakes, détente becomes intimately linked with popular feelings. This runs the risk of creating the conditions whereby the official process becomes a hostage to public opinion. Put crudely, 'what the people have given, the people can take away'.

Instead, the true impact of the earthquakes in Greece and Turkey has to be seen in terms of the way in which public opinion legitimised a process that was already underway. The outpouring of emotion shown by the two peoples was unprecedented and led to the rapid formation of contacts between groups and individuals in the two countries. However, all this would seem to suggest a latent desire for an improvement of relations. The questions, therefore, is whether rapprochement would have been able to come about otherwise? If there was a deep seated sense of hostility it is unlikely that the earthquakes could have fundamentally changed this. In this regard, it could be argued that the disasters provided the people of the two countries with a mechanism for expressing their hopes for a more stable and secure relationship. This seems to be supported by polling data. For instance, a poll taken in Greece in the autumn on 1997 showed that 63 per cent of Greeks favoured rapprochement with Turkey.[11]

In this sense, it would perhaps be wrong to suggest that the earthquakes created a wish for rapprochement. Instead, the quakes seemed to provide a catalyst for desires that already existed, albeit weakly, to come to the fore. An optimistic account of what happened, therefore, is that the earthquakes simply presented an opportunity for the people of the two countries to express a latent wish to put aside past differences and work together. Moreover, it is noticeable that even now, despite the failure of rapprochement to bring about solid political results, there appears to be no real wish to return to the rhetoric of the past. While the nationalist voices that became almost completely silent during the period after the earthquakes have since re-emerged, their prevalence and influence appears to have decreased. In this sense, the lasting legacy of the earthquakes is that they allowed the people of the two countries to escape from the language and stereotypes of the past and develop a new way of looking at one another.

In any event, in the case of Greece and Turkey, the use of the term 'disaster diplomacy' should not be used as a broad brush to describe the rapprochement that has taken place between Athens and Ankara. Instead it should be used more specifically. It should be seen as a way in which two peoples arrived at a point at which they wished put aside past prejudices. In doing so, this mutual recognition among Greeks and Turks of the equality and humanity of the other allowed the two governments to strengthen, and deepen, a process that had already been put in place. 'Disaster diplomacy', in the case of Greek-Turkish rapprochement, should therefore be seen as a process that allowed for a popular legitimisation of official diplomacy already underway and based on mutual interests. Correspondingly, it should not be used as term to describe the processes that led to the initiation of the policy of rapprochement.

The role of Ismail Cem and George Papandreou

Any discussion on Greek-Turkish rapprochement would be incomplete without an examination of the roles played by George Papandreou and İsmail Cem. Over the course of that year they became the public faces of the process. Indeed, rapprochement became intimately, if not inextricably, linked with the two foreign ministers. But perhaps the most important factor to take into account was the relative asymmetry that existed between the two men in terms of the degree of influence that they had over their respective governments. While many have held the two men responsible for the process of rapprochement, in reality it has been widely argued that the real driving force behind the process was in fact Papandreou.[12] Although it was İsmail Cem who initiated contact with his counterpart, and therefore took the vital first steps in the process, it soon became clear that the driving force for détente was to be found in Athens, rather than Ankara. There are several explanations for why this was the case.

In the first instance, and this is perhaps not widely appreciated, the process of rapprochement was built upon serious intellectual foundations. From the Greek perspective, it was not simply a diplomatic tactic. Instead, it was a political strategy. As noted earlier, within the Greek Foreign Ministry a number of senior figures had worked to provide a strong theoretical rationale for the policy based on a thorough understanding of the process of European Union integration. Over the course of the summer, efforts were made to develop a justification for reversing decades of Greek foreign policy that had been based on traditional balance-of-power thinking and had used EU accession as a tool of leverage against Turkey. Instead, the aim was to put in place an entirely new approach that would emphasise that long term stability could only be achieved by drawing Turkey closer to Europe and by building and cementing bilateral ties. The model of Franco-German relations in the aftermath of the Second World War became the model for Greek policy makers, who realised the need to create a pattern of interdependence that would make future conflict too costly for the two countries. Importantly, this foreign policy goal fit neatly with a general process of domestic political modernisation that had been initiated by Simitis several years earlier. And while the aim had always been to see such a process linked to Greek external relations, it was not until the arrival of Papandreou that this thinking really appeared to take root.

However, the significant affect Papandreou was able to have over the process as compared with Cem was also determined by the very different political circumstances within which the two foreign ministers operated. Without a doubt, Papandreou had the far easier environment within which to work. Most importantly, he enjoyed the confidence of Simitis. The two men were of the same mindset regarding the need for modernisation across the board. However, Simitis had always been more focused on domestic issues than on foreign policy. In this sense, Papandreou was fortunate not just to have the full support of a like-minded prime minister, but also to have the degree of latitude necessary to formulate a new approach that would mark a radical break with previous Greek foreign policy. This is not to say that it was altogether easy for Papandreou. There were clearly those within PASOK who objected to the developments taking place. However, their voices had been weakened to a certain degree following the Öcalan debacle. Moreover, Papandreou was to a certain extent shielded by the fact that he was the son of Andreas Papandreou, who was still the hero to many in the more nationalist sections of the party.

In contrast, Cem operated within a far more difficult political context. Although a senior member of DSP, Cem did not enjoy the same relationship with Ecevit as Papandreou had with Simitis. Moreover, Ecevit was known to be both interested in foreign policy, especially relations with Greece and the Cyprus issue. He was also far more resolute in his opinions on both matters than his Greek counterpart. Meanwhile, the nationalist elements within the DSP were far more influential than those in PASOK. For example, Şükrü Sina Gürel, a noted hard liner on Greek-Turkish relations, and another member of the DSP, served as the minister for Cyprus and government spokesman.[13] In this sense, even within the highest echelons of Cem's own party there were those who were instinctively suspicious, if not wholly opposed to, the process of rapprochement. On top of this, Cem was operating within the constraints of a coalition that included the MHP, which just a few years previously had been on the fringes of the extreme right and was still avowedly nationalist in its orientation. In this sense, the entire political situation encountered by Cem could not have been more different from that facing Papandreou.

However, the potential obstacles in front of Cem were not just limited to the political sphere. There was also the military to consider. As the ultimate guardians of state security, both in a domestic sense and in terms of external threats, no attempt at rapprochement could ever have taken place without at least the tacit consent of the military hierarchy. However, there was little real indication of exactly how they perceived the process. General Hüseyin Kıvrıkoğlu, the Chief of the General Staff, was known to be a hard-liner. However, it seems as though he and the other commanders of the various branches of the armed forces were nevertheless willing to go along with the process and see where it went.[14] For example, the reduced number of incursions of Greek airspace during the Nikiforos military exercise in Cyprus in early October 1999 indicated a willingness to contribute towards the lowering of tensions and the perpetuation of the goodwill that had developed. But balanced against this it is worth remembering that the Turkish Government did not make any significant gesture during the period under discussion, and therefore rapprochement was in one sense relative cost free for Turkey. Nevertheless, for all these reasons Papandreou had far more room to manoeuvre than his counterpart. In fact, when weighed against the political and institutional obstacles faced by Cem, it is to his credit that he was able to achieve as much as he did.

Aside from Cem and Papandreou, another important figure in the process was Yiannos Kranidiotis. His influence over the process was significant, both at an intellectual level and in practical terms. On the one hand he was one of the key architects of the idea. A leading expert on the European Union, and a former Greek MEP, he saw the opportunity to take the European model of Franco-German reconciliation and apply it to Greek-Turkish relations. But it was not until the appointment of Papandreou as minister, coupled with the overture from Cem, that an opportunity was presented to take this idea forward. In practical terms, however, his role was rather different. He had little to do with the actual course of discussions between the two ministers or the two delegations. Instead, his most significant contribution was managing relations with the Greek Cypriots.[15] As a Greek Cypriot himself – his father had been Cypriot Ambassador in Athens – Kranidiotis was both admired and trusted in Nicosia. This was especially important as many Greek Cypriots distrusted Papandreou, believing that he was too willing to reach an accommodation with Turkey and would give in on Cyprus too easily. Of course, the irony is that the process of rapprochement, which was treated with scepticism and suspicions by most Greek Cypriots, was in large part based on the ideas of

Kranidiotis. Nevertheless, his presence in the Greek Government served to reduce the concerns of the Greek Cypriots. This was seen in the aftermath of his death, when relations between Athens and Nicosia became visibly strained and Papandreou had to work with the Greek Cypriots directly.[16]

The future of rapprochement

The question that naturally arises – at least at the time of writing – is where does the process go in the future? The answer, rather unsurprisingly, is that it is difficult to say. While the rapprochement has been founded on the premise that Greece and Turkey share mutual concerns over matters beyond their bilateral relations, and that this should be the basis for a more cooperative relationship, both governments have insisted that a full normalisation of relations can only be achieved by resolving the outstanding disputes. To this extent the process must eventually deal with the Aegean, Cyprus and the other lesser issues that have blighted relations between the two countries. Yet the fact that the need to solve the issues is recognised does not mean that they can be solved overnight. Nor is it simply a case of finding the right political will, although this would certainly be helpful. Cyprus, in particular, presents substantial problems. Whereas the Aegean is a strictly bilateral issue, and can therefore be solved by the two governments in a mutually acceptable manner, the Cyprus issue is primarily shaped by the political leaders of the two communities. Certainly Athens cannot impose a solution on the Greek Cypriots, and Ankara, contrary to the belief of many Greek and Greek Cypriots, cannot just impose a settlement on the Turkish Cypriots.

There is also the question of Turkey's relationship with the EU. Conventional thinking is that if this process is interrupted, or even halted altogether, it could well lead to a resurgence of Greek-Turkish hostility. Certainly it is possible to see how such a development could lead to renewed tensions. However, it is sad to think that an improvement in Greek-Turkish relations can only be conceptualised in terms of Turkey's integration with Europe. Although important, there should be much more to regional relations than this. Neither Athens nor Ankara should forget that the underlying rationale of the talks was to find areas of common interest. This is no less the case if Turkey remains outside the European Union than if it joins. Likewise neither should forget that no matter how bad relations may become in future there will always be areas of mutual concern that are best handled by co-operation rather than confrontation. If in the future it appears as if tensions are again emerging, both governments should pause to consider whether the re-emergence of conflict can really be seen to serve their best interests. Is it really worth returning to the hostility of the past when the process initiated in 1999 has finally brought the two countries to the verge of a peaceful and sustainable coexistence?

APPENDIX A

CEM AND PAPANDREOU LETTERS

Letter from İsmail Cem to George Papandreou, 24 May 1999

Dear George,

I want to share with you my views on ameliorating our bilateral relations. As you also expressed a similar interest to me, I hope these ideas will help us to begin exploration of avenues for possibly moving our relations forward.

Our initial step should be to address the problem of what is perceived in Turkey as links that exist in Greece with terrorist organizations and their systematic encouragement. This is a matter of crucial importance for us and recent events have made it imperative that this issue be handled in an explicit manner and at the bilateral level between our two countries.

I, therefore, suggest that Turkey and Greece conclude an agreement to combat terrorism. Resolution of this issue would permit us to approach our known differences with greater confidence. The substance of this agreement may be inspired by accords we have already signed with some of our other neighbors, but is should also be specific to the nature of the problem as it affects our relations. We have some further ideas in this respect which we are ready to share with you.

I further suggest that parallel to the signing and implementation of such an agreement, we could also initiate a plan for reconciliation. For this purpose, we could benefit from the ideas I had forwarded to the EU in November 1997, emphasizing resort to all the peaceful means referred to in the UN Charter as well as those I placed on the table back in February-March 1998 that enjoyed positive echoes from international circles as being constructive and realistic. Certainly, we would be open to new ideas, too.

If you think we can proceed on these two categories of action, we might instruct our high officials to come together and have them meet and begin to discuss these matters in privacy.

Waiting for your response, I present my warm regards and best wishes.

İsmail Cem

Letter from George Papandreou to İsmail Cem, 25 June 1999

Dear İsmail,

Allow me once again to congratulate you on your reappointment as Foreign Minister of the Republic of Turkey. I am looking forward to continuing our friendly and constructive cooperation.

In this regard I would like to thank you for your letter dated 24 May 1999 and I wish to offer the following thoughts:

First of all I would like to welcome the expression of willingness from your side to improve our bilateral relations. This is also the sincere wish of the Greek side. Greece is willing to address the issues in our relations within the framework of International Law and Treaties. I strongly believe that we must adopt a realistic approach which will allow outstanding issues to be dealt with in sequence creating thus both a strengthening sense of confidence in our relations and a perspective of further steps along the way.

In parallel, we could also envisage resuming dialogue on issues, many of which we have attempted to deal with in the past. Cooperation in several fields of mutual interest such as culture, tourism, environment, crime, economic cooperation and ecological problems should be amongst the topics of our talks. Allow me to elaborate on these suggestions:

-- Tourism should become an area of cooperation. Closer cooperation between Greece and Turkey will enhance our competitiveness and strengthen the attraction of our two countries as tourist destinations. Important exchanges already exist between the local authorities, tourist organizations and chambers of commerce of the Greek islands of the Aegean and those on the western coast of Turkey. It is important we strengthen these contacts and examine into specific issues that will facilitate their cooperation therefore accrue multiple benefits for both our countries.

-- One of the most important resources our two countries possess is the beauty of our natural environments. Our two countries continue to remain comparatively unspoiled by the developments of modern economies. This however may not be so in a few years. The preservation and/or restoration of our natural surroundings, particularly when we speak of the Mediterranean, our coasts, our seas, our rivers and lakes must be a priority for both of us. Let us therefore explore the possibilities of cooperation on ecological issues that will not only preserve our tourist industry's prospects but also guarantee a better quality of life to our citizens.

-- Both Greece and Turkey have rich cultural traditions. Building a multicultural Europe means that we need to enhance our cultural identities and understand each other's specificity. Our cooperation in this field could involve such projects as the restoration of religious and cultural monuments. Mosques, churches, and cultural sites could be identified for this purpose in both our countries. Extremely important are of course live exchanges of artists, intellectuals and academics, but also groups that have formed non-governmental organizations. These exchanges could expand to journalists, women, youth, professionals as well as institutions such as those of tertiary education and many others. In this context complicated but important issues such as Balkan history books in our educational systems might be explored with other neighboring countries.

-- Dealing with organized crime, drug trafficking, illegal migration and terrorism are a priority for Greece and Turkey. Therefore cooperation in this field is a necessity. Such cooperation must obviously be compatible with our obligations as an EU member country. It must also respect our commitments arising from a number of international treaties and agreements signed by us. Furthermore, I hope you will agree it is essential that any form of cooperation on terrorism should also take into account the basic principles safeguarding human rights adopted by the Council of Europe, to which both our countries participate. In any case nothing prevents our two countries from exploring all avenues for cooperation in order to combat terrorism within the framework of relevant international agreements of which we are both part. I also suggest that we could examine our cooperation within the context of the recent SECI agreement to prevent and combat trans-border crime. In this context Greece also has important concerns with regard to drug trafficking and illegal migration. Many attempts have been made by drug dealers or illegal migrant traffickers to cross our common border. This has become a major issue of concern for our citizens and our cooperation here will be truly welcomed. Cooperation on all the above issues would also be of great interest to many nations in Europe as their cities are target destinations of these illegal activities.

-- Trade between our countries has greatly increased over the past years. Let us therefore see how we can enhance this momentum to our mutual benefit. Among other things we could examine the possibility of concluding bilateral economic agreements for instance an agreement on preventing double taxation. Our business communities, who have shown leadership in Greek-Turkish relations, could also contribute positively to our discussions on economic cooperation.

-- South East European Cooperation and the Black Sea Economic Cooperation – where we have already achieved a good record of successful collaboration – provide us with another field for cooperation. The recent crisis in Kosovo is a good example on how our two countries can coordinate their policies within a regional context. While the immediate crisis is over, much is yet to be done for reconciliation, reconstruction and stability in Kosovo, Yugoslavia and the region as a whole. The Stability Pact offers us a number of opportunities to coordinate and develop our joint efforts. I have always believed that close cooperation between Greece and Turkey in multilateral organizations will contribute to give greater impetus to wider stability in the region. Our cooperation in these areas should serve as an example for others. Keeping this in mind we could explore other areas of cooperation within SEEC and BSEC. The South East European Cooperation, SECI and the Black Sea Economic Cooperation, where we have already achieved a good record of collaboration, can become important areas of successful work between us.

The possibility of concluding bilateral, or even multilateral agreements, in the above mentioned fields could also be envisaged in the light of the progress of our cooperation.

In this context we could meet when the opportunity arises in order to have a sincere and constructive exchange of views. I have always been of the view that personal contacts between us can in many ways be productive. They particularly can be useful if we are to define common approaches, ways and means to address outstanding bilateral issues and enhance mutual confidence.

Hoping to hear from you soon, I send you my sincere wishes for success in your post.

George A. Papandreou

APPENDIX B

HELSINKI CONCLUSIONS

The enlargement process

3. The European Council confirms the importance of the enlargement process launched in Luxembourg in December 1997 for the stability and prosperity for the entire European continent. An efficient and credible enlargement process must be sustained.

4. The European Council reaffirms the inclusive nature of the accession process, which now comprises 13 candidate States within a single framework. The candidate States are participating in the accession process on an equal footing. They must share the values and objectives of the European Union as set out in the Treaties. In this respect the European Council stresses the principle of peaceful settlement of disputes in accordance with the United Nations Charter and urges candidate States to make every effort to resolve any outstanding border disputes and other related issues. Failing this they should within a reasonable time bring the dispute to the International Court of Justice. The European Council will review the situation relating to any outstanding disputes, in particular concerning the repercussions on the accession process and in order to promote their settlement through the International Court of Justice, at the latest by the end of 2004. Moreover, the European Council recalls that compliance with the political criteria laid down at the Copenhagen European Council is a prerequisite for the opening of accession negotiations and that compliance with all the Copenhagen criteria is the basis for accession to the Union.

5. The Union has made a firm political commitment to make every effort to complete the Intergovernmental Conference on institutional reform by December 2000, to be followed by ratification. After ratification of the results of that

Conference the Union should be in a position to welcome new Member States from the end of 2002 as soon as they have demonstrated their ability to assume the obligations of membership and once the negotiating process has been successfully completed.

6. The Commission has made a new detailed assessment of progress in the candidate States. This assessment shows progress towards fulfilling the accession criteria. At the same time, given that difficulties remain in certain sectors, candidate States are encouraged to continue and step up their efforts to comply with the accession criteria. It emerges that some candidates will not be in a position to meet all the Copenhagen criteria in the medium term. The Commission's intention is to report in early 2000 to the Council on progress by certain candidate States on fulfilling the Copenhagen economic criteria. The next regular progress reports will be presented in good time before the European Council in December 2000.

7. The European Council recalls the importance of high standards of nuclear safety in Central and Eastern Europe. It calls on the Council to consider how to address the issue of nuclear safety in the framework of the enlargement process in accordance with the relevant Council conclusions.

8. The European Council notes with satisfaction the substantive work undertaken and progress which has been achieved in accession negotiations with Cyprus, Hungary, Poland, Estonia, the Czech Republic and Slovenia.

9. (a) The European Council welcomes the launch of the talks aiming at a comprehensive settlement of the Cyprus problem on 3 December in New York and expresses its strong support for the UN Secretary-General's efforts to bring the process to a successful conclusion.
(b) The European Council underlines that a political settlement will facilitate the accession of Cyprus to the European Union. If no settlement has been reached by the completion of accession negotiations, the Council's decision on accession will be made without the above being a precondition. In this the Council will take account of all relevant factors.

10. Determined to lend a positive contribution to security and stability on the European continent and in the light of recent developments as well as the Commission's reports, the European Council has decided to convene bilateral intergovernmental conferences in February 2000 to begin negotiations with Romania, Slovakia, Latvia, Lithuania, Bulgaria and Malta on the conditions for their entry into the Union and the ensuing Treaty adjustments.

11. In the negotiations, each candidate State will be judged on its own merits. This principle will apply both to opening of the various negotiating chapters and to the

conduct of the negotiations. In order to maintain momentum in the negotiations, cumbersome procedures should be avoided. Candidate States which have now been brought into the negotiating process will have the possibility to catch up within a reasonable period of time with those already in negotiations if they have made sufficient progress in their preparations. Progress in negotiations must go hand in hand with progress in incorporating the acquis into legislation and actually implementing and enforcing it.

12. The European Council welcomes recent positive developments in Turkey as noted in the Commission's progress report, as well as its intention to continue its reforms towards complying with the Copenhagen criteria. Turkey is a candidate State destined to join the Union on the basis of the same criteria as applied to the other candidate States. Building on the existing European strategy, Turkey, like other candidate States, will benefit from a pre-accession strategy to stimulate and support its reforms. This will include enhanced political dialogue, with emphasis on progressing towards fulfilling the political criteria for accession with particular reference to the issue of human rights, as well as on the issues referred to in paragraphs 4 and 9(a). Turkey will also have the opportunity to participate in Community programmes and agencies and in meetings between candidate States and the Union in the context of the accession process. An accession partnership will be drawn up on the basis of previous European Council conclusions while containing priorities on which accession preparations must concentrate in the light of the political and economic criteria and the obligations of a Member State, combined with a national programme for the adoption of the acquis. Appropriate monitoring mechanisms will be established. With a view to intensifying the harmonisation of Turkey's legislation and practice with the acquis, the Commission is invited to prepare a process of analytical examination of the acquis. The European Council asks the Commission to present a single framework for coordinating all sources of European Union financial assistance for pre-accession.

13. The future of the European Conference will be reviewed in the light of the evolving situation and the decisions on the accession process taken at Helsinki. The forthcoming French Presidency has announced its intention to convene a meeting of the conference in the second half of 2000.

European Council, Helsinki European Council Presidency Conclusions, 10–11 December 1999

NOTES

Introduction

1 Jeremy Bowen, 'The Story of Ocalan's Arrest', *BBC News*, 28 May 1999.
2 Joshua Black, 'Greek Diplomacy and the Hunt for Abdullah Ocalan', *WWS Case Study 4/00*, Woodrow Wilson School for Public and International Affairs, Princeton University, 2000.
3 Philip H. Gordon, 'Post-Helsinki: Turkey, Greece and the European Union', *The Strategic Regional Report*, Brooking Institution, February 2000.
4 F. Stephen Larrabee, 'Turkish Foreign and Security Policy: New Dimensions and New Challenges', in Zalmay Khalilzad, Ian O. Lesser, F. Stephen Larrabee, *The Future of Turkish-Western Relations: Toward a Strategic Plan* (Santa Monica: RAND, 2000), p.24.
5 Ayten Gundogdu, 'Identities in Question: Greek-Turkish Relations in a Period of Transformation?', *Middle East Review of International Affairs* (MERIA), Volume 5, Number 1, March 2001.
6 For an excellent account of this see Claude Nicolet, *United States Policy towards Cyprus, 1954–1974: Removing the Greek-Turkish Bone of Contention* (Mannheim: Bibliopolis, 2001).
7 Dimitri Keridis, 'Political Culture and Foreign Policy: Greek-Turkish Relations in the Era of European Integration and Globalization', *A NATO Fellowship Final Report*, June 1999, p.7.
8 It is worth noting that the formal start of the relationship between Turkey and the EU preceded its application by almost a quarter of a century. An association agreement was signed between Turkey and the European Economic Community (EEC) in 1963.
9 Grigoriadis, Ioannis N. 'The Changing Role of the EU Factor in Greek-Turkish Relations', Symposium Paper, 'Current Social Science Research on Greece', *Paper Presented at the 1st PhD Symposium on Modern Greece*, Hellenic Observatory, London School Of Economics And Political Science, 21 June 2003, p.3.

10 Of course it would be wrong to suggest that the decision by Greece to veto Turkey's candidacy led to deep problems with all of its European partners. It was widely understood that Greece had the backing of a number of other member states, most notably Germany, which were opposed to Turkish membership but did not want to spark a bilateral crisis with Ankara.

11 Skouroliakou, Melina. 'The Theory That Never Turned Into Practice: Case Study from Eastern Mediterranean', *Paper for presentation at the ISA-South Conference*, Miami, 3–5 November 2005.

12 It is worth noting that Turkey does not contest the twelve mile limit as a limit under international law. Indeed, it has extended its own territorial waters to twelve miles in the Black Sea and the Mediterranean. Instead, it argues that any move by Greece to extend its territorial waters would effectively turn the Aegean Sea into a Greek lake. Süha Bölükbaşı, 'The Turco-Greek Dispute', in Clement H. Dodd (editor), *Turkish Foreign Policy: New Prospects*, Modern Turkish Studies Programme, School of Oriental and African Studies (Huntingdon: The Eothen Press, 1992), p.38.

13 Phaedon John Kozyris, 'The Legal Dimensions of the Current Greek-Turkish Conflict: A Greek View', in in Dimitris Keridis and Dimitrios Triantaphyllou (editors), *Greek-Turkish Relations in the Era of Globalization* (Virginia: Brassey's, 2001), p.106.

14 'Holbrooke: Greece, Turkey were on verge of battle', *CNN*, 31 January 1996.

15 Vincent Boland, 'Faith, Hope and Parity', *Financial Times*, 25 August 2005.

16 U.S. Department of State, *Turkey Country Report on Human Rights Practices for 1998*, Released by the Bureau of Democracy, Human Rights, and Labor, February 26, 1998.

17 For an overview of the situation just prior to rapprochement see Christopher Panico, 'Greece: The Turks of Western Thrace', *Human Rights Watch*, Volume 11, Number 1, January 1999.

18 There is an extensive body of literature on the Cyprus issue. For a broad cross-section of views and competing analyses see Oliver Richmond, *Mediating in Cyprus* (London: Frank Cass, 1998); Farid Mirbagheri, *Cyprus and International Peacemaking* (London: Hurst, 1987); Clement Dodd (ed.), *Cyprus: The Need for New Perspectives* (Huntingdon: The Eothen Press, 1999); Joseph S. Joseph, *Cyprus: Ethnic Conflict and International Politics: From Independence to the Threshold of the European Union* (Basingstoke: Macmillan, 1999); Michael Emerson and Natalie Tocci, *Cyprus as the Lighthouse of the East Mediterranean: Shaping EU Accession and Reunification Together* (Brussels: CEPS, 2002); David Hannay, *Cyprus: The Search for a Solution* (London: IB Tauris, 2005) and Claire Palley, *An International Relations Debacle: The UN Secretary-General's Mission of Good Offices in Cyprus, 1999–2004* (Oxford: Hart Publishing, 2005).

19 European Court of Human Rights, *Loizidou v. Turkey*, 15318/89 [1996], ECHR 70, 18 December 1996.

20 This point was made to by Richard Clogg during a conference on Greek-Turkish relations held at St Antony's College, Oxford University, in May 2004. South East European Studies Programme (SEESP), *SEESP Newsletter*, Number 2, European Studies Centre, St Antony's College, 2004, p.6.

21 For a review of the debate, see Olga Demetriou. 'The EU and the Cyprus Conflict: A Review of the Literature', *Working Paper Number 5*, EU Border Conflicts Studies, January 2004. See also Christopher Brewin, *European Union and Cyprus* (Huntingdon: The Eothen Press, 2000); Nathalie Tocci, *EU Accession Dynamics and Conflict Resolution: Catalysing Peace or Consolidating Partition in Cyprus?* (London: Ashgate, 2004); Christou, George. *The European Union and Enlargement: The Case of Cyprus* (Basingstoke: Palgrave Macmillan, 2004); and James Ker-Lindsay, *EU Accession and UN Peacemaking in Cyprus* (Basingstoke: Palgrave Macmillan, 2005).

22 Marc-Andre Gaudissart, 'Cyprus and the European Union: The Long Road to Accession', *The Cyprus Review*, Volume 8, Number 1, Spring 1996, p.27.

23 F. Stephen Larrabee, 'The EU Needs to Rethink its Cyprus Policy', *Survival*, Volume 40, Number 3, Autumn 1998, p.25.

24 David Barchard, *Turkey and the European Union* (London: Centre for European Reform, 1998), p.35.

25 For an examination of Denktaş's obstructive role in the Cyprus peace process over many years see David Hannay, *Cyprus: The Search for a Solution* (London: I.B. Tauris, 2005), pp.17–21.

26 A study published several years after the start of rapprochement noted that, 'there is a surprising scarcity in the literature of studies explicitly devoted to analysing the EU's impact on the Greco-Turkish conflict.' Bahar Rumelili, 'The European Union's Impact on the Greek-Turkish Conflict: A Review of the Literature', *Working Paper Number 6*, EU Border Conflicts Studies, January 2004, p.1.

27 'Iran quake could open door to Iran-USA ties', *AFP*, 30 December 2003.

28 'Earthquake Diplomacy in South Asia', *Washington Times*, 24 October 2005.

Chapter 1

1 Tozun Bahceli, *Greek-Turkish Relations Since 1955* (Boulder, Colorado: Westview Press, 1987), p.5.

2 Bruce Clark, *Twice a Stranger: How Mass Expulsion Forged Modern Greece and Turkey* (London: Granta, 2006), p.17.

3 Warren Treadgold, *A History of Byzantine State and Society* (Stanford: Stanford University Press, 1997), p.805.

4 For a review of some of the general problems and implications of ascribing an ethnic dimension to conflict see V.P. Gagnon, *The Myth of Ethnic War: Serbia and Croatia in the 1990s* (London: Cornell University Press, 2004).

5   Thanos Veremis, 'The Protracted Crisis', in Dimitris Keridis and Dimitrios Triantaphyllou (editors), *Greek-Turkish Relations in the Era of Globalization* (Virginia: Brassey's, 2001), p.42.
6   Leyla Bouton and Kerin Hope, 'Relations with Greece: Big issues have still to be resolved', Turkey Survey, *Financial Times*, 2000.
7   Bahceli, *Greek-Turkish Relations Since 1955*, p.1. For a review of the way in which Greeks and Turks perceive each other across a variety of contexts, see the special issue of *South European Society and Politics*, Volume 11, Number 1, March 2006. See also Hercules Millas, 'National Perceptions of the 'Other' and the Persistence of Some Images', in Mustafa Aydin and Kostas Ifantis (eds.), *Turkish-Greek Relations: Escaping from the Security Dilemma in the Aegean* (London: Routledge, 2004).
8   William Hale, *Turkish Politics and the Military* (London: Routledge, 1994), p.30.
9   For an account of the Asia Minor campaign, see Michael Llewellyn Smith, *Ionian Vision: Greece in Asia Minor, 1919–1922* (London: Hurst & Co, London, 1998).
10 Erik J. Zürcher, *Turkey: A Modern History* (London: I.B. Tauris, 1997), p.159.
11 An account of these events and the subsequent effect on Greece and Turkey can be found in Clark, Twice a Stranger, and Renée Hirschon (editor), *Crossing the Aegean: An Appraisal of the 1923 Compulsory Population Exchange between Greece and Turkey* (New York and Oxford: Berghahn Books, 2003).
12 Bahceli, *Greek-Turkish Relations Since 1955*, p.13.
13 C.M. Woodhouse, *Modern Greece: A Short History*, 2nd Edition (London: Faber and Faber, 1991), p.220.
14 Nicole and Hugh Pope, *Turkey Unveiled: Atatürk and After* (London: John Murray, 1997), p.115. Mustafa Kemal took the surname Atatürk, Father of the Turks, in 1934.
15 Convention Regarding the Regime of the Straits Signed at Montreux, July 20th, 1936.
16 Woodhouse, *Modern Greece*, p.234.
17 For a discussion on Turkey's foreign policy during the Second World War and an examination of why it did not join the war see Selim Deringil, *Turkish Foreign Policy During the Second World War: An Active Neutrality* (Cambridge University Press. Cambridge 1989).
18 However, as has been pointed out, the amount supplied was limited due to grain shortages in Turkey. Mark Mazower, *Inside Hitler's Greece: The Experience of Occupation, 1941–44* (New Haven and London: Yale University Press, 1993), p.47.
19 It was estimated that German forces could have occupied Istanbul within 48 hours. Pope, *Turkey Unveiled*, p.73.
20 Zürcher, *Turkey*, p.208.

21 Robert Holland and Diana Markides, *The British and the Hellenes: Struggles for Mastery in the Eastern Mediterranean 1850–1960* (Oxford: Oxford University Press, 2006), p.228.
22 See Speros Vryonis, *The Mechanism of Catastrophe: The Turkish pogrom of September 6–7, 1955, and the destruction of the Greek community of Istanbul* (New York: NY Greekworks.com, 2005).
23 Richard Clogg, 'Greek-Turkish Relations in the Post-1974 Period', in Dimitri Constas (editor), *Greek-Turkish Conflict in the 1990s: Domestic and External Influences* (Basingstoke: Macmillan, 1990), p.13.
24 Nicos Rolandis, 'The Twilight Zone', *Cyprus Mail*, 2 April 2006.
25 Pope, *Turkey Unveiled*, p.116.
26 UN Security Council Resolution 186 (1964), 4 March 1964. For an account of this period see Alan James, *Keeping the Peace in the Cyprus Crisis of 1963–64* (Basingstoke: Palgrave Macmillan, 2001); and James Ker-Lindsay, *Britain and the Cyprus Crisis, 1963–64* (Mannheim und Mohnsee: Bibliopolis, 2004).
27 John Reddaway, *Burdened with Cyprus: The British Connection* (London: Weidenfeld & Nicholson, 1986), p.184.
28 The most comprehensive and detailed account to date of the invasion and the peace talks, albeit told from a predominantly Turkish perspective, is Mehmet Ali Birand, *30 Hot Days* (Nicosia: Kemal Rustem, 1985).
29 Thanos Veremis, *The Military in Greek Politics: From Independence to Democracy* (London: Hurst, 1997), p.164.
30 Hale, *Turkish Politics and the Military*, p.217.
31 There is an extensive literature available on UN peacemaking activities in Cyprus from 1964. See, for example, Oliver Richmond, *Mediating in Cyprus* (London: Frank Cass, 1998); Farid Mirbagheri, *Cyprus and International Peacemaking* (London: Hurst, 1987) and, more recently, James Ker-Lindsay, 'From U Thant to Kofi Annan: UN Peacemaking in Cyprus, 1964–2004', *Occasional Paper 5/05*, South East European Studies at Oxford (SEESOX), St Antony's College, Oxford University, October 2005.
32 Hale, *Turkish Politics and the Military*, p.218.
33 Süha Bölükbaşı, 'The Turco-Greek Dispute: Issues, Policies and Prospects'; in Dodd, Clement (ed), *Turkish Foreign Policy: New Prospects* (Huntingdon: The Eothen Press, 1993), p.34.
34 Turkey in fact claimed that Greece had been conducting research and exploration since 1960. Bahceli, *Greek-Turkish Relations Since 1955*, p.130.
35 Arapoglou, Stergios, 'Dispute in the Aegean Sea: Imia/Kardak Crisis', Research Report, Air Command and Staff College, Air University, Maxwell Air Base, Alabama, April 2002, p.3.
36 Van Coufoudakis, 'Greek Political Party Attitudes towards Turkey: 1974–89', in Dimitri Constas (editor), *Greek-Turkish Conflict in the 1990s: Domestic and External Influences* (Basingstoke: Macmillan, 1990), p.44.
37 UN Security Council Resolution 395 (1976), 25 August 1976.

38 International Court of Justice, Aegean Sea Continental Shelf Case (Interim Protection), Order of 11 September 1976.
39 Bahar Rumelili, 'The European Union's Impact on the Greek-Turkish Conflict: A Review of the Literature', *Working Paper Number 6*, EU Border Conflicts Studies, January 2004, p.4.
40 North Atlantic Council, *Final Communiqué*, Brussels, 7–8 December 1978.
41 International Court of Justice, Greece v. Turkey, Aegean Sea Continental Shelf Case, Jurisdiction of the Court, Judgment, General List No. 62 [1978] ICJ 1, 19 December 1978.
42 Şükrü Elekdağ, 'Is Turkey Evading the Law?', Milliyet, 31 January 2000 as translated in the *Turkish Press Review*, Office of the Prime Minister, Directorate General of Press and Information, 31 January 2000.
43 *Keesing's Contemporary Archives*, 8 January 1982, p.31263.
44 Mehmet Ali Birand, 'Turkey and the 'Davos Process': Experiences and Prospects', in Dimitri Constas (editor), *Greek-Turkish Conflict in the 1990s: Domestic and External Influences* (Basingstoke: Macmillan, 1990), p.29.
45 Pope, *Turkey Unveiled*, p.123.
46 The results of this change were dramatic. In 1980 the number of Greeks visiting Turkey was 19,477. In 1990 the figure was 203,320. Joanna Apap, Sergio Carrera and Kemal Kirisci, 'Turkey in the European Area of Freedom, Security and Justice', *EU-Turkey Working Paper Number 3*, Centre for European Policy Studies, August 2004, p.33.
47 *Keesing's Contemporary Archives*, September 1986, p.34636.
48 Pope, *Turkey Unveiled*, p.193.
49 F. Stephen Larrabee and Ian O. Lesser, *Turkish Foreign Policy in an Age of Uncertainty* (Santa Monica: RAND 2003), p.74.
50 Bölükbaşı, 'The Turco-Greek Dispute: Issues, Policies and Prospects', p.38.
51 C.M. Woodhouse, *Modern Greece: A Short History*, 2nd Edition (London: Faber and Faber, 1991), p.308.
52 *Keesing's Contemporary Archives*, April 1987, p.35084.
53 *Keesing's Contemporary Archives*, May 1987, p.35129.
54 Pope, *Turkey Unveiled*, p.194; and Birand, 'Turkey and the 'Davos Process': Experiences and Prospects', p.32.
55 Coufoudakis, 'Greek Political Party Attitudes towards Turkey: 1974–89', p.50.
56 It has been said that the Davos Meeting was also significant insofar as Greece recognised, albeit privately, that there was room for improvement with regard to the treatment of the Muslim minority in Thrace. Bahceli, *Greek-Turkish Relations Since 1955*, p.184.
57 Bölükbaşı, 'The Turco-Greek Dispute: Issues, Policies and Prospects', p.27.
58 Richard Clogg, 'Greek-Turkish Relations in the Post-1974 Period', in Dimitri Constas (editor), *Greek-Turkish Conflict in the 1990s: Domestic and External Influences* (Basingstoke: Macmillan, 1990), p.21.

59 Woodhouse, *Modern Greece*, p.348.
60 Coufoudakis, 'Greek Political Party Attitudes Towards Turkey: 1974–89', p.51. As Coufoudakis also points out, this period marks a reversal in political opinions in Cyprus towards Papandreou. The small and more nationalist parties, EDEK and DIKO, which had supported Papandreou's hard-line towards Turkey in the past, now became more critical of his stance. Meanwhile, the steps taken by Papandreou were supported by both of the main Cypriot parties, DISY and AKEL, which are traditionally less nationalist and represent 60–70 per cent of the population.
61 Bölükbaşı, 'The Turco-Greek Dispute: Issues, Policies and Prospects', p.46.
62 Carol Migdalovitz, '86065: Greece and Turkey: Current Foreign Aid Issues', *CRS Issue Brief*, Congressional Research Service (CRS), 3 December 1996.
63 *Ibid.*
64 Madeleine Demetriou, 'On the Long Road to Europe and the Short Path to War: Issue-Linkage Politics and the Arms Build-up on Cyprus', *Mediterranean Politics*, Volume 3, Number 3, Winter 1998, p.43.
65 European Commission, *Regular Report on Turkey's Progress towards Accession*, 1998, p.6.
66 Ioannis N. Grigoriadis, 'The Changing Role of the EU Factor in Greek-Turkish Relations', Symposium Paper, 'Current Social Science Research on Greece', *1st PhD Symposium on Modern Greece*, Hellenic Observatory, London School Of Economics And Political Science, 21 June 2003, p.2.
67 Erkan Erdogdu, 'Turkey and Europe: Undivided but not United', *Middle East Review of International Affairs* (MERIA), Volume 6, Number 2, June 2002. The view that Greece undertook not to use its membership to disrupt relations is one that the author has heard stated by many Turkish academics and officials. However, there is no direct evidence that such an undertaken was ever given by Athens.
68 Thanos Veremis, 'The Protracted Crisis', in Dimitris Keridis and Dimitrios Triantaphyllou (editors), *Greek-Turkish Relations in the Era of Globalization* (Virginia: Brassey's, 2001), p.44.
69 Statement made by Murat Karayalçın, Foreign Minister of Turkey, on Greek Cypriot Application for EU Membership on 6 March, 1995 during the EU-Turkey Association Council in Brussels. However, it has been argued that the decision actually benefited Turkey as it de-linked the Cyprus issue from the customs union and, by extension, membership of the European Union. Stelios Stavridis, 'The European Union's Contribution to Peace and Stability in the Eastern Mediterranean (the So-Called Athens-Nicosia-Ankara Triangle): A Critique', Working Paper, *Fundacion SIP Zaragoza*, November 2005, p.16.
70 'Greek Territorial Waters and National Airspace', Website of the Hellenic Ministry of Foreign Affairs, accessed April 2006. Specifically, the Greek Government referred to Article 2, Paragraph 4 of the UN Charter, which

states, 'All Members shall refrain in their international relations from the threat or use of force against the territorial integrity or political independence of any state, or in any other manner inconsistent with the Purposes of the United Nations.'

71 'The Question of the Imia Islands: Turkish Allegations on "Grey Zones" in the Aegean Sea', *Website of the Greek Ministry of Foreign Affairs*, accessed April 2006.
72 Specifically, the Turkish Government argued that although the 1947 Treaty of Paris had ceded the Dodecanese and adjacent islets to Greece, the Kardak islets, as they are known in Turkish, were actually 5.5 nautical miles from the nearest Greek island, and only 3.8 nautical miles from the Turkish coast. In the view of the Turkish Government, they were not, therefore, adjacent and not, therefore, Greek territory.
73 Veremis, 'The Protracted Crisis', p.44.
74 For an analysis of the important role of the media during this crisis and in general see Katharina Hadjidimos, 'The role of the Media in Greek-Turkish Relations: ', Co-Production of a TV Programme Window by Greek and Turkish Journalists', *Robert Bosch Stiftung, Kolleg für Internationale Aufgaben*, Programm Jahr 1998/99.
75 *Statement by Ambassador Ömer Akbal, Spokesman of the Turkish Foreign Ministry*, 31 January 1996.
76 This was subsequently confirmed in a highly publicised interview given to Turkish television by Admiral Güven Erkaya, the Commander of the Turkish Navy at the time. He also said that Baykal had also favoured military action. *Athens News Agency*, 12 February 1998.
77 The elections had been won by the Islamist Welfare Party (RP), which obtained 158 seats in the 550-seat Grand National Assembly. However, Çiller's True Path Party (DYP) had come second with 135 seats and the Motherland Party (ANAP), third with 131 seats. The two other remaining parties represented in the Assembly were the Democratic Left Party (DSP), with 76 seats and the Republican People's Party (CHP) with 50 seats.
78 United Nations, *Press Release SG/SM/5887*, 30 January 1996.
79 Holbrook was of course best known as the prime mover behind the Dayton peace agreement, which had brought the Bosnian civil war to an end the previous year.
80 *Statement to Reuters*, 1 February 1996.
81 For a fuller analysis of the crisis see Ekavi Athanassopoulou, 'Blessing in Disguise? The Imia Crisis and Turkish-Greek Relations,' *Mediterranean Politics*, Volume 2, Number 3, Winter 1997.
82 'Greek Official Talks Plainly About Turks: Seeks 'Normal' Ties, Not 'Friendly' Ones', *The Washington Times*, 10 April 1996.
83 See Erdogdu, 'Turkey and Europe: Undivided but not United'.

84 For an analysis of the S-300 missile crisis see Demetriou, 'On the Long Road to Europe and the Short Path to War'.
85 By this point, Denktaş had also come to be seen as the main obstacle to a settlement by the international community. For an analysis of Denktaş's role by someone closely involved with the talks see David Hannay, *Cyprus: The Search for a Solution* (London: IB Tauris, 2005), pp.17–21.
86 In early 1999, the author had the opportunity to speak with a senior member of the Turkish General Staff who confirmed that plans for an air strike against the missiles had indeed been drawn up.
87 See, for example, Athanassopoulou, 'Blessing in Disguise? The Imia Crisis and Turkish-Greek Relations'; and Alexis Heraclides, 'Greek-Turkish Relations from Discord to Détente: A Preliminary Evaluation', *The Review of International Affairs*, Volume 1, Number 3, Spring 2002.
88 'New Phase Opens in Greek-Turkish Relations', *Greece: A News Review from the Embassy of Greece Press Office*, Volume 3, Number 7, July/August 1997.
89 'Agreement between the Government of the Republic of Turkey and the Turkish Republic of Northern Cyprus on the Establishment of an Association Council', 6 August 1997.
90 'Turkey Reneges on Madrid Agreement', *Greece: A News Review from the Embassy of Greece Press Office*, Volume 3, Number 8, September 1997.
91 *Athens News Agency*, Daily News Bulletin, 27 September 1997.
92 Veremis, 'The Protracted Crisis', p.46.
93 European Council, *Luxembourg European Council Presidency Conclusions*, 12–13 December 1997.
94 William Park, 'Turkey's European Union Candidacy: From Luxembourg to Helsinki – to Ankara?', *Mediterranean Politics*, Volume 5, Number 3, Autumn 2000, p.35.
95 European Commission, *Regular Report on Turkey's Progress towards Accession*, 1998, p.7.
96 James Ker-Lindsay, *EU Accession and UN Peacemaking in Cyprus* (Basingstoke: Palgrave Macmillan, 2005), p.22.

Chapter 2

1 For an analysis of the events of that period see Yüksel Sezgin, 'The October 1998 Crisis in Turkish-Syrian Relations: A Prospect Theory Approach', *Turkish Studies*, Volume 3, Number 2, Autumn 2002, p.45.
2 'Fugitive on the run: Ocalan mystery tour', *BBC News*, 16 February 1999.
3 'Greece dogged by Ocalan Affair', *BBC News*, 27 February 1999. It was not clear, however, whether he chose to leave the compound against Greek advice or whether, as he later claimed, he was tricked into doing so by Greek officials.

NOTES

4 Office of the Prime Minister, Directorate General of Press and Information, Statement by Prime Minister Ecevit, 16 February 1999, *Newspot 13*, January 1999.
5 'The Kurds aflame with rage', *Time*, 9 March 1999.
6 'The Ocalan Trial: Greece, Ocalan And The Shadow State', Institute for War and Peace Reporting (IWPR), *Balkan Crisis Report 5*, 4 March 1999.
7 'World Media Watch: Kurdish reaction to Ocalan's arrest', *BBC News*, 18 February 1999.
8 'Court revisits Ocalan nightmare', *Kathimerini* (English edition), 28 May 2003.
9 *Athens News Agency*, 17 February 1999.
10 'George Papandreou, flouting Greek tradition', *The Economist*, 1 May 1999.
11 *Athens News Agency*, 28 January 1997.
12 'Ocalan reportedly implicates Greeks in supporting PKK', *CNN*, 22 February 1999.
13 'Turkey shootout over Ocalan', *BBC News*, 19 February 1999.
14 'Turkey calls Greece an outlaw state', *BBC News*, 22 February 1999.
15 'Turkey warns Greece in Kurdish rebel case', *Washington Post*, 23 February 1999.
16 'Rebels funded by Greek churches" *BBC News*, 26 February 1999.
17 Nicole and Hugh Pope, *Turkey Unveiled: Ataturk and After* (London: John Murray, 1997), p.276.
18 Ahmet O. Evin, 'Changing Greek Perspectives on Turkey: An Assessment of the post-Earthquake Rapprochement', in Ali Carkoglu and Barry Rubin (eds.), Special Issue: Greek-Turkish Relations in an Era of Détente, *Turkish Studies*, Volume 5, Number 1, Spring 2004, p.7.
19 'Greece dogged by Ocalan affair', *BBC News*, 27 February 1999.
20 Yonca Poyraz Dogan, 'Ilter Turkmen: We concentrate on the common interests for both Greece and Turkey. That's our secret', *Greek-Turkish Synergy*, 30 March 2002. Perhaps the most prominent of these groups was a high-profile initiative that had been established several years earlier by leading business figures. Notably, the Greek-Turkish Forum was in fact one of the very few groups that continued to function during the crisis.
21 'Conflict shakes Greek tightrope', Associated Press, 20 April 1999.
22 'George Papandreou: A call for bolder vision in Balkans', *International Herald Tribune*, 22 May 1999.
23 *Anadolu Agency*, 25 March 1999.
24 *Athens News Agency*, 6 April 1999.
25 *Anadolu Agency*, 15 April 1999. Logan also noted that Turkey's refusal to engage with EU on issues such as Cyprus, human rights, and the Aegean was jeopardising its chances of candidacy.
26 *To Vima tis Kyriakis*, 11 April 1999.

27 *Ibid.* It was also expected that the two would discuss several other regional matters, including an invitation Simitis had issued Clinton to visit Greece while he was in the area for the OSCE summit in Istanbul in November.

28 In third place came the Virtue Party, an Islamist grouping that took fifteen per cent of the votes and 11 seats. The final two parties represented in the parliament would be the two traditional centre rights parties, Motherland Party (ANAP), which took 13 per cent of the vote and 86 seats and the True Path Party (DYP), which 12 per cent of the vote and 85 seats.

29 Alan Makovsky, 'Research Guide: Turkey's Election and New Government', *Middle East Review of International Affairs* (MERIA), 1999.

30 *Athens News Agency*, 20 April 1999.

31 *Kathimerini*, 21 April 1999.

32 *Athens News Agency*, 24 April 1999.

33 *Athens News Agency*, 20 April 1999.

34 *Sabah*, 26 April 1999.

35 *Athens News Agency*, 26 April 1999.

36 *Ibid.*

Chapter 3

1 *Athens News Agency*, 4 May 1999.

2 *CyBC Radio*, 6 May 1999.

3 *Anadolu Agency*, 6 May 1999.

4 *Anadolu Agency*, 6 May 1999.

5 *Anadolu Agency*, 14 May 1999.

6 *Ibid.*

7 *ERT Radio*, 15 May 1999.

8 *Anadolu Agency*, 14 May 1999.

9 *Hürriyet*, 2 June 1999.

10 *Athens News Agency*, 3 June 1999.

11 *Anadolu Agency*, 2 June 1999.

12 *Milliyet*, 3 June 1999.

13 *Hürriyet*, 2 June 1999.

14 *Athens News Agency*, 5 June 1999.

15 *Ibid.*

16 *Anadolu Agency*, 10 June 1999.

17 *Ibid.*

18 *Ibid.*

19 *Athens News Agency*, 12 June 1999.

20 The Cypriot Government Spokesman referred to Ecevit's 'medieval' views on the subject and asked why, if the Cyprus dispute had already been solved, were the, "UN, the European Union, the Group of Eight, the Non-Aligned Movement and the Commonwealth" involved in efforts to solve the issue. *Cyprus News Agency*, 13 July 1999.

21 *To Vima tis Kyriakis*, 20 June 1999.
22 *Reuters*, 12 July 1999.
23 *Cyprus News Agency*, 13 July 1999.
24 *TRT TV*, 26 June 1999.
25 Text of the Ocalan verdict', *BBC News*, 29 June 1999.
26 *Athens News Agency*, 30 June 1999.
27 'International community rejects Ocalan death penalty', *CNN*, 29 June 1999.
28 *Ta Nea*, 23 July 1999.
29 *Macedonian Press Agency*, 22 July 1999.
30 *Ibid.*
31 *Ta Nea*, 23 July 1999.
32 *Ibid.*
33 Rozakis was also the first co-ordinator of the Greek team on the Greek-Turkish Forum. However, he stepped down when he was appointed to the European Court of Human Rights (ECHR). See Yonca Poyraz Dogan, 'Costas Carras: Greek and Turkey do share the same understanding about the region and the world around us...', *Greek-Turkish Synergy*, 29 March 2002.
34 *Ependitis*, 10 July 1999.
35 *Ibid.*
36 *To Vima tis Kyriakis*, 11 July 1999.
37 *Anadolu Agency*, 26 July 1999.
38 *Anadolu Agency*, 28 July 1999.
39 'Greece/Turkey: 'Positive' Talks To Continue Today', *RFE/RL*, 29 July 1999.
40 *TRT TV*, 28 July 1999.
41 'Greece/Turkey: 'Positive' Talks To Continue Today', *RFE/RL*, 29 July 1999.
42 Cited in *Hürriyet*, 28 July 1999.
43 Cited in Greek Helsinki Monitor (GRM) and Minority Rights Group – Greece, 'Report about Compliance with the Principles of the Framework Convention for the Protection of National Minorities (along guidelines for state reports according to Article 25.1 of the Convention), Part I, 18 September 1999.
44 For a cross section of political views, see the reports in *Kathimerini* and *To Vima*, 30 July 1999.
45 *Kiriatiki Eleftherotypia*, 1 August 1999.
46 *Tipos tis Kyriakis*, 1 August 1999.

Chapter 4

1 *Athens News Agency*, 25 August 1999.
2 *Athens News Agency*, 18 August 1999.
3 The final death toll was over 15,000, meanwhile an estimated 200,000 had been made homeless in an area of devastation that was larger than Denmark

and Belgium combined. 'Address by Minister Of Foreign Affairs İsmail Cem at DEIK Meeting in London', *Turkish Ministry of Foreign Affairs*, September 3, 1999.
4. *Athens News Agency*, 18 August 1999.
5. *Sabah*, 23 August 1999.
6. *Athens News Agency*, 18 August 1999.
7. *Anatolia News Agency*, 20 August 1999.
8. *Cumhuriyet*, 27 July 1999.
9. *Athens News Agency*, 25 August 1999.
10. *Ibid.*
11. *Anadolu Agency*, 25 August 1999.
12. *Anadolu Agency*, 27 August 1999.
13. *Athens News Agency*, 31 August 1999.
14. *Sabah*, 23 August 1999.
15. Athens News Agency, 25 July 1999. She also praised Greece for it role in assisting refugees from Kosovo during the recent crisis.
16. Cyprus News Agency, 18 August 1999. Similar statements of sympathy were made by other senior officials. For instance, Spyros Kyprianou, the President of the House of Representatives, stated, 'Our thoughts are with the ordinary people who are suffering...our opponent is the official Turkish state and its expansionist policies'. Cyprus News Agency, 18 August 1999.
17. *Ibid.*
18. *Cyprus News Agency*, 25 August 1999.
19. Athens News Agency, 25 August 1999.
20. *To Vima tis Kyriakis*, 5 September 1999.
21. *Milliyet*, 27 August 1999.
22. This relationship preceded Dervişoğlu and Ioannides as there had in fact been good contacts between the senior commanders of the Greek and Turkish navies for a number of years. These had even produced tangible results in terms of building confidence and trust and had, on at least one occasion, avoided a crisis between the two countries. Admiral Güven Erkaya, the former commander of the Turkish Navy, discussion with the author.
23. 'Turkey appeals for bulldozers, body bags after 'disaster of century'', *CNN*, 24 August 1999.
24. *Hürriyet*, 24 August 1999.
25. *Hürriyet*, 24 August 1999.
26. *Kyriatiki Eleftherotypia*, 19 September 1999.
27. *Ibid.*
28. Apart from Durmuş, there were others within the Turkish Government who also took a sceptical view of what was happening. The author can recall a meeting in Ankara soon after the earthquakes between the Greek-Turkish Forum and a member of the Turkish Government who was a noted hard-liner on Greek-Turkish issues. He thanked Greece for all its support and

assistance over the previous few weeks, but promptly announced that, 'it changes nothing'. He then went on to explain that Greece was a nation built out of internal conflicts and that these had only been solved when Greece had decided to direct its aggression against Turkey. This was just hours after members of the Forum had met with Cem and other senior members of the Foreign Ministry and had been warmly welcomed at a lunch at the Grand National Assembly hosted by the deputy speaker.

29 *Eleftheros Typos*, 20 August 1999.
30 *Kyriatiki Eleftherotypia*, 19 September 1999.
31 'Address by Minister Of Foreign Affairs İsmail Cem at DEIK Meeting in London', *Turkish Ministry of Foreign Affairs*, September 3, 1999.
32 *To Vima* and *Kathimerini*, 22 August 1999.
33 *Eleftheros Typos*, 23 August 1999.
34 *Eleftheros Typos*, 27 August 1999.
35 *Ibid.*
36 *Milliyet*, 30 August 1999.
37 Ibid. Berberakis, a reporter for the Turkish newspaper *Milliyet* in Greece, had previously been heavily criticised by Greek nationalists for trying to discredit Greece. As a result, the organisation *Reporters sans frontières* had even asked the Greek Government to assure his safety. Athens News Agency, 22 July 1995.
38 Pantayias published another editorial piece in another major newspaper later in the year in which he also explained that relations between states needed to include other non-governmental components. 'The Seismic Rapprochement', *To Vima tis Kyriakis*, 10 October 1999.
39 *Eleftheros Typos*, 9 September 1999.
40 *Eleftheros Typos*, 23 August 1999.
41 *Anadolu Agency*, 24 August 1999.
42 *Athens News Agency*, 31 August 1999.
43 Haralambopoulos, who had been foreign minister from 1981–85, had also been minister of defence and deputy prime minister and had also been a contender in the 1996 party leadership race won by Simitis. Papoulias, who succeeded him in the post, served from 1985–89. In 2005, following nomination by the New Democracy administration, Papoulias was elected President by the parliament.
44 *Athens News Agency*, 31 August 1999.
45 *Ta Nea*, 30 August 1999.
46 Panayotis Dimitras, '"People's Diplomacy" Spearhead of Greek-Turkish Rapprochement', *AIM Athens*, 13 October 1999.
47 *Athens News Agency*, 31 August 1999.
48 *Ibid.*
49 *Hellenic Radio* (ERA), 31 August 1999.
50 *To Vima tis Kyriakis*, 29 August 1999.
51 *Ibid.*

52 *Kyriatiki Eleftherotypia*, 29 August 1999.
53 *Sabah*, 30 August 1999.
54 *Athens News Agency*, 31 August 1999.
55 *TRT*, 7 September 1999.
56 *Anadolu Agency*, 7 September 1999.
57 'Death toll rising in Greek earthquake', *CNN*, 7 September 1999.
58 *Milliyet*, 10 September 1999.
59 *Anadolu Agency*, 7 September 1999.
60 *Milliyet*, 10 September 1999.
61 *Anadolu Agency*, 7 September 1999.
62 *Hurriyet*, 9 September 1999.
63 *Ibid.*
64 *Anadolu Agency*, 10 September 1999.
65 *Ibid.*
66 *Milliyet*, 10 September 1999.
67 Turkey had consistently refused top sign such a pact in the past. One Greek academic recounted a conversation he once had with a former foreign minister of Turkey in which he asked why Ankara resisted signing such an agreement. He was told that doing so, 'would be disadvantageous to Turkey because it would deprive the country of its most important bargaining chip – its military might as a way of putting pressure on Greece.' Thanos Veremis, 'The Protracted Crisis', in Dimitris Keridis and Dimitrios Triantaphyllou (editors), *Greek-Turkish Relations in the Era of Globalization* (Virginia: Brassey's, 2001), p.43.
68 *Eleftherotypia*, 14 September 1999.
69 *Anadolu Agency*, 6 September 1999.
70 *Athens News Agency*, 10 September 1999. Prior to the meeting, on Monday 6 September, İnal Batu, the deputy leader of the Republican Peoples Party (CHP) met with Korkmaz Haktanır, the Undersecretary of the Foreign Minister, to discuss the meeting, stating that, 'We are not in the Government but if we have proposals for solution, we convey them. There have been remarkable and obvious positive developments in the relations between the two countries since George Papandreou became Greek Foreign Minister. We want to contribute to this and we want them to be more positive.' *Anadolu Agency*, 6 September 1999.
71 *Anadolu Agency*, 19 September 1999.
72 *Anadolu Agency*, 20 September 1999.
73 *Eleftherotypia*, 22 September 1999.
74 *Anadolu Agency*, 15 September 1999.
75 *Sabah*, 10 September 1999.
76 For an analysis of the types of activity that grew in the aftermath of the earthquakes see Bahar Rumelili, 'The EU and Cultural Change in Greek

Turkish Relations', *Working Paper Number 17*, EU Border Conflicts Studies, April 2005.

Chapter 5

1. *Anadolu Agency*, 12 September 1999.
2. *Eleftherotypia*, 11 September 1999.
3. This initiative was also a product of the realisation of the need for regional co-operation in the aftermath of Kosovo. As the Greek head of the Force's Political-Military Committee, Ambassador Nikos Dimadis, stated, 'After Kosovo, the NATO and EU member states realised that there can be no distinction between different areas in Europe and that the Balkans can become a source of stability'. *Eleftherotypia*, 13 September 1999.
4. *Anadolu Agency*, 11 September 1999; *Eleftherotypia*, 13 September 1999.
5. *TRT TV*, 12 September 1999.
6. In addition to Kranidiotis, several others travelling on the plane were killed, including his son. 'Plane accident kills Greek minister', BBC News, 15 September 1999. In a mark of respect, the meeting was postponed. As it happens, Kranidiotis was not originally scheduled to have been on the flight. He had only decided to attend the meeting in Romania that morning. Greek foreign ministry official in conversation with the author.
7. *Athens News Agency*, 15 September 1999.
8. *Ibid.*
9. Despite this view, Kranidiotis apparently had no intention of becoming involved in Cypriot politics. Despite his commitment to Cyprus and the Cyprus issue, he always saw himself as a Greek politician. This was confirmed to the author by two sources who knew the minister well.
10. *Cyprus News Agency*, 15 September 1999.
11. *Cyprus Broadcasting Corporation* (CyBC), 15 September 1999.
12. *Anadolu Agency*, 15 September 1999.
13. *Athens News Agency*, 21 September 1999.
14. *Anadolu Agency*, 15 September 1999.
15. *Anadolu Agency*, 16 September 1999.
16. *Joint Communique signed after the meeting of high officials of the Foreign Ministries of Turkey and Greece*, September 16, 1999.
17. *Eleftherotypia*, 22 September 1999.
18. This was an extremely serious issue of concern for the Greek Government. It is worth noting that the following year it brought the matter to international attention. Athens News Agency, 15 July 2000. Less than two weeks later the project was put on indefinite hold by Prime Minister Ecevit.
19. *Eleftherotypia*, 22 September 1999.
20. *Anadolu Agency*, 24 September 1999.
21. *Athens News Agency*, 25 September 1999.
22. *Ibid.*

23 'Letter dated 23 September 1999 from the Permanent Representatives of China, France, the Russian Federation, the United Kingdom of Great Britain and Northern Ireland and the United States of America to the United Nations Addressed to the Secretary-General', *United Nations Security Council Document S/1999/996*, 23 September 1999, para.27.
24 *Athens News Agency*, 25 September 1999.
25 *Ta Nea*, 5 October 1999. The poll was carried out between 17–29 September and had used 1,170 interviews. Meanwhile, another poll carried out in Athens for Mega Channel showed that 37 per cent of respondents had a better view of Turkey and that only 3 per cent had a worse view. Moreover, 40 per cent believed that both countries had the responsibility to work together to improve relations. This was in contrast to the 49 per cent who believed that Turkey should make the first move, and the 4 per cent who believed that Athens should take the initiative. Cited in Panayotis Dimitras, '"People's Diplomacy" Spearhead of Greek-Turkish Rapprochement', *AIM Athens*, 13 October 1999.
26 *Anadolu Agency*, 1 October 1999.
27 *Ta Nea*, 27 September 1999.
28 *Anadolu Agency*, 30 September 1999.
29 *TRT*, 3 October 1999.
30 *Anadolu Agency*, 3 October 1999.
31 *NET TV*, 4 October 1999.
32 *Anadolu Agency*, 4 October 1999.
33 It is worth noting that the Greek Government effectively draws a distinction between an incursion and an invasion of Greek airspace and a violation of Greek airspace. Tacitly recognising the ambiguity of having 10 nautical miles of airspace and 6 nautical miles of territorial waters (although entitled to twelve miles in both cases), anything between the 6–10 miles is regarded as an incursion. Anything within the 6 mile limit, which is recognised by Turkey, is an invasion of Greek airspace. As stated to the author by a leading Greek specialist on the issue.
34 *Athens News Agency*, 4 October 1999.
35 *Ta Nea*, 2 November 1999.
36 *Cyprus News Agency*, 4 October 1999.
37 *Ta Nea*, 2 November 1999.
38 *O Logos*, 13 October 1999.
39 *Athens News Agency*, 14 October 1999.
40 *Macedonian Press Agency*, 16 October 1999.
41 *Athens News Agency*, 13 October 1999. Apart form his visits to EU member states, it was also announced that he would visit Canada, the United States and Russia, before attending the OSCE summit in Istanbul on 19–20 November.
42 *Ta Nea*, 21 October 1999.

43 'Edited Transcript of a Doorstep Interview Given by the Foreign Secretary, Robin Cook, and the Greek Foreign Minister, George Papandreou', London, Monday 18 October 1999.
44 *Athens News Agency*, 21 October 1999.
45 *Athens News Agency*, 12 October 1999. The letter was delivered by Korantis during a meeting with Ecevit.
46 *Ta Nea*, 21 October 1999.
47 *Athens News Agency*, 20 October 1999.
48 *Ta Nea*, 22 October 1999.
49 The report was in fact filed by a well-known Turkish journalist who had participated in a meeting between Papandreou and the Greek-Turkish Forum, held on 25 October at the Greek Foreign Ministry (and where the author was also present). Needless to say, the fact that such a meeting had forced the Ministry to issue a written denial of the claims proved to be extremely embarrassing for the Forum.
50 *Athens News Agency*, 19 October 1999.
51 *Anadolu Agency*, 27 October 1999.
52 *Ibid.*
53 *Anadolu Agency*, 26 October 1999.
54 *Macedonian Press Agency*, 16 October 1999.
55 *Athens News*, 3 November 1999.
56 It is worth noting that Mitsotakis was not a hard-liner by any means. In fact, in 1997, he had been awarded the prestigious İpekçi Award for his efforts to promote better relations between the two countries.
57 *Athens News*, 3 November 1999.
58 *Ibid.*
59 *Ibid.*

Chapter 6

1 *CyBC Radio*, 4 November 1999.
2 *Anadolu Agency*, 15 November 1999.
3 *Milliyet*, 17 November 1999.
4 *Ibid.*
5 'Secretary-General Says Proximity Talks on Cyprus Will Start 3 December', *United Nations Press Release UNIS/SG/2443*, 16 November 1999.
6 *To Vima tis Kyriakis*, 21 November 1999.
7 *Ibid.*
8 'White House shortens Clinton visit to Greece for security reasons', *CNN*, 10 November 1999.
9 'Violence greets Clinton visit', *BBC News*, 20 November 1999.
10 *Milliyet*, 21 November 1999.
11 *Anadolu Agency*, 20 November 1999.
12 *Athens News Agency*, 18 November 1999.

13 *Athens News Agency*, 12 November 1999.
14 *Ibid*. He also used the opportunity to reinforce the message, in the aftermath of Kosovo, that there should be no territorial readjustments in the Balkans.
15 'Remarks by President Bill Clinton and Prime Minister Simitis of Greece to the Government of Greece, Business and Community Leaders, Inter-Continental Hotel, Athens, Greece', November 20, 1999.
16 *Ta Nea*, 25 November 1999.
17 *Athens News Agency*, 23 November 1999.
18 *Athens News Agency*, 21 November 1999.
19 *Milliyet*, 21 November 1999.
20 *Cyprus News Agency*, 18 November 1999.
21 *CyBC TV*, 25 November 1999.
22 *Ibid*.
23 *Athens News Agency*, 30 November 1999.
24 *Ta Nea*, 27 November 1999.
25 *Anadolu Agency*, 3 December 1999.
26 *Ibid*.
27 *Cumhuriyet*, 5 December 1999.
28 *Ankara News Agency*, 13 December 1999.
29 European Council, *Helsinki European Council Presidency Conclusions*, 10–11 December 1999.
30 'Analysis: Greek stumbling block', *BBC News*, 10 December 1999.
31 The events of that evening were recounted by Ecevit in a later interview with a Finnish newspaper. 'Ecevit recalls dramatic events in HS interview', *Helsingen Sanomat* (International Edition), 13 November 2004.
32 *Milliyet*, 13 December 1999.
33 *Athens News Agency*, 11 December 1999.
34 *Athens News Agency*, 14 December 1999.
35 *Athens News Agency*, 13 December 1999.
36 *Anadolu Agency*, 2 December 1999.
37 *Anadolu Agency*, 14 December 1999.
38 *Anadolu Agency*, 16 December 1999.
39 *Athens News Agency*, 18 December 1999.

Epilogue

1 *Athens News Agency*, 21 January 2000.
2 East West Institute, *Press Release*, 6 April 2000.
3 The number of visitors to Turkey from Greece in 1996 was 147,553. In 2000 the total was 218,092. But by 2003 the number of visitors had risen to 368,425. Joanna Apap, Sergio Carrera and Kemal Kirisci, 'Turkey in the European Area of Freedom, Security and Justice', *EU-Turkey Working Paper Number 3*, Centre for European Policy Studies, August 2004, p.33.

NOTES

4   'Despite Turkish-Greek Thaw, Cyprus Quarrel Is Not Melting', *New York Times*, 18 December 2000.
5   Ali Carkoglu and Kemal Kirisci, 'The View from Turkey: Perceptions of Greeks and Greek-Turkish Rapprochement by the Turkish Public', in Ali Carkoglu and Barry Rubin (eds.), Special Issue: Greek-Turkish Relations in an Era of Détente, *Turkish Studies*, Volume 5, Number 1, Spring 2004, p.117.
6   'Greece and Turkey in Euro 2008 bid', *BBC News*, 17 September 2000.
7   In fact, the film was criticised by many Greek Cypriots as it appeared to lay part of the blame for the expulsion of Greeks from Istanbul on Archbishop Makarios.
8   Ali Carkoglu and Kemal Kirisci, 'The View from Turkey', p.117.
9   Larrabee, F. Stephen and Ian O. Lesser, *Turkish Foreign Policy in an Age of Uncertainty* (Santa Monica: RAND2003), p.85.
10 'Greek-Turkish Relations Questioned', *Associated Press*, 26 October 2000.
11 Kostas Ifantis, 'Strategic Imperatives and Regional Upheavals: On the US Factor in Greek-Turkish Relations', in Ali Carkoglu and Barry Rubin (eds.), Special Issue: Greek-Turkish Relations in an Era of Détente, *Turkish Studies*, Volume 5, Number 1, Spring 2004, p.36.
12 See *Athens News Agency*, 23 October 2004.
13 'Turkish military alarms Athens', *Athens News*, 29 October 2004.
14 For a review of this subject see Othon Anastasakis, 'Greece and Turkey in the Balkans: Cooperation or Rivalry?', in Ali Carkoglu and Barry Rubin (eds.), Special Issue: Greek-Turkish Relations in an Era of Détente, *Turkish Studies*, Volume 5, Number 1, Spring 2004.
15 *Athens News Agency*, 5 July 2005.
16 Bilateral Relations (The Rapprochement Process), *Website of the Hellenic Ministry of Foreign Affairs*, <www.mfa.gr>
17 *Ibid.*
18 Carkoglu and Kirisci, 'The View from Turkey', p.118.
19 'Greeks and Turks need to bury the hatchet', *Guardian*, 12 February 2002.
20 *Milliyet*, 4 November 2001.
21 David Hannay, *Cyprus: The Search for a Solution* (London: IB Tauris, 2005), p.155.
22 James Ker-Lindsay, *EU Accession and UN Peacemaking in Cyprus* (Basingstoke: Palgrave Macmillan, 2005), p.36.
23 76 per cent of Greek Cypriots rejected the agreement, as opposed to the 64 per cent of Turkish Cypriots who supported the plan. A full analysis of the peace talks can be found in Ker-Lindsay, EU Accession and UN Peacemaking in Cyprus.
24 'Greek socialists name Papandreou', *BBC News*, 9 February 2004.
25 Greek official, conversation with the author. Having said this, Yiannis Valinakis, the Alternate Foreign Minister, was one of the country's leading

professors of international relations. However, his influence over foreign policy formation and implementation was seen to be limited.
26 *Reuters*, 11 July 2004.
27 'Greek leader to make Turkey visit', *BBC News*, 3 July 2005. The last Greek prime minister to visit Turkey was his uncle, Constantine Karamanlis, in 1959.
28 For an analysis of Greek attitudes towards Turkish EU accession, especially in comparison with those of Cyprus, see James Ker-Lindsay, 'The Attitudes of Greece and Cyprus towards Turkey's EU accession', *Turkish Studies*, Volume 8, Number 1, March 2007.
29 'Newsmaker: Karamanlis', Online Newshour, *PBS*, 21 May 2004.
30 'No state visit can hide our growing isolation', *Cyprus Mail*, 25 October 2005.
31 'Papoulias leaves with a message of unity', *Cyprus Mail*, 20 October 2005.
32 All this has led one Greek Cypriot commentator to write, in November 2005, that, 'the Greek government in turn is keeping such a low profile on the Cyprus problem that if it got any lower it would be invisible.' Nick Pittas, 'Who really wants to solve the Cyprus problem?', *Cyprus Mail*, 6 November 2005.
33 Western diplomat, comments to the author, March 2006.
34 Ifantis, 'Strategic Imperatives and Regional Upheavals', p.35.
35 See Carkoglu and Kirisci, 'The View from Turkey'.

Conclusion

1 For an overview of civic initiatives before and after 1999 see Bahar Rumelili, 'The Talkers and the Silent Ones: The EU and Change in Greek Turkish Relations', *Working Paper Number 10*, EU Border Conflicts Studies, October 2004.
2 Ronald Meinardus, 'Third-Party Involvement in Greek-Turkish Disputes', in Constas, Dimitri (ed.), *Greek-Turkish Conflict in the 1990s: Domestic and External Influences* (Basingstoke: Macmillan, 1990), p.163.
3 Constantine Stephanou and Charalambos Tsardanides, 'The EC Factor in Greece-Turkey-Cyprus Triangle', in Constas, Dimitri (ed.), *Greek-Turkish Conflict in the 1990s: Domestic and External Influences* (Basingstoke: Macmillan, 1990), p.226.
4 Philip H. Gordon, 'Post-Helsinki: Turkey, Greece and the European Union', *The Strategic Regional Report*, Brooking Institution, February 2000.
5 Byron Theodoropoulos, 'Peremptory Reasoning', in Dimitris Keridis and Dimitrios Triantaphyllou (editors), *Greek-Turkish Relations in the Era of Globalization* (Virginia: Brassey's, 2001), pp.ix-x.
6 Kostas Ifantis, 'Strategic Imperatives and Regional Upheavals: On the US Factor in Greek-Turkish Relations', in Ali Carkoglu and Barry Rubin (eds.), Special Issue: Greek-Turkish Relations in an Era of Détente, *Turkish Studies*, Volume 5, Number 1, Spring 2004, p.32. This also seems to have been

accepted by US decision-makers. The author can recall a conference held in Athens in early December 2000 at which Nicholas Burns, the then US Ambassador to Greece, remarked that Greece should not invest too much faith in the European Union. In the view of many in attendance, the remark seemed to be less a warning and more a call for Greece to remain engaged with the US. In this regard, it was seen by many as an indication that the US understood that it was no longer the force in the country that it had once been.

7   There is a growing literature on the subject of disaster diplomacy. See, for example, Ilan Kelman and Theo Koukis (editors) 'Disaster Diplomacy' (special section), *Cambridge Review of International Affairs*, Volume XIV, Number 1, pp. 214–294. For more material on the issue of disaster diplomacy see <www.disasterdiplomacy.org>.

8   See also James Ker-Lindsay, 'The Role of "Disaster Diplomacy" in the Greek-Turkish Rapprochement', *Cambridge Review of International Affairs*, Volume XIV, Number 1, Autumn 2000.

9   See, for example, Dimitri Keridis, 'Political Culture and Foreign Policy: Greek-Turkish Relations in the Era of European integration and Globalization', *A NATO Fellowship Final Report*, June 1999, p.6; Heinz-Jurgen Axt, 'Avoiding a Casus Belli in Cyprus', *Internationale Politik*, Volume 2, Number 1, Spring 2001, p.71.

10 This has been recognised by several other analysts, such as Ayten Gundogdu, 'Identities in Question: Greek-Turkish Relations in a Period of Transformation?', *Middle East Review of International Affairs* (MERIA), Volume 5, Number 1, March 2001; F. Stephen Larrabee, 'Turkish Foreign and Security Policy: New Dimensions and New Challenges', in Zalmay Khalilzad, Ian O. Lesser, and F. Stephen Larrabee, *The Future of Turkish-Western Relations: Toward a Strategic Plan* (Santa Monica: RAND, 2000), p.23.

11 'Most Greeks Want Rapprochement with Turkey', *Reuters*, 30 October 1997.

12 Gordon, 'Post-Helsinki: Turkey, Greece and the European Union'. The importance of Greece in the process is also recognised by Larrabee, 'Turkish Foreign and Security Policy', p.21. See also, F. Stephen Larrabee and Ian O. Lesser, *Turkish Foreign Policy in an Age of Uncertainty* (Santa Monica: RAND2003), p.87.

13 Gurel replaced Cem as foreign minister in 2002.

14 It is worth noting that the General Staff were well aware of the work of the Greek-Turkish Forum by virtue of the participation of Admiral Güven Erkaya, who was actually the co-ordinator of the Turkish team until ill-health forced him to hand over to Ilter Turkmen, a former Turkish Foreign Minister. (See Yonca Poyraz Dogan, 'Ilter Turkmen: We concentrate on the common interests for both Greece and Turkey. That's our secret', *Greek-Turkish Synergy*, 30 March 2002.) Even in retirement Erkaya was held in very high esteem in military circles by virtue of the fact that he had been the

commander of the Turkish Navy during the 1996 Imia-Kardak incident and because of his central role in forcing the Islamist Erbakan government from power in 1997. (See Gareth Jenkins, 'Chip off the old block', *Al-Ahram Weekly*, 6–12 July 2000) In retirement, he was also an advisor to the Prime Minister. It was therefore notable that even in the immediate aftermath of the Öcalan crisis, Erkaya continued to support the work of the Forum. Although some may argue that his participation was little more than an attempt by the armed forces to keep an eye on what was happening, there are good reasons to argue against this view. The clearest evidence for this came in late 2000 when reports appeared suggesting that he had recommended a sizeable reduction in Turkish military forces along the Aegean coast. Despite being seriously ill at the time, he was worried that these reports might be denied. He therefore called journalists into his hospital room to confirm that he had indeed made the recommendations and that he stood by them. He died soon afterwards. The proposals were seen as highly significant and widely reported internationally. See, for instance, Stephen Kinzer, 'Turkey Considers Scaling Back Military Challenge to Greece', *New York Times*, 8 June 2000.

15 Senior Greek official, conversation with the author, spring 2006.
16 Although Nicosia was prepared to deal with an alternate foreign minister who was one of their own, if Papandreou had sent Kranidiotis's replacement, Christos Rokofyllos, to Cyprus it would have been taken as a grave insult. It would have been read as a clear signal that Papandreou had downgraded the Greek Cypriots, and therefore served to confirm all the suspicions that had developed.

BIBLIOGRAPHY

Aydin, Mustafa and Kostas Ifantis (editors), *Turkish-Greek Relations: Escaping from the Security Dilemma in the Aegean* (London: Routledge, 2004)

Bahcheli, Tozun, *Greek-Turkish Relations Since 1955* (Boulder, Colorado: Westview Press, 1987)

Barchard, David, *Turkey and the European Union* (London: Centre for European Reform, 1998)

Birand, Mehmet Ali, *30 Hot Days* (Nicosia: Kemal Rustem, 1985)

Brewin, Christopher, *Cyprus and the European Union* (Huntingdon: The Eothen Press, 2000)

Carkoglu, Ali and Barry Rubin (editors), *Greek-Turkish Relations in an Era of Détente* (London: Routledge Curzon, 2005)

Chircop, Aldo, Andre Gerolymatos and John O. Iatrides (editors). *The Aegean Sea after the Cold War: Security and Law-of-the-Sea Issues* (Basingstoke: Palgrave Macmillan, 2003)

Christou, George, *The European Union and Enlargement: The Case of Cyprus* (Basingstoke: Palgrave Macmillan, 2004)

Clark, Bruce, *Twice a Stranger: How Mass Expulsion Forged Modern Greece and Turkey* (London: Granta, 2006)

Constas, Dimitri (editor), *Greek-Turkish Conflict in the 1990s: Domestic and External Influences* (Basingstoke: Macmillan, 1990)

Couloumbis, Theodore A., Photini Bellou and Theodore C. Kariotis (editors). *Greece in the Twentieth Century* (London: Frank Cass, 2003)

Deringil, Selim, *Turkish Foreign Policy during the Second World War: An Active Neutrality* (Cambridge University Press. Cambridge 1989)

Diez, Thomas (editor), *The European Union and the Cyprus Conflict: Modern Conflict, Postmodern Union* (Manchester: Manchester University Press, 2002)

Dodd, Clement H. (editor), *Turkish Foreign Policy: New Prospects', Modern Turkish Studies Programme, School of Oriental and African Studies* (Huntingdon: The Eothen Press, 1992)

Dodd, Clement H. (editor), *Cyprus: The Need for New Perspectives* (Huntingdon: The Eothen Press, 1999)

Emerson, Michael and Natalie Tocci, *Cyprus as the Lighthouse of the East Mediterranean: Shaping EU Accession and Reunification Together* (Brussels: CEPS, 2002)

Featherstone, Kevin and Kostas Ifantis (editors), *Greece in a Changing Europe: Between European Integration and Balkan Disintegration* (Manchester: Manchester University Press, 1996)

Gagnon, V.P., *The Myth of Ethnic War: Serbia and Croatia in the 1990s* (London: Cornell University Press, 2004)

Hale, William, *Turkish Politics and the Military* (London: Routledge, 1994)

Hale, William, *Turkish Foreign Policy 1774–2000* (London: Frank Cass, 2000)

Hannay, David, *Cyprus: The Search for a Solution* (London: IB Tauris, 2005)

Hirschon, Renée (editor), *Crossing the Aegean: An Appraisal of the 1923 Compulsory Population Exchange between Greece and Turkey* (New York and Oxford: Berghahn Books, 2003)

Holland, Robert, *Britain and the Revolt in Cyprus, 1954–59* (Oxford: OUP, 1998)

James, Alan, *Keeping the Peace in the Cyprus Crisis of 1963–64* (Basingstoke: Palgrave Macmillan, 2001)

Joseph, Joseph S., *Cyprus: Ethnic Conflict and International Politics: From Independence to the Threshold of the European Union* (Basingstoke: Macmillan, 1999)

Kelman, Ilan and Theo Koukis (editors), 'Disaster Diplomacy' (special section), *Cambridge Review of International Affairs*, Volume XIV, Number 1, Autumn 2000

Keridis, Dimitris and Dimitrios Triantaphyllou (editors), *Greek-Turkish Relations in the Era of Globalization* (Virginia: Brassey's, 2001)

Ker-Lindsay, James, *Britain and the Cyprus Crisis, 1963–64* (Mannheim und Möhnesee: Bibliopolis, 2004)

Ker-Lindsay, James, *EU Accession and UN Peacemaking in Cyprus* (Basingstoke: Palgrave Macmillan, 2005)

Khalilzad, Zalmay, Ian O. Lesser, F. Stephen Larrabee, *The Future of Turkish-Western Relations: Toward a Strategic Plan* (Santa Monica: RAND, 2000)

Larrabee, F. Stephen and Ian O. Lesser, *Turkish Foreign Policy in an Age of Uncertainty* (Santa Monica: RAND2003)

Lesser, Ian O., F. Stephen Larrabee, Michele Zanini and Katia Vlachos, *Greece's New Geopolitics* (Santa Monica: RAND, 2001)

Llewellyn Smith, Michael, *Ionian Vision: Greece in Asia Minor, 1919–1922* (London: Hurst & Co, London, 1998)

Markides, Diana Weston, *Cyprus 1957–1963: From Colonial Conflict to Constitutional Crisis* (Minneapolis, Minnesota: University of Minnesota, 2001)

Mazower, Mark, *Inside Hitler's Greece: The Experience of Occupation, 1941–44* (New Haven and London: Yale University Press, 1993)

Mirbagheri, Farid, *Cyprus and International Peacemaking* (London: Hurst, 1989)

Moustakis, Fotios, *The Greek-Turkish Relationship and NATO* (London: Frank Cass, 2003)

Pope, Nicole and Hugh, *Turkey Unveiled: Atatürk and After* (London: John Murray, 1997)

Reddaway, John, *Burdened with Cyprus: The British Connection* (London: Weidenfeld & Nicholson, 1986)

Richmond, Oliver P., *Mediating in Cyprus: The Cypriot Communities and the United Nations* (London: Frank Cass, 1998)

Sanguineti, Vittorio, *The Enlargement of the European Union: Turkey: The Controversial Road to a Wrong Candidacy* (Biblioteca Della "Rivista di Studi Politici Internazionali": Firenze, 1999)

Tocci, Nathalie, *EU Accession Dynamics and Conflict Resolution: Catalysing Peace or Consolidating Partition in Cyprus?* (Aldershot: Ashgate, 2004)

Veremis, Thanos, *The Military in Greek Politics: From Independence to Democracy* (London: Hurst, 1997)

Vryonis, Speros, *The Mechanism of Catastrophe: The Turkish Pogrom of September 6–7, 1955, and the Destruction of the Greek Community of Istanbul* (New York: NY Greekworks.com, 2005)

Wilson, Andrew, The Aegean Question, *Adelphi Papers*, Number 155, London, 1979

Woodhouse, C.M., *Modern Greece: A Short History*, 2nd Edition (London: Faber & Faber, 1991)

Zürcher, Erik J., *Turkey: A Modern History* (London: I.B. Tauris, 1997)

Articles, Chapter and Papers

Acer, Yucel, 'Recent Developments and Prospects for the Settlement of the Aegean Disputes', *Turkish Studies*, Volume 3, Number 2, Autumn 2002

Apap, Joanna, Sergio Carrera and Kemal Kirisci, 'Turkey in the European Area of Freedom, Security and Justice', *EU-Turkey Working Paper Number 3*, Centre for European Policy Studies, August 2004

Anastasakis, Othon, 'Greece and Turkey in the Balkans: Cooperation or Rivalry?', in Ali Carkoglu and Barry Rubin (editors), *Greek-Turkish Relations in an Era of Détente* (London: Routledge, 2005)

Arapoglou, Stergios, 'Dispute in the Aegean Sea: Imia/Kardak Crisis', *Research Report*, Air Command and Staff College, Air University, Maxwell Air Base, Alabama, April 2002

Athanassopoulou, Ekavi, 'Blessing in Disguise? The Imia Crisis and Turkish-Greek Relations,' *Mediterranean Politics*, Volume 2, Number 3, Winter 1997

Axt, Heinz-Jürgen, 'Avoiding a Casus Belli in Cyprus', *Internationale Politik*, Volume 2, Number 1, Spring 2001

Axt, Heinz-Jürgen, 'Relations with Turkey and Their Impact on the European Union', *Southeast European and Black Sea Studies*, Volume 5, Number 3, September 2005

Bahcheli, Tozun, Theodore A. Couloumbis and Patricia Carley, Greek-Turkish Relations and US Foreign Policy: Cyprus, the Aegean, and Regional Stability, *Peaceworks No.17*, August 1997, United States Institute for Peace

Bahceli, Tozun, 'Turning a New Page in Turkey's Relations with Greece? The Challenge of Reconciling Vital Interests', in Mustafa Aydin and Kostas Ifantis (editors) *Turkish-Greek Relations: Escaping from the Security Dilemma in the Aegean* (London: Routledge, 2004)

Birand, Mehmet Ali, 'Turkey and the 'Davos Process': Experiences and Prospects', in Dimitri Constas (editor) *Greek-Turkish Conflict in the 1990s: Domestic and External Influences* (Basingstoke: Macmillan, 1990)

Black, Joshua, 'Greek Diplomacy and the Hunt for Abdullah Ocalan', *WWS Case Study 4/00*, Woodrow Wilson School for Public and International Affairs, Princeton University, 2000

Bölükbaşı, Süha, 'The Turco-Greek Dispute', in Clement H. Dodd (editor), *Turkish Foreign Policy: New Prospects*, Modern Turkish Studies Programme, School of Oriental and African Studies (Huntingdon: The Eothen Press, 1992)

Carkoglu, Ali and Kemal Kirisci, 'The View from Turkey: Perceptions of Greeks and Greek-Turkish Rapprochement by the Turkish Public', in Ali Carkoglu and Barry Rubin (editors), Special Issue: Greek-Turkish Relations in an Era of Détente, *Turkish Studies*, Volume 5, Number 1, Spring 2004

Clogg, Richard, 'Greek-Turkish Relations in the Post-1974 Period', in Dimitri Constas (editor) *Greek-Turkish Conflict in the 1990s: Domestic and External Influences* (Basingstoke: Macmillan, 1990)

Coufoudakis, Van, 'Greek Political Party Attitudes Towards Turkey: 1974–89', in Dimitri Constas (editor) *Greek-Turkish Conflict in the 1990s: Domestic and External Influences* (Basingstoke: Macmillan, 1990)

Demetriou, Madeleine. 'On the Long Road to Europe and the Short Path to War: issue-Linkage Politics and the Arms Build-up on Cyprus', *Mediterranean Politics*, Volume 3, Number 3, Winter 1998

Demetriou, Olga. 'The EU and the Cyprus Conflict: A Review of the Literature', *Working Paper Number 5*, EU Border Conflicts Studies, January 2004.

Dogan, Yonca Poyraz, 'Costas Carras: Greek and Turkey do share the same understanding about the region and the world around us...', *Greek-Turkish Synergy*, 29 March 2002.

Dogan, Yonca Poyraz, 'Ilter Turkmen: We concentrate on the common interests for both Greece and Turkey. That's our secret', *Greek-Turkish Synergy*, 30 March 2002.

Erdogdu, Erkan, 'Turkey and Europe: Undivided but not United', *Middle East Review of International Affairs* (MERIA), Volume 6, Number 2, June 2002

Evin, Ahmet O., 'Changing Greek Perspectives on Turkey: An Assessment of the Post-Earthquake Rapprochement', in Ali Carkoglu and Barry Rubin (editors), Special Issue: Greek-Turkish Relations in an Era of Détente, *Turkish Studies*, Volume 5, Number 1, Spring 2004

Evin, Ahmet O., 'The Future of Greek-Turkish Relations', *Southeast European and Black Sea Studies*, Volume 5, Number 3, September 2005

Gaudissart, Marc-Andre, 'Cyprus and the European Union: The Long Road to Accession', *The Cyprus Review*, Volume 8, Number 1, Spring 1996

Gordon, Philip H., 'Post-Helsinki: Turkey, Greece and the European Union', *The Strategic Regional Report*, Brooking Institution, February 2000.

Greek Helsinki Monitor (GRM) and Minority Rights Group – Greece, 'Report about Compliance with the Principles of the Framework Convention for the Protection of National Minorities (Along Guidelines for State Reports According to Article 25.1 of the Convention), Part I, 18 September 1999

Grigoriadis, Ioannis N., 'The Changing Role of the EU Factor in Greek-Turkish Relations', Symposium Paper, 'Current Social Science Research on Greece', *Paper Presented at the 1st PhD Symposium on Modern Greece*, Hellenic Observatory, London School Of Economics And Political Science, 21 June 2003

Gundogdu, Ayten, 'Identities in Question: Greek-Turkish Relations in a Period of Transformation?', *Middle East Review of International Affairs* (MERIA), Volume 5, Number 1, March 2001

Gunduz, Aslan, 'Greek-Turkish Disputes: How to Resolve Them?', in Dimitris Keridis and Dimitrios Triantaphyllou (editors), *Greek-Turkish Relations in the Era of Globalization* (Virginia: Brassey's, 2001)

Hadjidimos, Katharina, 'The role of the Media in Greek-Turkish Relations: Co-Production of a TV Programme Window by Greek and Turkish Journalists', *Robert Bosch Stiftungkolleg fur Internationale Aufgaben*, Programm Jahr 1998/99

Heraclides, Alexis, 'Greek-Turkish Relations from Discord to Détente: A Preliminary Evaluation', *The Review of International Affairs*, Volume 1, Number 3, Spring 2002

Heraclides, Alexis, 'The Greek-Turkish Conflict: Towards Resolution and Reconciliation', in Mustafa Aydin and Kostas Ifantis (editors), *Turkish-Greek Relations: Escaping from the Security Dilemma in the Aegean* (London: Routledge, 2004)

Ifantis, Kostas, 'Strategic Imperatives and Regional Upheavals: On the US Factor in Greek-Turkish Relations', in Ali Carkoglu and Barry Rubin (editors), Special Issue: Greek-Turkish Relations in an Era of Détente, *Turkish Studies*, Volume 5, Number 1, Spring 2004

Ifantis, Kostas, 'Greece's Turkish Dilemmas: There and Back Again...', *Southeast European and Black Sea Studies*, Volume 5, Number 3, September 2005

Jenkins, Gareth, 'Turkey's Changing Domestic Politics', in Dimitris Keridis and Dimitrios Triantaphyllou (editors), *Greek-Turkish Relations in the Era of Globalization* (Virginia: Brassey's, 2001)

Keridis, Dimitri, 'Political Culture and Foreign Policy: Greek-Turkish Relations in the Era of European integration and Globalization', *A NATO Fellowship Final Report*, June 1999

Keridis, Dimitri, 'Domestic Developments and Foreign policy: Greek Policy Towards Turkey', in Dimitris Keridis and Dimitrios Triantaphyllou (editors), *Greek-Turkish Relations in the Era of Globalization* (Virginia: Brassey's, 2001)

Ker-Lindsay, James, 'The Role of "Disaster Diplomacy" in the Greek-Turkish Rapprochement', *Cambridge Review of International Affairs*, Volume XIV, Number 1, Autumn 2000

Ker-Lindsay, James, 'From U Thant to Kofi Annan: UN Peacemaking in Cyprus, 1964–2004', *Occasional Paper 5/05*, South East European Studies at Oxford (SEESOX), St Antony's College, Oxford University, October 2005

Ker-Lindsay, James, 'The Attitudes of Greece and Cyprus towards Turkey's EU Accession', *Turkish Studies*, Volume 8, Number 1, March 2007.

Kirisci, Kemal, 'The "Enduring Rivalry" between Greece and Turkey: Can 'Democratic Peace' Break It?', *Alternatives Journal*, Volume 1, Number 1, Spring 2002

Kozyris, Phaedon John, 'The Legal Dimensions of the Current Greek-Turkish Conflict: A Greek View', in Dimitris Keridis and Dimitrios Triantaphyllou (editors), *Greek-Turkish Relations in the Era of Globalization* (Virginia: Brassey's, 2001)

Larrabee, F. Stephen, 'The EU Needs to Rethink its Cyprus Policy', *Survival*, Volume 40, Number 3, Autumn 1998

Larrabee, F. Stephen, 'Turkish Foreign and Security Policy: New Dimensions and New Challenges', in Zalmay Khalilzad, Ian O. Lesser, F. Stephen Larrabee, *The Future of Turkish-Western Relations: Toward a Strategic Plan* (Santa Monica: RAND, 2000)

Larrabee, F. Stephen, 'Security in The Eastern Mediterranean: Transatlantic Challenges and Perspectives', in Dimitris Keridis and Dimitrios Triantaphyllou (editors), *Greek-Turkish Relations in the Era of Globalization* (Virginia: Brassey's, 2001)

Makovsky, Alan, 'Research Guide: Turkey's Election and New Government', *Middle East Review of International Affairs* (MERIA), 1999

Meinardus, Ronald, 'Third-Party Involvement in Greek-Turkish Disputes', in Constas, Dimitri (editor) *Greek-Turkish Conflict in the 1990s: Domestic and External Influences* (Basingstoke: Macmillan, 1990)

Migdalovitz, Carol, '86065: Greece and Turkey: Current Foreign Aid Issues', *CRS Issue Brief*, Congressional Research Service (CRS), 3 December 1996

Millas, Hercules, 'National Perceptions of the 'Other' and the Persistence of Some Images', in Mustafa Aydin and Kostas Ifantis (editors) *Turkish-Greek Relations: Escaping from the Security Dilemma in the Aegean* (London: Routledge, 2004)

Niarchos, Georgos, 'Continuity and Change in the Minority Policies of Greece and Turkey', *Paper Presented at the 1st PhD Symposium on Modern Greece: Current Social Science Research on Greece*, London School of Economics and Political Science, 21 June 2003.

Nicolaidis, Kalypso, 'Europe's Tainted Mirror: Reflections on Turkey's Candidacy after Helsinki', in Dimitris Keridis and Dimitrios Triantaphyllou (editors), *Greek-Turkish Relations in the Era of Globalization* (Virginia: Brassey's, 2001)

Oguzlu, Tarik, 'Is the latest Turkish-Greek détente promising for the future?', *European Security*, Volume 12, Number 2, June 2003

Onis, Ziya, 'Greek-Turkish Relations and the European Union: A Critical Perspective', *Mediterranean Politics*, Volume 6, Number 3, Fall 2001

Özel, Soli, 'Rapprochement on Non-Governmental Level: The Story of the Turkish-Greek Forum', in Mustafa Aydin and Kostas Ifantis (editors), *Turkish-Greek Relations: Escaping from the Security Dilemma in the Aegean* (London: Routledge, 2004)

Panico, Christopher, 'Greece: The Turks of Western Thrace', *Human Rights Watch*, Volume 11, Number 1, January 1999.

Park, William, 'Turkey's European Union Candidacy: From Luxembourg to Helsinki – to Ankara?', *Mediterranean Politics*, Volume 5, Number 3, Autumn 2000

Reuter, Jürgen, 'Reshaping Greek-Turkish Relations: Developments before and after the EU Summit in Helsinki', *Occasional Paper 00.01*, Hellenic Foundation for European and Foreign Policy (ELIAMEP), 2000

Rumelili, Bahar, 'The European Union's Impact on the Greek-Turkish Conflict: A Review of the Literature', *Working Paper Number 6*, EU Border Conflicts Studies, January 2004

Rumelili, Bahar, 'The Talkers and the Silent Ones: The EU and Change in Greek Turkish Relations', *Working Paper Number 10*, EU Border Conflicts Studies, October 2004

Rumelili, Bahar, 'The EU and Cultural Change in Greek-Turkish Relations', *Working Paper Number 17*, EU Border Conflicts Studies, April 2005

Sezgin, Yuksel, 'The October 1998 Crisis in Turkish-Syrian Relations: A Prospect Theory Approach', *Turkish Studies*, Volume 3, Number 2, Autumn 2002.

Skouroliakou, Melina, 'The Theory That Never Turned Into Practice: Case Study from Eastern Mediterranean', *Paper for Presentation at the ISA-South Conference*, Miami, 3–5 November 2005

Stavridis, Stelios, 'The European Union's Contribution to Peace and Stability in the Eastern Mediterranean (the So-Called Athens-Nicosia-Ankara Triangle): A Critique', *Working Paper*, Fundacion SIP Zaragoza, November 2005

Stearns, Monteagle, 'The Security Domain: A US Perspective', in in Dimitris Keridis and Dimitrios Triantaphyllou (editors), *Greek-Turkish Relations in the Era of Globalization* (Virginia: Brassey's, 2001)

South East European Studies Programme (SEESP), *SEESP Newsletter*, Number 2, European Studies Centre, St Antony's College, 2004

Stephanou, Constantine and Charalambos Tsardanides, 'The EC Factor in Greece-Turkey-Cyprus Triangle', in Constas, Dimitri (editor) *Greek-Turkish Conflict in the 1990s: Domestic and External Influences* (Basingstoke: Macmillan, 1990)

Theodoropoulos, Byron, 'Preface: Peremptory Reasoning', in Dimitris Keridis and Dimitrios Triantaphyllou (editors), *Greek-Turkish Relations in the Era of Globalization* (Virginia: Brassey's, 2001)

Tsakonas, Panayiotis, 'Turkey's Post-Helsinki Turbulence: Implications for Greece and the Cyprus Issue', *Turkish Studies*, Volume 2, Number 2, Fall 2001

Veremis, Thanos, 'The Protracted Crisis', in Dimitris Keridis and Dimitrios Triantaphyllou (editors), *Greek-Turkish Relations in the Era of Globalization* (Virginia: Brassey's, 2001)

Zahariadis, Nikolaos, 'A Framework for Improving Greek-Turkish Relations', *Mediterranean Quarterly*, Volume 11, Number 4, Fall 2000

Official Documents

Convention Regarding the Regime of the Straits Signed at Montreux, 20 July 1936.

European Commission, *Commission Opinion on Turkey's Request for Accession to the Community*, 20 December 1989

European Commission, *Regular Report on Turkey's Progress towards Accession*, 1998

European Council, *Luxembourg European Council Presidency Conclusions*, 12–13 December 1997

European Council, *Helsinki European Council Presidency Conclusions*, 10–11 December 1999
European Court of Human Rights, *Loizidou v. Turkey*, 15318/89 [1996], ECHR 70, 18 December 1996
Foreign and Commonwealth Office, *Edited Transcript of a Doorstep Interview Given by the Foreign Secretary, Robin Cook, and the Greek Foreign Minister, George Papandreou*, London, Monday 18 October 1999
Hellenic Republic, 'The Question of the Imia Islands: Turkish Allegations on "Grey zones" in the Aegean Sea', *Website of the Ministry of Foreign Affairs* (accessed April 2006)
Hellenic Republic, 'Greek Territorial Waters and National Airspace', *Website of the Ministry of Foreign Affairs* (accessed April 2006)
Hellenic Republic, 'Bilateral Relations (The Rapprochement Process), *Website of the Ministry of Foreign Affairs* (accessed April 2006)
International Court of Justice, *Greece v. Turkey, Aegean Sea Continental Shelf Case (Interim Protection)*, Order of 11 September 1976
International Court of Justice, *Greece v. Turkey, Aegean Sea Continental Shelf Case, Jurisdiction of the Court, Judgment*, General List No. 62 [1978] ICJ 1, 19 December 1978
Joint Communiqué signed by President Demirel of Turkey and Prime Minister Simitis of Greece, Madrid, 8 July 1997
Joint Communiqué signed after the meeting of high officials of the Foreign Ministries of Turkey and Greece, 16 September 1999
North Atlantic Treaty Organisation (NATO), *North Atlantic Council, Final Communiqué*, Brussels, 7–8 December 1978
Republic of Turkey, Ministry of Foreign Affairs, *Statement made by Murat Karayalcin, Foreign Minister of Turkey*, on Greek Cypriot Application for EU Membership on 6 March, 1995 during the EU-Turkey Association Council in Brussels
Republic of Turkey, Ministry of Foreign Affairs, *Statement by Ambassador Ömer Akbal, Spokesman of the Turkish Foreign Ministry*, 31 January 1996
Republic of Turkey, Ministry of Foreign Affairs, *Agreement between the Government of the Republic of Turkey and the Turkish Republic of Northern Cyprus on the Establishment of an Association Council*, 6 August 1997.
Republic of Turkey, Office of the Prime Minister, Directorate General of Press and Information, Statement by Prime Minister Ecevit, 16 February 1999, *Newspot* 13, January 1999
Republic of Turkey, Ministry of Foreign Affairs, *Interview by Minister of Foreign Affairs İsmail Cem to Journalist Murat Birsel on the Program 'Gündemdekiler' on NTV Television*, June 7, 1999
Republic of Turkey, Ministry of Foreign Affairs, *Address by Minister of Foreign Affairs İsmail Cem at DEIK Meeting in London*, September 3, 1999
United Nations, *Security Council Resolution 186 (1964)*, 4 March 1964.

United Nations, *Security Council Resolution 395 (1976)*, 25 August 1976.
United Nations, *United Nations Convention on the Law of the Sea*, 10 December 1982
United Nations, *Press Release, SG/SM/5887*, 30 January 1996
United Nations, 'Letter dated 23 September 1999 from the Permanent Representatives of China, France, the Russian Federation, the United Kingdom of Great Britain and Northern Ireland and the United States of America to the United Nations Addressed to the Secretary-General', *United Nations Security Council Document S/1999/996*, 23 September 1999
United Nations, 'Secretary-General Says Proximity Talks on Cyprus Will Start 3 December', *Press Release UNIS/SG/2443*, 16 November 1999
United States, Department of State, *Turkey Country Report on Human Rights Practices for 1998*, Released by the Bureau of Democracy, Human Rights, and Labor, February 26, 1998
United States, *Remarks by President Bill Clinton and Prime Minister Simitis of Greece to the Government of Greece, Business and Community Leaders, Inter-Continental Hotel, Athens, Greece*, November 20, 1999.

News Sources

Al-Ahram Weekly, Anadolu Agency, Associated Press, Athens News, Athens News Agency, BBC News, CNN, Cyprus Broadcasting Corporation (CyBC), Cyprus Mail, Cyprus News Agency, The Economist, Eleftherotypia, Financial Times, The Guardian, Keesing's Contemporary Archives, Kyriatiki Eleftherotypia, Eleftheros Typos, Hellenic Radio, Hurriyet, Kathimerini, Kyriatiki Eleftherotypia, Macedonian Press Agency, Milliyet, O Logos, Reuters, Sabah, Ta Nea, New York Times, To Vima tis Kyriakis, Turkish Radio and Television, Turkish Daily News, The Washington Times

INDEX

Aegean Crisis (1976), 20, 111
Aegean Crisis (1987), 3, 24, 26, 111
Aga, Mehmet Emin, 100-1
Agrapidis, Christos, 59
airspace, 5, 27, 111
airspace violations, 4-5, 23, 97, 104
Akbulut, Yıldırım, 58
AKUT, 68-9, 102, 113
Akyol, Nihat, 65
Albania, 40, 74
Albright, Madeleine, 41, 90
Ankara Convention, 14
Annan Plan, 7, 107
Annan, Kofi, 50, 106
Aslanis, Costas, 59
Atacanlı, Sermet, 44, 86
Athens earthquake, 9, 68-9, 112
Avramopoulos, Dimitri, 58-9, 71

Bahçeli, Devlet, 41-2
Balkan Entente, 14
Balkan Pact, 15
Balkan Wars, 13
Balkan, Mithat, 54
Bartholomew, Patriarch, 90
Batu, İnal, 144
Benos, Stavros, 65
Berberakis, Takis, 65
Berne Declaration, 21-5
Bilateral Agreements, 102

Black Sea Economic Cooperation (BSEC), 86, 126
Bosnia-Herzegovina, 40, 116
Bostancıoğlu, Metin, 74
Britain, 6, 12-18, 84, 106, 117
Bulgaria, 13, 56, 74
Burns, Nicholas, 89, 151
Byzantine Empire, 11

Çakir, Erol, 81
Çakmakoğlu, Sabahattin, 58, 74, 88, 101
Capital Tax (*Varlık Vergisi*), 15
Cassoulides, Ioannis, 61, 83, 94
Casus Belli resolution, 5, 29, 85, 90
Caucasus, 82, 117
Celasin, Ergin, 97
Cem, Ismail
  Aegean islets, 45; Albright, 90; Athens, 102; Athens earthquake, 69; Cyprus, 77-8; financial aid from Greece, 66; Greece and terrorism, 48; Greek-Turkish Forum, 143; Helsinki European Council, 99; Izmit earthquake, 57; Kosovo, 40; Papandreou, 40, 43, 45-7, 50, 52, 73, 76-7, 82, 86, 112; rapprochement, 2, 9, 47, 115, 119-21; resignation, 105-6, 151; Turkey's EU candidacy, 85, 96

Christides, Michael, 45
Christodoulos, Archbishop, 59
Çiller, Tansu, 30
Clerides, Glafkos, 60-1, 75, 93, 105-6
Clinton, Bill, 30, 83, 89-93, 100, 117
Cold War, 2-3
continental shelf, 4, 19, 22, 26-7, 53, 110
Cook, Robin, 84
Council of Europe, 125
Council on Foreign and Defence Affairs (Kysea), 30
Croatia, 116
Cyprus
 1963 Crisis, 17; anti-occupation protests, 31; British rule, 15; Davos Process, 26-7; Kranidiotis, 75; EOKA Campaign, 16; EU accession, 4, 8, 28, 32, 33, 49; EU membership, 109; Greek policy since 1974, 6, 19; Greek-Turkish relations, 2; Guarantor Powers, 6; High Level Agreements, 33; independence, 16, 110; Izmit earthquake, 60-1; Mitsotakis, 27; non-recognition by Turkey, 108; Öcalan, 38; Paphos Air Base, 44; peace talks, 32, 90, 105-6; rapprochement, 82-3; referendum, 106-7; Turkish invasion, 1, 3, 6, 18, 20-1, 110

Dalaras, George, 60
Davos Process, 26-28, 102, 111
demilitarisation, 111
Demirel, Suleyman
 1976 Aegean Crisis, 20; Athens earthquake, 68; Clinton, 90, 92; Helsinki European Council, 100; Kranidiotis, 75; Mitsotakis, 27; Öcalan, 38; Simitis, 32, 41, 43
Demirtaş, Ekrem, 85

Democratic Left Party (DSP), 41-2, 46, 54, 99, 105, 120, 137
Democratic Social Movement (DIKKI), 67
Denktaş, Rauf R., 32-3, 78, 95, 105-6, 138
Dervişoğlu, Selim, 62, 142
Dimadis, Nikos, 145
direct talks, 51, 54-5, 73-6, 112-3
Disaster Diplomacy, 9-10, 118-9
Dodecanese, 15, 137
Durmuş, Osman, 62-4, 142

East-West Institute, 102
Ecevit, Bulent
 Aegean islets, 45; Athens earthquake, 68-9; Clinton, 90; Cologne European Council, 48; Cyprus, 78, 87, 94, 105; Cyprus invasion, 18; Greek television interview, 49; Gurel, 106; Helsinki European Council, 99, 114; Izmit earthquake, 63; Korantis, 147; Montreux meeting (1978), 21; Öcalan, 37; rapprochement, 54, 81, 117, 120; Simitis, 84, 89-91; Turkey's EU candidacy, 94, 97; Turkish elections, 41-2, 46
Egypt, 15
EMAK, 57-8, 69, 81, 102, 113
Enosis, 15-18
EOKA, 16
Erdoğan, Recep Tayyip, 106-7
Erkaya, Guven, 137, 142, 151
European Commission, 28, 106
European Convention on Human Rights, 101
European Council
 Cologne (1999), 47-8, 79; Corfu (1994), 28; Helsinki (1999), 8, 79, 97, 99, 102, 114, 116; Luxembourg (1997), 4, 33, 53, 112

European Court of Human Rights (ECHR), 6, 100
European Union (EU)
  Cyprus issue, 7; Greek accession, 22; Greek membership, 4; Greek-Turkish relations, 4, 9, 32, 117; rapprochement, 7, 115; Turkey Association Agreement, 27-8; Turkish candidacy, 2, 4, 8, 28, 47, 49, 79, 109, 113-4; Turkish membership application, 28

First World War, 13
Floratos, Evangelos, 59
Fourth Financial Protocol, 4, 28, 31
France, 3, 12-13, 84
Franco-German rapprochement, 3, 120
Germany, 3, 14, 84
Germen, Acar, 81
Greek independence, 12
Greek Intelligence Service (EYP), 37
Greek minority in Turkey, 5, 13, 15, 24, 81, 105, 111
Greek Orthodox Church, 38
Greek-Turkish Business Council, 65
Greek-Turkish Forum, 139, 141, 142, 147, 151
Grey Wolves, 31, 42
Grey Zones, 5, 88
Gürel, Şükrü Sina, 106, 120, 151
Gürtuna, Ali Müfit, 59, 71, 81

Haktanır, Korkmaz, 144
Halki Theological School, 5, 85, 90, 101
Halonen, Tarja, 66
Haralambopoulos, Ionannis, 66
Hasikos, Socrates, 93
Holbrooke, Richard, 30

Imia-Kardak Crisis, 5, 29-31, 45, 56, 111, 117, 152

India, 10
İnönü, İsmet, 17
International Court of Justice (ICJ), 20-2, 25-6, 49, 53, 84, 90-1, 95, 97, 114
Ioannides, Georgios, 62
İpekçi Award, 37, 102
Iran, 10
İrtemçelik, Mehmet Ali, 99
Israel, 36
Istanbul Riots (1955), 16
Italy, 13-15, 35, 74, 84
Izmit earthquake, 9, 57, 112

Joint Transportation Committee, 76
Justice and Development Party (AKP), 106

Kalamanis, Apostolos, 58
Kapsis, Yiannis, 87
Karamanlis, Constantine, 67, 92, 100, 107-8
Karamanlis, Constantine (1907-1998), 18, 20, 107, 150
Kardak. *See* Imia-Kardak Crisis
Katrivanos, Dimitris, 57
Kemal, Mustafa (Atatürk), 13-14, 17, 133
Kenya, 1, 35
Kıvrıkoğlu, Huseyin, 45, 121
KKE (Greek Communist Party), 91, 100
Koç, Rahmi, 60
Konstantopoulos, Nikos, 71, 93
Korantis, Ioannis, 48, 52, 57, 68, 70, 76, 147
Korea, 15
Köse, İsmail, 70
Kosovo, 39-43, 47, 50, 54, 65, 82, 112, 126, 142, 145
Koutsikos, Panayiotis, 60

Kranidiotis, Yiannos, 42, 49, 53-4, 58, 71, 74-5, 79, 82, 121-2, 145, 152
Ksidas, Fotis, 59
Kumbul, Bekin, 72
Kyprianou, Spyros, 142

Lebanon, 35
Lipponen, Paavo, 100
Logan, David, 41, 139
Loğoğlu, Faruk, 52
Loizidou Case, 6

Macedonia (FYROM), 40, 74, 116
Madrid Declaration, 32-3
Mahruki, Nasruh, 69
Makarios III, Archbishop, 16-18, 88, 110
Megali Idea, 13
Middle East, 82
Mitsotakis, Constantine, 27, 66, 87, 100, 147
Molyviatis, Petros, 107
Montenegro, 13
Montreux Convention, 14
Montreux meeting (1978), 21
Motherland Party (ANAP), 42, 46, 63, 99, 137, 140
Muslim minority in Greece, 5, 13, 72, 101, 105, 111

National Action Party (MHP), 41-2, 46, 49, 62, 70, 121
NATO
  1987 Aegean Crisis, 25; Cyprus, 17; Greece and Turkey, 3-4, 15, 21, 104, 110; Imia-Kardak Crisis, 30; Kosovo, 40; Madrid Summit (1997), 32; Washington Summit (1999), 41
Netherlands, 84
New Democracy, 22, 27, 67, 100, 107

Nicolaou, Yiannis, 46
Nikiforos (military exercise), 121
North Aegean Petroleum Company (NAPC), 24

Öcalan, Abdullah, 1, 34-9, 49, 51, 112, 152
OSCE Istanbul Summit, 73, 89
Ottoman Empire, 11-15, 47
Özal, Turgut, 23-8, 107, 111
Pakistan, 10
Pandayias, George, 65, 67
Pangalos, General Theodore (1878-1952), 14
Pangalos, Theodore, 31, 33, 37, 43, 47, 66, 87
Panteleras, Petros, 60
Papadopoulos, Alekos, 37
Papadopoulos, Tassos, 106
Papageorgopoulos, Vassilis, 59
Papandreou, Andreas, 22-9, 37, 111, 120
Papandreou, George
  Ankara, 102; appointed foreign minister, 37; Athens earthquake, 69; Britain, 84; Cem, 40, 46-7, 50, 52, 73, 76-7, 82, 86, 112; Clinton, 92; Cologne European Council, 47-8; criticism, 87; Cyprus, 78, 93, 94, 121, 152; Cyprus issue, 82-3; financial aid to Turkey, 66; France, 84; Greek-Turkish Forum, 147; Italy, 84; Izmit earthquake, 57; Kranidiotis, 74, 152; minority issues, 101; Mitsotakis, 66; Muslim minority in Greece, 55-6; NATO Summit (1999), 41; Öcalan, 37; PASOK leader, 107; rapprochement, 2, 9, 42, 55, 66, 77-80, 101, 115, 119-22; Turkey's EU candidacy, 79-80, 84-6, 94-5; United States, 43; visit to Turkey, 80-1

Index

Papandreou, George (1888-1968), 17
Papandreou, Vasso, 67
Papapetrou, Michael, 83, 89
Papoulias, Karolos, 27, 66, 108, 143
Paris peace conference, 13
PASOK, 22, 27, 37, 66, 71, 75, 87, 107, 120
Patriarchate of Constantinople, 5-6, 24
Petsalnikos, Philipos, 37
PKK, 1, 34-9, 44, 46, 70, 77
Plaza Lasso, Galo, 17
Pomaks, 55
Population exchange, 14, 110
Prinos oil field, 22, 24

Red Cross, 61
Reppas, Dimitri, 44-5, 48, 66, 88, 94
Republican Peoples Party (CHP), 71
Republican Turkish Party (CTP), 106
Rodriquez, Florinda Rojas, 60
Rokofyllos, Christos, 75, 83, 87, 152
Roma (Gypsies), 55
Romania, 14, 56, 74
Rozakis, Christos, 53, 141
Russia, 12, 35

S-300 Crisis, 31-4, 83, 111
Samaras, Antonis, 67
Samson, Nicos, 18
Second World War, 14, 120
Seljuk Empire, 11
Serbia, 13, 39, 40, 116
Şerif, İbrahim, 101
Simitis, Constantine
  Athens earthquake, 68; Clerides, 93; Clinton, 92; Cologne European Council, 48, 79; criticisms, 100; Cyprus issue, 83 Demirel, 32, 41, 43; Ecevit, 89-91; Helsinki European Council, 98, 100; Imia-Kardak Crisis, 29-30; Izmit earthquake, 58; Kranidiotis, 74-5; Öcalan, 36-7, 51; OSCE Summit, 93; Papandreou, 87; PASOK, 143; rapprochement, 85, 120; retirement, 107; Turkey's EU candidacy, 80, 84-5, 95, 114
Skopelitis, Anastasios, 54
Solana, Javier, 99
South East Europe Peacekeeping Brigade (SEEBRIG), 74
Southeast European Cooperation Initiative (SECI), 125-6
Soviet Union, 3
Spain, 84
Spiliotopoulos, Aris, 42
Stability Pact, 126
Stavrakakis, Charalambos, 37
Stephanopoulos, Constantine, 58, 68, 92
Synaspismos, 71
Syria, 34, 35

Taksim, 16-17
Tara, Şarik, 60
territorial waters, 5, 19, 27, 77, 111
Theodorakis, Mikis, 59
Theodoropoulos, Byron, 116
Tito, Josip Broz, 15
TPAO, 20
Treaty of Lausanne, 5, 13-16, 19, 55, 110
Treaty of Paris, 15, 137
TRNC, 23, 29, 32
True Path Party (DYP), 68, 137, 140
Tsilas, Loucas, 65, 80
Tsitsas, Thanasis, 63
Tsovolas, Dimitri, 66
Türkeş, Alparslan, 42
Turkish Grand National Assembly, 5, 18, 29
Turkish War of Independence, 13
Turkish-EU Association Council, 31
Turkmen, Ilter, 151

Tütüncüoğlu, Faik, 60
Tuygan, Ali, 58
Tzohadzopoulos, Akis, 52, 58, 74, 88, 93

Ulusu, Bülend, 23
United Nations
  Cem-Papandreou meeting, 51; Charter, 21, 29; Conference on the Law of the Sea, 19, 24; Convention on the Law of the Sea, 5, 19, 29; Cyprus peace talks, 17, 53; General Assembly, 54, 73, 75, 77; Imia Kardak Crisis, 30; joint rescue team proposal, 77; Peacekeeping Force in Cyprus (UNFICYP), 17, 110; Security Council, 21
United States
  1987 Aegean Crisis, 25; arms embargo on Turkey, 21; Cyprus issue, 18; Greek-Turkish relations, 3-4, 32, 117; Helsinki European Council, 97; Imia-Kardak Crisis, 30, 111; relations with Iran, 10; Kosovo, 40; Turkey's EU candidacy, 113
US Congress, 6

Valinakis, Yiannis, 149
Vardinoyianni, Vardis, 58
Venizelos, Eleftherios, 13-14, 17
Verheugen, Günter, 99

World Economic Forum, 26
World Health Organisation (WHO), 63

Yılmaz, Mesut, 27
Yugoslavia, 14, 40

Zisi, Rodoula, 65
Zurich-London Agreements (1959), 16